Forgiven

of Murder ...

A True Story

by Denise Mountenay

TOGETHER FOR LIFE!

Copyright © 2007 by Denise Mountenay

ISBN 0-9685056-0-0

Fourth printing, January 2007

Canadian Cataloguing in Publication Data
Mountenay, Denise, 1957-
Forgiven of murder ... A True Story
Includes selected bibliographical references.
ISBN 0-9685056-0-0
1. Autobiography.   2. Abortion-Canada   3. Women's Issues
I. Title
HQ767.5.C2M69   1999   363.46   C99-900394-1

PUBLISHED and DISTRIBUTED by
C. REALITY PUBLISHERS
Price $20.00 & S & H
Together for Life Ministries
107 Discovery Ave., Morinville, AB, Canada T8R 1N1
Phone (780) 939-5774
Also, available at Life Cycle Books:
1-800-214-5849, www.lifecyclebooks.com

Typesetting by PATRICK GLENN and ART DESIGN
Front cover design by Herbert Ratsch, ART DESIGN
Printing production by ART DESIGN PRINTING INC.
Edmonton, Alberta, Canada

Disclaimer:

This publication is designed to provide accurate and personal information. It is sold with the understanding that the publishers are not engaged in rendering legal, psychological or other professionals advise. If advice or assistance is required, the services of a competent professional, such as a Pastor, Priest, Pregnancy Crisis Counselling Centre, or Pro Life group is recommended.

The analysis contained herein represents the experiences and opinions of the author. The author and publishers are not responsible for the results of any action taken from information in this work, unless it saves the lives of Preborn children.

Names and places have been changed to protect the identity of some characters. Emphasis in bold italics is the author's. Biblical references are taken from the King James, New Kings James, Amplified, and New International versions.

WARNING: Some descriptions of actual events are graphic, and may not be suitable for youth under the age of 14. Details have been included to reveal the seriousness of the subject matter.

Forword

by Rev. Ken Campbell

"Choose Life Canada"

It was at "The Way" Inn, a Christian pro-life counselling ministry to women in crisis pregnancies that I was first introduced to Denise. Recognizing that God was preparing a rare "handmaiden of the Lord" for front-line service in this battle for the soul of a society and the souls of men!

Abortion is the pivotal issue on which the destiny of our nation will be determined. No one can read Denise's book and not be overwhelmed by God's amazing grace in her life, which has brought her to Himself, and sent her out as a soul liberated from sin, self, and "spewable," self-indulgent Christianity.

Christians ought to read this book for the revival of authentic Christian discipleship.

Non-Christians should read it to be introduced to the grace of God.

Politicians should read it to awaken their consciences to recognize and to fulfill the duty of the State, to protect the humanity of every person from conception to natural death!

It is with profound thanksgiving to God for His grace in Denise's life, that I commend this book to all who would know the God of all grace, through Jesus Christ, and who would serve their generation-as does Denise-by the will of God!

Dedication

This book of memoirs is dedicated to my first three children Jennifer, Daniel and Rebecca who were violently killed and taken from me. Although we never got to hold hands, cuddle or laugh together, I love you, and one day I will be with you in heaven.

Also, I would like to dedicate this work to my beloved parent's Ruth and Hans. They always loved and encouraged me. They have been an inspiration and good example of unconditional love, integrity and honour. These are aspirations we all need to grow and thrive as a prosperous society.

Special thanks to GOD, and all of my wonderful friends for life, who supported the printing of this book: Mom & Dad, Tante Mila, Pastor Rob & Carroll, Dana & Rhonda, Rev. Ken Campbell, Beverly Hadland, Peggy, Marlene & Eric, Bob, Brian, Rick & Willy, Patricia, Carol, Myrna, Barbara, Diane, James & Roberta, Cynthia, Brian & Wendy, Royce & Susan, Laura, Sue, Thelma, Linda, Denise, Lionel, Hilda, Agnes, Phyllis, Maureen, Roy & Shelley Beyer, Ron & Veronica , Darka, Carole May, all the prayer warriors & my best friends Kim, Charlene, Erika and Joanne. Great appreciation to my husband Paul for his fantastic computer help and support.

Introduction

This book began as an inspiration in 1987. However, it has taken more than twelve years to complete. The intense pain of remorseful recollections, the distractions of life and the time and energy required to fulfill this vision has been spent.

Although, emotional and difficult, I have been speaking publicly about my personal experiences to students, young adults, women's groups and the public for more than eleven years now. It has become obvious that the perspective I share is unique, and diversified. The subject matters are most controversial and are a great podium for debate. The absolute truth and information contained in this book should end the dispute once and for all.

It is my intention to expose the rhetoric and euphemisms that have become common place, as well as convey the facts in a simple format. Over the years I have spoken to thousands of women who have shared similar experiences. They have thanked me for having the courage to speak out, because they could not.

Most important, my motivation is to illuminate what is being done in the dark regions around this world. We pray that precious lives will be saved, as well as women spared the eternal suffering of lost souls and damaged emotions.

Contents

Chapter 1

"Defiled"

Once again with a heavy heart, genuine tears streamed down my cheeks as I relived and retold my story. This time it was in front of a Bio-Ethics class of students at a College in Edmonton, Alberta. Were they hearing my profound remorse? Could they comprehend the truth, or were their minds so polluted with deception and preconceived ideas, that it did not matter? Although difficult and humiliating for me, this story must be heralded. It is a matter of life and death! *If it makes the difference to save one life, it is worth it!*

We all have our own original life story. Each journey includes times of euphoria and times of discouragement, times of love and times of sorrow, times of joy, and times of despair. This is my unique story.

A big hand pressed hard over my mouth. Fear gripped me. I couldn't scream; I could hardly breathe. What was happening? The covers were brazenly pulled down to my ankles. Who was doing this? A strange, naked heavy weight thumped down on top of me, forcing my legs apart. I tried to holler while pushing against this oppressive heaviness. With my heart racing, I struggled and squirmed against him, but it was no use. He was much too strong.

I was helpless. This is difficult for me to write but I must go on. Pain seared below as he repeatedly thrust himself into me. Then he fled, without a word. Alone, in shock, pain and fear, I wept quietly in torment that he might reappear. **I was only thirteen years old.**

This tragic rape subconsciously changed the course of my entire life forever. We assumed I was safe and secure at my girlfriend's house. Cindy had invited me to come and sleep over at her house, she didn't know. Sadly, my parents could have done nothing, to prevent this attack. They were unable to protect me from this secret pedophile.

Cindy's brother, who was about twenty-four years old at the time, invited us to play pool with him and his buddy Terry, in their basement. We played pool and listened to the Miss American Pie record. Cindy and I giggled and laughed at everything, we were so young and naive. The men smoked and drank a few beers.

Cindy and I left to go and phone some boys from our class for fun. We did, and giggled and laughed some more. It was getting late. I was tired. Back in our room, we changed into our flannelette nightgowns, and I snuggled into my single cot. She said that she was going to go and say good night to Terry, who she thought was cute. Our room looked more like a built in summer porch, an extension to the house, on the far end. Two single beds sat across from each other, a dresser, night table and throw rugs on the floor. After turning out the light, and shutting the door at the foot of my bed, I started to fall into a deep sleep.

Startled, I heard the door creak open. Squinting my eyes, I could see the hall light shining into the room. A tall, dark outline of a stark-naked man silently crept over to my bedside. He scared the heck out of me, I gasped, "Uhhh!" He put one hand over my mouth. That is when my innocence was taken away.

I wanted to yell out for Cindy. Her brother was the intruder. Where was she? She still had not come back from her visit with Terry. I was too afraid to move in case he would return. Upset and hurt, I just cried myself back to sleep.

The next morning Cindy's Mom was calling from the kitchen to get us up. "Breakfast is ready." She was in such a hurry to get us out of bed. I felt sick, depressed, and defiled not wanting to move. It was as if everything was in slow motion now. I couldn't talk, I felt so degraded and ashamed! As if paralysed, I forced myself to try to be normal. I couldn't tell anyone what happened, because I felt so horrible. As I strolled into the kitchen, there sat the whole family. Everyone was seated, and waiting for me. They all looked up when I walked into the kitchen, and there he sat, with a big grin on his face. I looked down. It was unbearable even to glance at him. My head hung low. What humiliation and embarrassment.

From this tragic day on, my life and personality drastically changed for the worse. It took almost 17 years before I could even talk about it. Should I report it to police now, after all these years? How many other young girls did he violate? These questions often haunt me. Could my exposing his repulsive deeds perhaps save another young girls' innocence? Is it too late?

Chapter 2

"Back To The Beginning"

My beginning on earth started when my Mom and Dad were intimate with each other and God allowed my conception to take place. It was sometime in April of 1956. The precise moment was when one of my Dad's sperm engaged with one of my Mother's eggs that I came into being. **Just like you!** It was like a computer microchip. The fact that I was a female, and would look like I do. The whole genetic code was there. Awesome.

My birthday was on January 17, 1957 in Toronto's Mount Sinai Hospital, a present for an amazing lady, my beloved Mother, Ruth and Father, Hans. My Mom is a special treasure from Switzerland, and my Dad, an arduous working mechanic from Germany. They met in a crowded restaurant in downtown Toronto. Both of them had been feeling lonely, and struggling to learn the English language in a new and strange land.

They had escaped the ravages of Europe after an ugly war, suffering from the aftershock, but glad to be alive. My Dad was recuperating from the cruelty and brutality of World War II. He had lost his Dad in this War. His mother, brother and twin sister were forced to flee their home in Liegnitz, because the Russians were coming. Dad had volunteered to join the Navy so he would not be forced to join the notorious "SS." He was only 17. They had relinquished everything. Food was scarce.

My Mother was fleeing the consequences and shame of having sex before marriage, and getting caught. While under the influence of alcohol, she lost her inhibitions, and reluctantly gave in to a man. Her virginity was lost, and she conceived. She refused to have her baby aborted or marry the man who took advantage of her. The stigma of single Moms was cruel back then. Mom gave birth to my beautiful sister Rita. Please know that God does not have "accidents" or make "mistakes!" He created everyone for a purpose. We thank God for Rita, who is so precious, and for all the love she shares.

Feeling humiliated and condemned by the church, Mom fled to Canada to start a new life. Although very emotional for Mom, she left Rita to be well-taken care of by her Grandparents and loving Aunts. It was many years before Mom and Rita would reunite.

My Dad is a very handsome fellow, and quite the serious type. He being an intelligent, studious and confident man, won my mother's heart. My Mom admired the fact that he was temperate, ambitious and not afraid to work.

Only three days after their first encounter, they went to Toronto City Hall and made arrangements to be married. It was a quick romance. They were mature and ready to settle down. The security and companionship they shared, took away most of the fears and pain of isolation away from family. They had many obstacles and challenges to overcome being in a new, foreign country. Shortly thereafter, I was conceived, and born.

Both my parents were very hard-working, honest people. My Mom, a jubilant musician arrived in Canada as an authentic Swiss yodeler! She played the accordion well, a bright red, all button "Record" model that her step-Father gave her as a going away present.

Seeing an ad in the paper, she entered a 'Talent Show' at the old 'El Mocambo,' night club, on Spadina Avenue in downtown Toronto. Paper litter and garbage clutter this road. China town thrives in this area with many fresh fruit and vegetable markets. It has this foul smell, and you can spot dead ducks and chickens hanging in steamy restaurant windows. Spadina Avenue was close to the University of Toronto as well.

The stench and clouds of smoke, the aroma of beer and strong liquor in the nightclub swelled. Loud, drunken patrons roared with clatter, but Mom was used to it. She had lived and worked hard in her Grandfathers' Hotel in Switzerland. She had become an expert on how to handle boisterous drunks. The raunchy atmosphere did not intimidate her one bit.

Mom gleefully sang, and her fingers danced on that bright shiny red accordion. Swiss music is very joyful and upbeat. It makes you tap your feet, prompting you to get up and dance the polka. She wore an authentic Swiss costume complete with fancy strings, bows and puffy white sleeves. Mom won first prize that night. After the show, the owner approached her. With tears in his eyes, he shook her hand, congratulating her. He began to explain, "You look just like an old girlfriend I used to have in Austria, some thirty years ago."

He was from Gleichenberg, Austria where my great-uncle once owned a Swiss Milk Bar. "Oh, did your old girlfriend's name happen to be Lena?" Mom asked. "Why yes, that was her name," he replied in astonishment. They decided to write a letter to my Grandmother of the discovery. Was this merely a coincidence, or was this a divine appointment?

After several attempts to contact the CBC radio for a job, my mother got another lead. They told her to call Ivan Romanoff a man who was airing a radio program called "Song of my people." It just so happened that they were looking for a Swiss yodeler! She was immediately hired, and began singing on the air. Soon she would produce two records and be a guest on the entertainment program entitled, "Holiday Ranch." Mom got the occasional spots to sing in various Night clubs around the city.

Just two years and five days after my birth, my little brother Tommy, was born. He was so cute and chubby. Yet, I just wanted to pinch him. Extremely jealous, I threw a temper tantrum the first time I laid eyes on him, Mom reported.

As preschoolers we used to live in 'Cabbage-town' Toronto, an older residential downtown area. Most houses were three storeys high, very narrow, and joined together in a row. With no front yards to speak of, and very tiny back yards, we were a bit cramped for style. It was a very tough area. We often played with our neighbours, Karen and Moe who would join us in the tiny backyard pool. Karen's background is a mystery to me, but Moe was Chinese, and his parents owned a dry cleaner's store a couple of doors away. They couldn't speak a word of English, but we somehow communicated well with Moe.

For some odd reason, Tommy and I would end up playing across the street in an abandoned parking lot. The attraction was the many beautiful round glistening stones to play with over there. One really hot, humid summer day I found a glass cola bottle. It was about half full. After taking a whiff, decided this was *yucky*. Little Tommy who was about thirty months old, kept motioning and grunting that he wanted the bottle. So I said, "Okay, here you go, you can have it then." With that he grabbed the bottle and whooped it down in a flash. He must have been truly thirsty.

The next thing you know, he starts gasping for air like he couldn't breathe. He doubled over coughing, gagging and choking. It was terrible. He smelled awful too! Scared now, I ran over to tell Mommy that something was the matter with Tommy. She said, "Oh my God," dropped everything and went running across the road. She swept him off the ground. Tommy was still gasping and starting to go into convulsions. She looked at me, demanding, and frantic, "What did you do, What happened, what did he eat, what did he drink?" At that I replied, "Oh I just gave him some Pop here." Really scared now, I reached for the bottle on the ground. Mom quickly grabbed it from me, smelled the top and said, "Let's go, we have to take him right to the hospital, Come on, hurry!"

It turned out that the bottle was full of an oil and gas combination. Not good for the lungs or digestive tract. They had to pump his stomach and keep him in for observation. This was Tommy's first close call with death. Thank God he made it.

As the years went on Tommy and I fought very hard, sibling rivalry prevailed. We would have great battles while in the car as passengers going about town with Mom. We were always getting into trouble. When we would make a mess or break something and get caught, of course I would blame him totally. We would argue over who got Brownie, (our beloved dog) to sleep in their bed.

My parents had bought a Rooming House in Cabbage-town, in the heart of Toronto. Mom was strict with her tenants, yet she always had a soft spot. Often she took in old folks that came to the door begging for food or asking for money. She couldn't afford to give them any money, but she would invite them in for a cup of hot tea and a cold sandwich. Everyone was welcome. It was an open door policy.

Chapter 3

"Out Of The Ashes"

Mom and Dad decided to head north, out of the big city of Toronto when I was five. The air pollution back then was due to huge amounts of coal being used as fuel. This was causing problems with our breathing. After selling the rooming house we moved to a pleasant little home near Lake Wilcox, just north of Toronto. The air was fresh. There were big trees all around, lots of green grass, and vibrant colours. We got a cute little puppy named Brownie. She was a Heinz-57 variety. She had the most loving brown eyes. We trained her to sit, shake a paw and be obedient.

Tommy and I loved her so much. She was our best friend. Some fond memories include playing ball, skipping and playing 'hide n seek' with friends. Sometimes we would pick wild rhubarb from the neighbour's garden, and dip it in lots of sugar. We also used to go for hot family saunas'.

Life was quite good, until calamity hit us. This particular day I had offered to help the teacher sharpen pencils after school. I was in Grade one now. While busy at the pencil sharpener, one of my girlfriends, a neighbour from across the road from where we lived, arrived. She was a couple of years older than I and attended another school. To my great surprise she interrupted my teacher who was working at her desk. Suzie whispered something in her ear. Suddenly my teacher turned with great concern. "That is enough Denise, you can go along with your friend now," the teacher responded. "But I'm not finished." I announced.

Suzie quickly grabbed my hand, sternly pulling me along. She said, "We have to hurry and go to someone's house." She insisted that we go the long way around, instead of the shortcut that I usually took. I kept asking her, "Why did you come to my school and get me?' What is the hurry? What is going on?" Suzie refused to give me an answer. She just kept pulling me onward.

To my shock and bewilderment, I could see and smell thick, heavy smoke. Then I realized that it was bellowing from our house. "I want to go home" I began to cry. When I started to question things again, she insisted that I stay at this neighbours house until my parents got there. Frantic, I was afraid that our little dog, Brownie, might be in the flames. I tried to escape from this strange woman a few times. Then finally I broke away. Running out of her house as fast I could, the woman shouted, "Get back here!" Ignoring her shouts, I just kept running toward our house now engulfed in huge flames and clouds of dense smoke. By this time the fire trucks and firefighters were on the scene.

In a flash, I saw my little puppy, waging her tail and running all around. It was autumn. There were lots of dry leaves on the ground. She was delighted to be outside among all the commotions.

My little brother Tommy, on the other hand was giving the firefighters a hard time. He was in the house, trying to put out the blazing flames, with little cups of water. They managed to drag him out, but when they turned their backs, he would run right back in to try to save the house. What a hero! Finally, they took him away from the scene. Another close call for Tom.

The inspectors discovered and declared that the cause of the fire was due to faulty wiring. My parents had just had all new plumbing installed, and spent a small fortune on fixing up the place. We lost family photos, furniture, appliances, bedding, everything. We got out with just the clothes on our backs. The house was totally destroyed. We were invited to stay at a neighbours' home until we found another place to live. For a while Tommy and I slept at the feet of Mom and Dad on a pull out couch. This was such a difficult time for my parents. They were heartbroken!

The unfortunate thing was that my parents were underinsured. They were never able to recover this great loss of material goods. They were however, extremely grateful that Tommy and I were safe! ~

We were forced to move. With little money, my Dad rented a small house on the grounds where he worked as a diesel mechanic for a big potato chip factory. Dad would bring home these humungous clear plastic bags full of fresh crispy potato chips.

This move also meant new school and new friends. One day while playing baseball with a new girlfriend Pauline, I ended up getting a big whack in the forehead with her baseball bat. Standing poised, like the professionals, ready for action, back-catcher, then whack! Obviously standing too close behind her, Right in the head! That incident cost me four stitches and a few tears. Perhaps it knocked a little more sense into me, or did I lose some?

We had lived at Federal Farms for a couple of years; when my Mom, fed up with her obesity, requested to be admitted into the hospital. This tightly controlled facility would force her to lose weight. She had gotten quite over weight and needed to do something drastic. After the birth of my brother Tommy, she just seemed to let herself go. The constant stress of financial worries, along with the demands of raising two small children, and working out of the home some, definitely contributed.

Most of all there was the hereditary factor, since her Mom was over-weight, and her Grandmother, and some of her relatives. When stress abounded, she fed her stomach instead of her soul, hoping to fill the gaps with food instead of the bread of life.

However, we all must resist the temptation to over indulge, especially me. The doctors decided to put Mom on a starvation diet of just water, tea or coffee. Sure, this obtained quick results, but it was only temporary. Eventually the weight would creep back on.

While in hospital, Mom got a new roommate, a kind lady from Mapleville. Mom shared her dream of owning a home for the elderly one day, with this lady. After working in some terribly run nursing homes over the years, she wanted to make a difference. Mom just could not get over the abuse and neglect going on in many of these institutions. It was deplorable. Mom loved the old folks, they reminded her of her Grand-parents who raised her. She had a big heart of compassion.

Then Mrs. Sydor told her about this big gorgeous home in Mapleville that was up for sale. Mom confided that she really did not have any money. However, she thought that she could always make inquiries. It might be worth a try, even if the owner just rented her the house. All enthusiastic now, Mom got out of the hospital and headed straight up to see this place.

She met with Dr. Bennett, the long time owner. He was a well-established dentist, kind and sympathetic. After hearing Mom's concern, and sensing her determination, Dr. Bennett agreed to rent this outstanding property to establish a lovely senior's home. Now we could move in, with option to buy at a very reasonable price. He even left some furniture. Mom was confident that she could run a "Home away from Home" for older folks in need of tender loving care. With only $100.00 in her bank account, Mom had the guts to take a chance, and go for it.

My parents took the risk, and purchased this grandiose home, they named it "Maple Lodge." This picturesque property on the main road into town, included a waterway, with an island. It was complete with a white bridge, towering windmill and rustic artificial well. Gigantic weeping willow trees overhung the waters that flowed around the island. Truly, this was one of the most prestigious properties in the area.

Tommy and I thought we were on fantasy island. My brother and I had landed in paradise as children. On about 3/4 of an acre of land, they had creatively decorated the backyard and side of the huge house. The landscape was sprinkled with a multitude and extraordinary array of colours, flowers, plants and shrubs of every description. The magnificent fragrance of lilacs in early spring, MMMmmm! Hyacinths, roses, petunias, Wow! Towering cedar hedges divided the back yard into sections. Brownie just loved to trot under and through those bushes enjoying the cool shade.

It was exceptional as children to have all these neat places to hide out and discover. We would invite friends over to play great 'Hide n Seek' and adventure games. The grounds had been well kept with immaculate care. Giant blue spruce trees, arrayed the front yard enveloped by the paved circular driveway. We were on top of the world now.

I was about nine years old, and my brother seven when we moved to this enchanting place. Filled with compassion, Mom wanted to nurture and care for the dear souls who needed it with dignity. She always bought and cooked the best of food. She ensured that all the nurses and staff were of like mind and quality. Mom was quite proud of her accomplishments, and made a good reputation for herself and her work.

Our family lived in the basement, which was cool in the summer, and cozy in the winter. We had these two big fancy stone fireplaces, one on the main floor, and one in our basement living room. Still, Mom would never allow us to light them. She was in constant fear of another fire starting.

My job was to help Mom by serving the old folks their meals on individual trays. Often I would cut the grass on the large lawn, without complaint. Dad worked full time as a diesel mechanic. After a while, Mom bought a little tractor to mow the lawn, now that was fun! Tommy and I now fought over who could cut the grass.

Mom would buy cute little yellow ducklings in the spring for the pond. However, darkness loomed. By winter, the local teenage vandals were shooting them down in the night. It was heart breaking to see all the blood on the snow and ice where they had slaughtered and stolen the grown ducks. Obscurity hung about.

After coming home from work Dad would typically relax on his lounging chair feet up, and dive into his books. My Dad was the epitome of a book worm. He would sit and read for hours at a stretch, not at all aware of the things or conversations going on around him. Most of the time he was consumed in the thralls of the Encyclopedia Britannica, devouring sections on wars, politics and the history of wars.

Chapter 4

"Six Months To Live"

Soon trepidation and sickness would endeavour to spoil the happiness of moving into our new home and business. Shortly after arriving in Mapleville at the age of nine, I was unexpectedly overcome with high fevers of up to 105°. My distraught parents would rush me to the nearest Doctor's office. On occasion they would refer me to the nearest hospital for treatment. My Dad would tenderly wrap me in a soft blanket and carry me out to the car. My body so weak at times I could hardly walk.

After treating the symptoms with aspirins and antibiotics, the fevers would fiercely return. Laying in Mom and Dad's bed, brought a certain amount of comfort. The extreme heat from the fevers would burn me up, then icy cold chills would force me to shiver and shake uncontrollably. No appetite, just aches and pains in by bones. The continuous cycle of visiting doctors was getting ridiculous, and it was really scaring my parents.

These high fevers persisted for over a year, accompanied by sharp stabbing pains in my lower back and side. They would just pump me full of drugs, and send me home. It was useless. This was apparently more than a simple flu. Then one day, my Mom insisted they take x-rays to get to the root of the problem.

There was great weight loss. My complexion was stark white. I began to look more like a frail skeleton. The fevers kept attacking with persistency. First I was admitted to "York County Hospital" in Newmarket. Here they abstracted bone marrow from my collar bone and breastbone for biopsies. They were looking for cancer, or Tuberculosis or some other disease. These exploratory surgeries have left their ugly scars on my collar bone and chest.

After countless needles, oodles of antibiotics and various tests, the doctors decided to send me to 'The Hospital for Sick Children' in downtown Toronto. This famous hospital is a renowned world training centre for MD's, Specialists and Pediatricians. For months I was forced to remain there. Day after day, needle after painful needle, test after test. They crammed large doses of penicillin into my thin arms attempting to keep me alive. Forever on intravenous tubes, hands and arms swelled from the needles. Feeling more like a guinea pig then a young girl, enduring it was difficult at times, but my spirit was good.

The various symptoms, were problematic for the doctors as some thought that I had cancer, then Tuberculosis. Finally they came to a conclusion. Without a miraculous improvement, I would not survive another six months. There was nothing else the Doctors could do! My condition was deteriorating. They hung an impending death sentence on me. My parents were distraught.

Throughout this whole ordeal I never felt afraid, or very lonely. It was always such a thrill to hear Mom's wonderful voice say "Haallooo Denise." She has such a big heart, her love for me just exploded into my soul, and room. Secure and truly loved, I never felt alarmed, she gave me strength, and vitality. Mom was always very affectionate and caring. Inside, I knew there was hope. Soon I would be out of there, somehow.

As a young child, living in the hospital was more like an escapade to me. Regularly I would visit the other kids, hang out with the nurses and offer to help them when I could. Occupying my time, I tried to keep busy. Mom always brought me a cute little doll, or some Libby's deep brown beans, my favourite. During the day, and into the evenings my small transistor radio played the latest hits of the 60's.

The doctors agreed to transfer me to another hospital called the 'Princess Margaret Hospital.' This hospital specializes in cancer treatment and therapy. However, being admitted to this hospital brought on much more anxiety and distress to my parents, as many patients never made it out of there alive. The city smelled rancid with pollution, and it appeared so cold and concrete outside my window. Yet, love surrounded me.

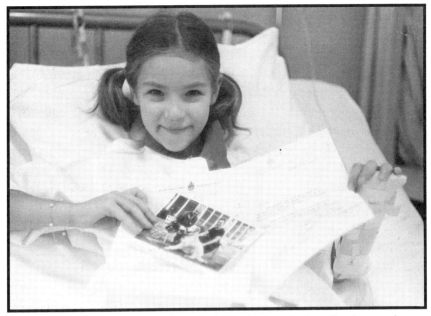

Nine years old and six months to live! The day I received my first letter and picture of the Hon. John Diefenbaker, former Prime Minister of Canada.

My Mom will never forget the drive home from the Princess Margaret one weekend visit. I matter of factly instructed her of my wishes, "When I die, I want you to give all of my organs to another little girl, so she can live." I had heard that there was always a need for organs. Mom got so upset and disturbed at this request that she had to take tranquilizers to calm herself down. This was so hard on my Mom. No one ever told me that I was dying.

Often, in the middle of the night I would suddenly wake up, with this incredible urge to make myself toast and honey. Sneaking into the hospital kitchenette, I helped myself. It tasted so good, succulent, delicious.

We never went to church because my Mom had a frightening experience with a Priest in Switzerland when she was thirteen. He was a sex pervert. My Dad has a hard time believing, especially when he can't see God face to face. But, I was dying! Nevertheless, I thank God that one night, my Mother in desperation, actually cried out to God and asked for His help. This was the most important thing that she ever did. God heard her cry and saved me.

The doctors were at a standstill, there was nothing else they could do. They only gave me a few months to live. As I grow and mature in the things of God, I have come to realize that God has a purpose and a plan for our lives. Sometimes, what the devil means for evil, God will turn it around for good. God prepares us for the road ahead. The Bible says in Romans 8:28 *"All things work together for good to those who are in Christ Jesus, and called according to his purposes and plans."* Life does have its fluctuations and there are repercussions to every free choice we make.

Miraculously, quite by fluke, or was it 'Divine' intervention? The doctors finally discovered a tumour. It was the size of a 'tennis-ball' they reported, and it was found deep in my lung. They had given me a bronchiscoptical, (that's what it sounded like) and had 'accidentally' punctured this tumour. This was the culprit trying to kill me. Thank God it was not malignant either. It just disappeared in time, no reoccurrences either! God had other plans for my life as we will see.

In grade three we had an assignment to compose and then speak in front of the class about what we wanted to become in the future. My essay was entitled "My Dream;" it was regarding the notion that I hoped to be a lady lawyer when I grew up. My aim was to defend the innocent, and talk about jurisprudence (the philosophy of law). With the help of Dad's encyclopedias everyone thought it was well written. Nonetheless I was unable to deliver it as I had hoped because of being a patient in the hospital.

My dear Mom took it upon herself to mail a copy of it to the Right Hon. John Diefenbaker, a former Prime Minister of Canada, and Judy LaMarsh a lady lawyer. Mr. Diefenbaker received my letters with joy, and so began our relationship as pen-pals. He invited our family to come and visit him on Parliament Hill.

Mom jumped at the opportunity, and packed up Tommy and me, while Dad worked. We headed to Ottawa. It was an exciting trip. We stayed at the luxurious 'Chateau Laurier Hotel.' It was posh, with very high ceilings and small windows. Mr. Diefenbaker gave us a personal tour of the Parliament Buildings. Then he presented me with a copy of the Canadian Charter of Rights and Freedoms which he autographed, and his working pen. He was a kind good man. It was an honour to meet and speak with this great politician.

The Hon. John Diefenbaker even called us, "His very special friends." My brother, Mom and I were quite thrilled to be treated so royally. Somehow, the media caught wind of my plight, and the Toronto Star, Telegram and Ottawa Citizen published articles on "Dief saves dying girl." It was very exciting to get all of his letters. Some of them were even hand written.

Probably, one reason that I have always had such a zeal for life, and a cheery outlook was because I had spent so much time confined in hospitals. At this age, and in grade three now, I had a couple of close girlfriends, Brenda and Cheryl. We were quite the team, as we would sing and pretend that we were a music group; we would gleefully bounce around the school playground, arms embracing each other, singing our hearts out. Some of our favourites included "These boots are made for walk'n," "Sixteen Tons," and "We all live in a Yellow Submarine." Do you remember these oldies?

My evenings were spent helping Mom upstairs in our Maple Lodge Nursing Home. Sometimes I would read letters or articles to Katie, a blind lady who was a patient. I really enjoyed helping Mom out wherever I could, with these dear old souls. You know what? With more than forty patients who lived in our home over the years, no one ever told me about the gospel of Jesus Christ. Now that is so startling to me now.

When playing games with Tom, we would cheat and fight. Once we were playing darts in the basement of the Nursing Home my parents owned. Tommy must have been about seven years' old. Since I hated to lose, I moved a dart closer to the center. "Oops," he caught me. Tom was upset. We started yelling and screaming at each other. I went running as fast as I could up the stairs as a dart flew toward me. Swoosh! It landed right into my right arm. "Ahhhhh, he got me!" I hollered. It was sticking out, and it hurt. He got quite a spanking from Dad for that one.

CANADA

LEADER OF THE OPPOSITION – CHEF DE L'OPPOSITION

O t t a w a,
August 25th, 1966.

Dear Denise,

 Your mother has sent me a copy of
your essay entitled "My Dream" and it is a
very well-written piece of work, particularly
for a nine-year old.

 When I was a small boy I decided to be
a lawyer and worked long and hard to achieve
that end.

 When I commenced the study of law there
were few women in the profession but things have
changed and there are today many women practising
law.

 Hoping that you will soon be returning
home, and that you will come to see me in Ottawa
one day,

   I am,

   With warmest good wishes,

Denise Wiche,
5th Floor D,
Hospital for Sick Children,
Toronto,
Ontario.

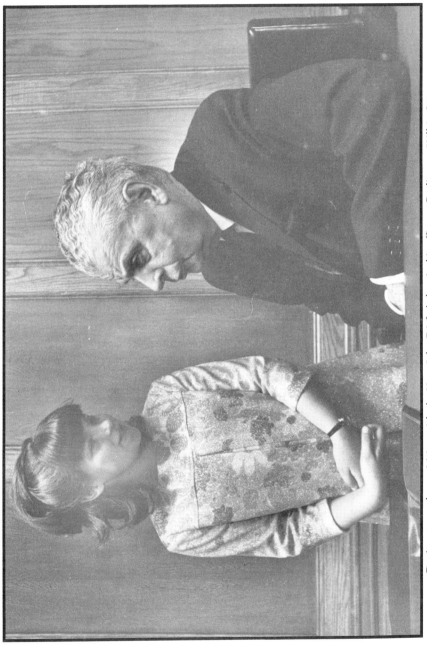

Denise at age eleven visiting with the Hon. John Diefenbaker, in his office on Parliament Hill in Ottawa.

We really fought like "Dog and Cat," until one significant day. Tom's masculinity appeared. Suddenly he was bigger and stronger than I. With no hope of winning again, I gave up. No more fighting with my younger brother, from now on we would just be friends.

Chapter 5

"The Cycle Of Shame ..."

Straightaway after the secret rape at the age of thirteen, I began to indulge in drugs, alcohol, and cigarettes. Most victims of rape or incest will turn to addictive substances as a form of escape from their pain. The shame and loss of self-respect and self-worth had consumed me. I totally let myself go. With no respect or dignity left for myself, I was headed for disaster.

Believing now, that *I was totally ruined, no decent man would ever want to marry me. I was just like a piece of garbage, so I might as well try to get back at men.* From this time on I became promiscuous, wanting to control men. Always getting hurt, ending up used and abused. Pain sears through my heart as I write these words. ***Because of being a rape victim, I endured many days, weeks, months and years of self-destructive behaviour.***

Of course the more I drank and did drugs the more I would lose my inhibitions. The more I let myself go, the more I needed to deaden and numb the guilt and remorse. So alcohol and other drugs became my anaesthetic. The vicious cycle of addictions overcame me. Dependent on these substances to function and relate, I would jump from one bad relationship to another. Most of the men just had sex in mind, and could easily take advantage of my inebriation, emotional distress and insecurity. The good men who really cared about me, I dumped. Because I felt so unworthy of them, they were too good for me. When would this roller coaster end?

By the time I was fifteen years old, I had developed into quite an attractive young woman. With a shapely body, I got much attention. By this time I had totally lost all interest in any academic training. Drugs became my god, getting high was my goal in life, and so there was no desire to go to school. Thus, I dropped out of High School with the "No God" mentality.

It was getting ever more difficult to function in a straight environment when so spaced out on chemicals. My sights were set on getting my drivers licence, getting a car, getting a job and getting my own apartment. Get, get, get ... This would provide complete freedom and independence from my parents. Rebellion was becoming a stronghold in my character, with an 'I don't care,' bad attitude. Detaching and withdrawing emotionally from my Mom and Dad, and appearing quite independent and mature for my age, I got away with murder.

One night "Surprise," my Dad was waiting up for me when I came home late from a party. Very high on 'LSD' a strong, mind-altering hallucinogenic drug, this turned out to be a very bad "trip." He was furious that I was drunk and stoned. (Today, I sure couldn't blame him). Anyway, he smacked me across the face and called me a "Swine" in that deep German accent. That hurt. I did not argue. Soon my Mother appeared, coming to my rescue.

Associating with people much older than I had its bad influence on me. These new friends of mine were the town derelicts. They were the hard core Speed freaks, the women who had bad reputations. The vagrants who swore constantly, and partied like animals. No conscience, no rules. Just anarchy. The 'If it feels good, do it,' attitude. The rough, tough bunch of drug addicts and alcoholics. So selfish, and so self-centred we were.

Today I am curious about their childhood conditions, and wonder about their backgrounds. What abuse and neglect did they have to endure as children and young teens, how many of them had been sexually abused, raped or beaten profusely? How many of their parents were alcoholics and self-centred?

For some strange reason, I never took up repeating their foul language. Still, I indulged in everything else they did, except hitting up with needles. Yuch, I had enough of the needles being jabbed into my veins as a 9-year-old, so there was no way I was going to shoot up! Thank

God or I probably would have died of an overdose. In the book of Proverbs it says that *'bad company corrupts character'*. Proverbs. 16:29; 24:1

One night two of my girlfriends and I were in a car with Jackie's Mom. Her Mom's boyfriend was driving. We were on the highway going about 60 miles an hour. We happened to be right in front of that garage where I had been raped. An unknown vehicle, without warning, suddenly pulled out in front of us. As we tried to veer around him, he idiotically turned left, and hit us on the side.

We went flying in the air! A deafening crash, bang, crunch the noise of heavy steel hitting and smashing. It was as if we were in slow motion inside that large vehicle. Like rag dolls in a gigantic dryer. Our limp helpless bodies tossed back and forth. Our car spun around, landing on the opposite side of the road, facing the opposite way, with the car on its side. Back then we were not wearing seatbelts either. Whew!

When I came to, Sheila, my other friend was tugging and pushing to get me out of the car. We could hear voices from the outside screaming at us, "Hurry up and get out of the car before it catches on fire!" After we had all gotten out safely, we just hugged each other, and thanked God that we were all alive. That was a miracle. Although I had a black eye and some big bruises, it was a wonder that no one was killed. The driver of the other car vanished, never to be found.

At the age of fifteen, I started going out with Barry. He was about twenty-one, blond, and very handsome. I fell in love with him. It was actually infatuation and obsession. I had to know where he was all the time and who he was with. I just wanted to be with him every minute. He became another god. He was my first real love. Barry's Dad had died of a heart attack when he was quite young. Barry was a heavy drinker. We were intimate. Eventually, his old girlfriend Lundy came back into the picture. She was older than I. Barry decided to dump me, and go back with her. I was severely heartbroken. Perhaps, it was a blessing in disguise.

Soon after our breakup my parents sent me to Switzerland. My mother thought that it would be good for me to get away from Barry and all those bad characters for a while. She knew how crushed I was over our break up. Every time I saw a yellow Camaro, or a man who looked like him in the slightest, my heart would jump.

Switzerland is one of the most pulchritudinous countries in the world. The houses are architecturally unique and most have extravagant wood carvings. My Grandfather owned a licensed Restaurant amidst the landscape. They called it the "Loewen," translated Lion. It was on a main street, in a small village, in a huge valley. Out the front door, and from my window you could see the most gigantic towering rocky mountains above, and rolling pastures below. It was breath taking to observe their majesty. The people are most friendly and hospitable. The air fresh. The food was excellent. Usually breakfast consisted of a variety of Swiss cheeses, meat, fresh rye bread, butter and jams. Lunches are the major meals in Europe. They were the largest meal of the day, and dinner was light. Everything was always tasty and delicious. Love those tasty wiener schnitzels, knackwurst, sauerkraut, noodles, goulash … Getting hungry?

My aunt Sami is a fantastic chef. The smell of the deep fryer cooking crispy battered chicken and chips were enticing. She married a bit later in life, her husband helped with the Restaurant, and he worked as a guard in the local prison. My Mom had four sisters, no brothers. One of her sisters was suddenly killed in a car accident when she was in her early twenties. That tragic event shook everyone up. My aunts are wonderful. They have always been kind and generous to me. They had helped to raise Rita too.

My Grandmother had died some years earlier. Aunt Sami ran the restaurant business. The initial plan was that I would be a waitress there, and learn to speak the German language. My parents urged me to enroll in a private school there and make something of myself. However, I just wanted to make money and get high.

Not many days after my arrival I started to feel nauseous. My aunt made an appointment for me to visit the local doctor. He took a urine sample and informed me in German, a language I hardly knew, that I was going to have a "baby." Shocked, and upset, I went for a long walk up into the Swiss Alps. I cried and cried, in anguish. I had never felt so isolated.

Aunt Sami was also pregnant with her first child, Marcos. She had been getting all kinds of delightful baby clothes, and baby stuff. So I thought, *Well, I am just going to work as long as I can work, have the baby and go on with life.* It was not possible for me to tell anyone I was pregnant. Ashamed, and afraid of rejection, I kept silent. My Aunt was getting a huge stock of baby clothes, so I began stealing and stashing some cute little outfits for my baby, and the getaway day.

One day a customer who owned a bar in Liechtenstein came to have lunch at our Restaurant. We started a conversation, and he offered me a job at his Hotel. He told me that he got many American customers, and was looking for someone who spoke fluent English. He promised that I would make a lot more money at his place. So I felt things were set. I would save as much money as I could. Have the baby, and write my parents a letter of congratulations announcing the birth of their new Grandchild. This was my plan, but still I knew my parents would be very disappointed.

Some of those regular drunks in the 'Loewen' would get so obnoxious. I enjoyed getting out of there occasionally. One cool, drizzly day I took my Grandfather's moped for a ride. Coming around the sharpest corner I had ever seen, I lost control. The motor bike went right over the center line of the narrow road and into the on coming lane. Crashing, then flying off the bike, smack dab up into the windshield of this white van. The two men held their arms up in self defence and shock as they watched me smash into the windshield head first. "Oohh" Bang! Down like a fly I went. They never ran me over, thank God.

Part of me rejoiced, thinking that I might have a miscarriage, and that would solve my dilemma. Another part of me was so scared, afraid and lonely. How could I ever repay for the damage to the moped, the embarrassment to my relatives and save face?

Astonishingly, like the Bionic woman, I didn't even have a scratch. Divine protection I'd say. The bike was totalled. When I got back to the Restaurant, this was the opportunity I had to call my Mom. I had to tell her that I had wrecked Grandad's moped. Upon hearing her familiar voice, when she answered the phone, I began to cry uncontrollably. Barely able to utter a word, she understood that I was in a bike accident and that I was physically unhurt. Yet my emotions were just tearing apart inside. Of course my Mom sensed that there was something seriously wrong. She kept asking me if I were okay? "Yeah, I'm okay," I sobbed reluctantly. She caught the next direct flight from Toronto to Zurich.

The next day she was there! So radiant, loving and kind. But, "Oh, what dread?" *Should I tell her I was pregnant? How could I tell her that I was pregnant? She would be so hurt, and disappointed. Dad would flip, for sure he would go into a rage, and it would bring so much shame to our family.* Mom was so proud of her children, and her accomplishments as a successful business woman. She had even run for Counsellor in our Ward, and had dreams of becoming a great Politician. I was convinced that this news would ruin everything. An emotional wreck, under so much turmoil, should I tell her, or shouldn't I?

A couple of days later, a regular drunk, reached over and lifted up my skirt with his hand. Incensed, I just turned around and belted him right across the head with a loud 'smack'. "You creep!" I shouted. Then frustrated and humiliated, I ran out of the restaurant, up the stairs to my room, and began to cry hysterically. My mother had witnessed the event and she took off after me to find out why I was so overly upset. She tried to comfort me. Sitting next to me on the bed, she cradled me in her arms, as I cried in agony.

Now she knew after fifteen minutes of unmanageable anguish that there was something more to why I was crying so much. Mom kept asking, "Denise, what is the matter? Tell me what is wrong, You can tell me, I love you." So slowly and with hesitation I began to tell her that I was pregnant. She then wept with me and said, "Well what do you want to do?" " Well," I responded, like I think any 16-year-old would under the circumstances, I said "Well, Mom, I don't know, I guess I'm gonna have a baby."

My Mother based her advice to me from her own experience of being an illegitimate child. In addition she also went through the ordeal of having a child out of wedlock herself. Mom instructed, "Denise, you are only sixteen, you have your whole life ahead of you. I want to take you back home, so you can see a good Doctor who is a real professional specialist, and they can just give you an operation. You are still so young.

Just come back home with me, and we will go from there. This'll be the best thing for you."

So I thought, *Well, if my Mom thinks its OK, and the doctors think its OK to have this operation, then it must be OK.* A few days later we headed back to Canada. I knew that Barry was the father of this baby, and I let him know it. He tried to deny it, claiming that he had prostate troubles. I told him not to worry, that I was going to have an operation to end it anyway. He was relieved. Surprisingly, he came to visit me while I was in the hospital. He brought me some flowers and a magazine. It was a thrill to see him. Unfortunately, he did not stay long. There I was, alone again.

Rationalizing, I denied any personhood to this pregnancy. It was all a matter of fact, business-like, quick and easy, no questions asked. They did the abortion in York County Hospital, in Newmarket, Ontario. I just wanted to put this episode behind me and go on with my life.

However, 'going on' meant to continue getting drunk, taking drugs and being a promiscuous young woman. My drinking and substance abuse became a lot worse after the abortion. I had absolutely no respect for myself. I just craved attention, and let myself go while under the influence of alcohol. I just did not care anymore about what happened to me, I deserved the worse. I was a wretched tramp.

A shocking event happened while away in Europe. A good friend of mine, Jimmy, only sixteen years old had committed suicide. His girlfriend, Julie and I had been good friends also. Jimmy and I rode the school bus together. They were at one of those notorious bush parties that we used to go to, flowing with beer and drugs for underage teens. Julie was found talking to some other guy. Jimmy was hurt. He got so inebriated. They said, he calmly went home, walked up the stairs into his bedroom, got the shot gun out of the cupboard, and shot himself in the head. Teen suicide, what a total waste. What a crime! Jimmy was such a nice guy. He never mouthed off, or tried to prove himself. He was tall, lanky and good looking too. We never heard about his real Dad, but his new step father was an alcoholic though. A precious life snatched again by alcohol.

Many emotions and terrible thoughts must have cascaded through his mind under the poisonous influence of alcohol that night. This book is for you too, Jimmy. I am so sorry that you took your own life. The instigator to your death I am sure, was all that booze you drank. Life is a blessing and we can make it through anything with God's help!

At the age of sixteen, I too was a mess, emotionally. Nevertheless, fooling everyone with a self-confident mask. A drop out now, my education meant nothing to me it just seemed like a total waste of time. Feeling like an adult, thinking school was for kids, I had to find a way to make money. With the help of my wonderful Mom, I got my first job working for her lawyer in Aurora. Here I learned some basic filing and reception work.

Every Wednesday I became his private chauffeur, driving him to downtown Toronto. He would instruct me to go shopping or do whatever I wanted, as long as I met him back at his small office or the dingy bar downstairs at a certain time. Then drive him safely back to the office or home because he would be so disgustingly drunk. When drunk, he became very loud and obnoxious. He was miserable and would slobber all over the place. The booze ended up killing him as it destroyed his liver, his reputation, his marriage and God knows what else … Wonder what the root causes to his addictions were?

Chapter 6

"Life In The Fast Lanes"

My personality was developing into quite the assertive, self-confident woman, and I genuinely liked people. In actuality, I had just become tougher and bolder too. With delight I had purchased my first car at sixteen from a friend of Barry's. Mom cosigned, I was working for the lawyer, had a tiny little apartment and now my very own car, a 1973 orange Toyota. This possession really boosted my independence and ego.

After scouting through the classified ads for a good opportunity to try something new, and make more money, I decided to try sales.

Sold shoes for a few months, that was boring! The wages were the minimum. Then I began to work in a bar with a girlfriend. Here we made really big tips, and it was the party life. We had money for booze and drugs. I loved to travel and somehow managed to save some money for trips to Switzerland over the years. At the age of nineteen, I booked myself a cruise to the Mediterranean Sea. After flying to Torrimolinos, Spain and getting on the ship there, we cruised to Casablanca, Morocco, Tangiers, Tunis, Sicily, Naples, Rome, Cannes-France and then back to Spain. It was fascinating, and quite the adventure. The ship was enormous.

Making hasty acquaintances, we drank, gambled, and toured together. Pompeii was hot, sandy and desolate, especially after a heavy night of drunkenness. Dehydration city! The huge corroding pillars marked another period in time when ungodliness reigned. They had destroyed, deserted, and abandoned this place. Total desolation. Casablanca was hustling with snake charmers and merchants greedy for your money. Morocco, Tangiers and Tunis were dirty, and smelly from camels and many strange aromas.

Sicily was beautiful, and much more civilized. Naples colourful and they had the best ice cream. Rome was fascinating! We visited the Trevi fountain, the Colosseum and best of all St. Peter's Basilica. This is the largest church building in the world. The moment you entered this sacred place you could feel an awesome presence. The architecture and the art were so exuberating. The history and significance of this church building of Jesus Christ were inspiring. Real Michael Angelo sculptures and paintings arrayed the cathedral. There was a magnificently crafted life size statue of Jesus Christ.

The annoying thing was that after I returned home, I could not stop scratching. Before I went berserk, or cracked up, I rushed to the doctor's office. He then referred me to a skin specialist. The prognosis, 'scabies'. It felt much worse after the doctor explained to me what scabies were. These little microscopic insects that crawl right under your skin and lay their eggs inside your flesh, causing terrific itching and scratching. Thank God for the soaps and creams that wiped out those little vermin.

Looking for love in all the wrong places, going from one bad relationship to another. This vicious cycle of love'em and leave'em, heart break after heart break, went on for many years. It is a marvel that I never contracted the HIV/AIDS virus.

At the age of 21, Debbie, a girlfriend and I took a wild trip out to Long Beach California. I drove my used 1977 bright green Mazda GLC. We rented a small apartment for a month. It was cheap. This city is where we were first introduced to cocaine. As I reflect on my turbulent past, it behooves me how often I was shielded from death and serious injury. We played Russian roulette with our lives. The number of times I was intoxicated and stoned while driving, is scary. The number of times I was in the arms of strange men who could have easily mutilated me is creepy. Several times I could have died of drug overdoses and alcoholic poisoning. God sure had his protective hand on me. His mercy endures forever.

Not caring at all about my health condition, or the misuse my body daily underwent while consuming vast amounts of drugs. Acid, THC, smoking drugs, drinking booze and whatever else we could get high on, began to take its toll. This stuff is out to destroy you.

My parents were going through difficult times as well. They had given up the Nursing Home years earlier, and moved up to the family cottage near Parry Sound. My Mom had gotten quite discouraged and stressed out about all the new Nursing Home Regulations. It was going to cost thousands of dollars to renovate to new government specifications. To top it off, rumours about my Dad having an affair with one of the staff, were scandalous. Fed up and emotionally drained, Mom practically gave the home away, owing thousands of dollars in back debts. She just wanted out of there and far away from that small town. Dad still worked as an auto mechanic and Mom got a job at a local Department store. Moving back to Ontario and in with my parents up near Parry Sound was peaceful.

Working as a bartender and cocktail waitress up in Northern Ontario, I can barely recall driving home that 25 mile stretch most of the time. After binges of drinking and smoking drugs I would fight with all my strength just to stay awake while driving. Many nights I barely made that course. Was it not for the flashing lights of a snow plough, or angels on chariots guiding my way home I would not be here today?

The pace was far too slow for me up in the great white northern country. It was too isolated. I decided to move to Newmarket. More people, more parties, better working opportunities and old friends. One cold winter stormy day I was driving out to Bolton from Newmarket to work in a bar, with my good friend Cathy. Alone in my car, and as was usual at the time, lit up a joint and began to get very high. The roads were so snow covered and icy, on which I decided to drive with my 4-way emergency flashers. Now that is bad driving conditions.

Then suddenly, without warning my back tires lost control and I began to drive up the middle of the highway. Sideways. A car was quickly approaching. Head on. At the last minute I knew we were going to crash. Letting go of the steering wheel. I put my arms up over my head. Then crash, boom, bash, the car went flying off the road and right into a big field. I thank God there happened to be NO fences, poles, rivers, rocks or obstacles in my path at the particular spot where my car flew. Another miracle!

When I came to, the Pablo Cruz tape was blaring aloud. All the windows were smashed or missing. The brisk, cold air and snow were blowing in my face. The passenger's door was now crunched right up next to me. Quickly, automatically, I reached down to make sure my legs and body were still intact. Yes, slowly I got out of the car shaking, and shivering.

The thought never even occurred to me to see how the people were in the other car. How self-centred, how stoned, how disgusting? Abruptly, a kind gentleman appeared from nowhere, asking me if I were all right. "OKAY … I think, " I replied, disoriented and shook up. Then he said, "Maybe you better come with me, you are bleeding from the head." Now petrified and paranoid, I climbed into his pick-up truck. The Good Samaritan drove me to the nearest Hospital for treatment. I still do not know who this man was. Again, by God's grace I was not seriously injured.

Deciding that I did not really want to be a bartender and cocktail waitress for the rest of my life, I took the challenge to sell cars. Determined, and ambitious as their first saleswoman, I got right into it and sold vehicles. Sales were exciting, I have always loved meeting new people, I enjoyed the business world. After a few months I thought that perhaps I should get my Real Estate Licence and sell properties to make more money instead. So I did. Enrolling in Humber College, I completed and passed the courses and sought a Realtor to take me on as a Rookie.

Back up North, my parents renovated and settled into what used to be our summer cottage, situated on the shores of beautiful Bluerock Lake. This home is on a spectacular piece of property with 60 feet of water frontage. Close to the dusty gravel road, there stood the old log cabin, which used to be the old 'ice hut' many years ago. Herb and Agnes, old family friends, used to store huge blocks of ice in there for the refrigerators. Mom, the creative artist, painted cute little red hearts on the windows' shutters, and I moved in. Heading back to Parry Sound, was exuberating, the air fresh, the peace, the security to be with my loving family, again.

The timing was bad on this move, however, as the Real Estate market crashed. Mortgage rates skyrocketed and it was a joke trying to sell vacation properties during this time. No one was buying vacation properties while interest rates skyrocketed. After a couple of years of struggling financially and only a few sales to my credit, it was time to move on. A young woman with potential, headed for the big city of Toronto.

My first position was landing a job for a Ski Resort at Blue Mountain. As the rental agent in their Toronto office, I had access to a higher class of people. Beginning to grow up, and mature, a part of me really wanted to become a respectable decent woman.

After a couple of years of renting out chalets, it was time to move up the ladder. After checking the newspaper for work I applied as an Insurance Agent to sell all lines of insurance: Home, Commercial, Life, Disability, Travel, Group and Auto. This was a great leap forward. They gave me a brand-new company car, an elegant silver 1982 Chevy Malibu-Classic with soft burgundy interior. After rigorous studies and technical exams I obtained the three Government licences required to sell insurance in Ontario.

Studying about life insurance, fiscal responsibilities, contemplating the future and financial planning, forced me to examine myself. I began to slow down somewhat. With the God-given talents to persuade people, and sincerely concerned about their future, I became a very successful saleswoman at the age of twenty-five. In a short while, with determination I was becoming 'Sales Person of the Month', and keeping very busy. Certificates of achievement and trophies began to cover my wall. Things were looking up. However, in private, I was still leading a wild life, still addicted to alcohol and other drugs.

In the winter of 1982/83 my Mom and I got this brain storm and decided to take a risk and open a small Restaurant and Catering business. The building was stuccoed white, with a slanted roof, it was situated right in the middle of a European type Village, at the base of Blue Mountain. Here stood about forty Swiss-style chalets that slept anywhere from 4-40 guests. These chalets included large stone fireplaces, a sauna and dishwashers. With my Swiss Mom as Chief cook, and me as the promotional director and assistant we did quite well. On weekends I would go up to Blue Mountain with Joyce, Joanne or one of my other girlfriends to cater food, ski, and help Mom. We had a lot of fun meeting people, and going skiing. We always ended up drinking in the bars or chalet parties.

It was a great winter up at Blue Mountain, but when the spring came, it died up there. My courageous Mom, tried to make a go of it in the summer, with the prospects of catering for a summer Tennis Camp. It was here that I met the most handsome, wonderful, kind, man and doctor.

Benn, an ear, nose and throat Specialist, had come up to the Tennis Camp to get some fresh air, instruction, and exercise. His wife, also a doctor, had recently left him for another man, who also happened to be a doctor. Sounds like the soap opera "General Hospital?" This news really surprised me.

How could any woman want to leave this incredible looking, successful and wonderful man? They had two very young girls, a two year old and the other about five years old. Benn was heartbroken that his wife had left him for someone else.

We really got along well, had fun, and I fell in love with him overnight. My parents were impressed. Benn was perfect for me. A dream comes true! A really nice, prestigious and respectable guy! He was my knight in shining armour? I was ready to settle down.

After a very short time of dating, Benn asked me to come and live with him. It was a two-hour drive from Toronto. Wow, how could I refuse? He treated me with respect. He had class, played the violin, and his parents were in the Salvation Army. Benn owned a large beautiful white painted home, situated on a large lot with big trees. There were big windows. It was bright. He soon bought me the most beautiful engagement ring and promised to marry me, once his divorce came through. Too good to be true.

Without any hesitation, and after being with the insurance company about a year and a half, I took a leave of absence. Giving up my apartment, I moved in with Benn. Everything had happened so fast. We started dating July 4, 1983 on July 25 he presented me with an engagement ring, and by Aug. 6th I had moved into his house. We were in a whirlwind of love and intrigue. The excitement and attractiveness to each other were so strong. Yet, oddly, there was something missing. The house was cluttered with things. It was very still and quiet. His nanny would come to clean and take care of the girls, so I felt a little out of place.

After a week of living with him, I discovered that I was pregnant. The terrible dilemma that I faced now, was that this could not be Benn's baby. The timing was off. He had just given me the most awesome diamond engagement ring, 3/4 of a carat with three marquis diamonds on each side of the large stone. I could not lie to Benn and pretend that he was the father. Besides he was a doctor. Frantic, I called my dear Mom with the perplexity. She exhorted me to just go and have another abortion. "Benn will surely leave you, if he finds out you're pregnant with someone else's kid," she warned. Then I called Sue, a close girlfriend who was studying to be a nurse to see what she thought. She confirmed my mothers prompting and urgency to have an abortion and get rid of the problem. When I hesitated, Sue told me that she would come with me, offering to drive a few miles over to Buffalo. This way no one would ever know …

Again I believed, *if it is okay with my Mom and friends. It is okay with the doctors, and it is okay with the government, than it must be all right!* Jim, a man whom I respected and admired, was a successful young computer giant on his way to the top. He was the biological father to this baby. We had dated for about a year, off and on. Jim had introduced me to his parents, but I was not good enough for him. Our relationship had again ended, for a while. Jim just wanted to be friends now. What a ridiculous statement people make, after having intimate relationships pretending to continue as casual friends. He was not interested in committing to me. Like most men, he just wanted a casual sexual relationship with no strings attached. Typical hedonism for selfish gratification. That is when I met Benn.

Making a trip to Toronto, I had to face Jim with the news of my pregnancy. After all he was partly responsible for getting me pregnant. In turmoil, and in fear I confronted Jim with the news. He became extremely angry and upset. "You better have an abortion," he demanded. "I do not love you, and I never want to see you again!" He shouted. He insisted I get out of his house. Slowly, immensely crushed, and exiled again, I left, as he slammed the door after me. Never had I felt so rejected, ashamed, and alone, or had I?

Chapter 7

"The Paid Assassins"

"Have nothing to do with the fruitless deeds of darkness, but rather expose them." Ephesians. 5:11

Tears roll down my cheeks as I begin to uncover the most horrendous detail of one of the most diabolical procedures practiced by so called, 'Doctors' today.

It was with such ease, one simple telephone call. An appointment was made to "end" this pregnancy. It was too easy! No questions asked. No alternatives or options given or even mentioned. No counselling, nothing! We told Benn we were going shopping or something. My friend Sue offered to accompany me across the American border, it was closest. We came to High Street in Buffalo, up to the elevator to the 6th floor. They had instructed me to bring cash in US. dollars to pay for the procedure. Jim had sent me the $200.00 US for the abortion. The receptionist quickly took the money and told me to sit and wait until they called my name. Nervously, I grabbed a People's magazine and began to flip through it. I could not concentrate on anything, yet I did not want to think about why I was there.

Fear began to grip my heart and feelings of panic twinged through my body. The room was packed with other women. One by one another woman would go off down the hall.

Jumping, when they called my name, my heart raced. A woman had me follow her to a tiny room off the reception area. She had me sit down. Then she asked me two questions, "Any allergies?" and "Do you know why you are here?" "Yeah, I guess so," I replied. This was the sum of my 'counselling' or so called, 'informed consent'. Then she said, "Ok, follow me." She gave me a hospital gown, told me to put it on, and let her know when I was ready. Slowly I changed my clothes as if numb. Then this woman led me down a long corridor to another much smaller waiting room. About five other women were sitting in gowns, glaring into magazines in this dark, gloomy room. We were all smoking cigarettes.

After a few minutes a nurse came in and asked if any of us would like some Tylenols? "Yeah, can I have two bottles?" I asked. She said of course not, and handed me two tablets in a tiny paper cup. I will never forget the one woman, who looked to be in her late 30's, refuse to take any. I could not believe it. It was as if she wanted to feel all the pain, as if to punish herself, like she deserved to suffer. The air was thick and putrid. There really was an atmosphere of reluctancy and death. Yet, one by one the other women went before me. Then came the anxiety of my name being called, it was my turn. The nurse escorted me down another long corridor to a room with a surgical table, a big machine and bright lights.

A woman had me lie down and put my feet up in the cold, steel, stirrups, spread eagle. The doctor was wearing a mask, surgical hat and rubber gloves. He just said "How far are you?" Rather mundanely. "I am not sure. I feel nervous" I replied. "This will only take a few minutes. The machine is a bit loud, just squeeze her hand." He then stuck his fingers up my vagina, and felt my abdomen. Telling the nurse, "She's about ten weeks, or so." He turned on this loud machine and began to lunge it in and out of my womb. While wide awake during the whole procedure, excruciating pain, like no other pierced my insides. Immediately, I began to scream, and yell moving my body up, cringing and trying to close my legs. I begged him to "Please STOP!"

The pain was so severe, it really hurt, I could not stand it! "Please stop, please stop?" I pleaded with him. He just kept repeating, "It is almost over." But he still kept on plunging. It felt like he was ripping and tearing me apart from the inside out, like a razor slashing my insides. Fiercely, I gripped and squeezed the nurse's hand like it was a sponge. I could not believe the intensity of the pain. It was unbearable and seemed to last forever. Twelve or so minutes of this agony seemed like two hours. "*Aghhh ...* " *Oh my God*, I began to think, *What have I done?* When he was finished, I completely curled up into the fetal position on the table, and my brain seemed to go blank. I was in shock! Then I snapped, and thought, *This is it, I am now a vegetable and I will never be the same, it is over, my life is over.* Thoughts of: *put me into an insane asylum* echoed into my conscience. The nurse just wanted to get me out of there. I could not talk anymore.

She mechanically slapped a big pad between my legs and ordered me to get up and get going. They had my money, and my baby, it was over now. She treated me like a piece of meat. It really disturbed me. She started nudging me off the table; complaining that I was taking too long. "Hurry and get up, we have many other people waiting." She sure did not care about how I felt, and the so called "doctor" was nowhere in sight. It was like going in slow motion, like after I had been raped. I began to move slowly and force myself up. It took every ounce of strength to manoeuver. The aftershock was intense. I felt like a zombie, numb.

It became obvious to me years later why the reception area was so far away from where the actual abortions took place. They certainly would not want the women waiting to have their babies aborted hear the screams and cries of those women going through that horrid experience while WIDE AWAKE!

Sue greeted me with a sigh of relief, and said "I am hungry, let's go get something to eat." Still in shock, and hardly able to talk or walk, I leaned against the wall and whispered, "Go ahead, but I am definitely NOT hungry. That was just the most horrible experience I have ever had in my whole life!" Stunned, I just walked along mesmerized, an episode that would go on to haunt me. A traumatic event which would inspire me to risk arrest to warn other women of this horrible procedure. Women need to know the whole truth and aftermath of abortion.

The intense cramping and pain persisted. Feeling exhausted and depressed, I just wanted to lie down and go to sleep. Sue went back to Toronto, and I went back to Benn. Of course I never told him about the abortion, what shame, disgust and horror. However, strangely now, there seemed to be a little tension and distance between us. He had brought me to meet his Christian parents. Benn had asked me not to smoke in their house. He never smoked. Respectfully, I even sacrificed not smoking for him. This was a challenge for me, since I was so addicted to cigarettes.

A few days later, I could feel Benn withdrawing from me. Out of nowhere he announced that he needed, "more time." He felt things were happening too fast, and he hoped that I would understand. He walked out. He said he was going to a bar to meet some of his friends and left me alone in the house. Devastated by this news, and feeling totally rejected, AGAIN. I desperately looked for that bottle of rum. I needed to anaesthetize myself. Overwhelmed with emotions about how I had given up my job for him, given up my apartment for him, and given up this pregnancy for him overwhelmed me.

I began drinking rum and coke, very hurt and distraught. While half bombed and crying I poured myself a hot bath, got a candle, turned out the lights and soaked in the water. Tears streaming down my face.

This was the icing on the cake. Earlier that day, I had driven myself to the nearest hospital emergency because of severe abdominal pains and bloating. The doctor asked me what happened. I told him that I had just had an abortion a few days earlier. He discovered that I had a **bad infection** in my uterus caused by that clinic abortion. He immediately put me on antibiotics, and told me to take it easy. There is NO such thing as a 'safe abortion'! Thoughts of suicide ran through my mind. I was a loser, an idiot, a wretch, useless and no good for nothing!

When Benn arrived home, I was a drunken slob. Surely now, he would see the pig that I really was. Again, I too pushed him away. Shame, guilt, remorse, self-pity, and anguish penetrated my soul. How else can I describe the pain? The next morning I just packed up and left. Crushed, lonely and depressed, I drove back to Toronto. In the deepest despair of my life, at the age of 26 I booked myself into a room in the YWCA. This was the lowest point that I had ever reached. The YWCA offered a very modest small room, cheap. My room came equipped with a cot, a sink, small window and a brown vinyl chair. My view consisted of ugly grey concrete blocks. I shared the dormitory like bathroom, living room, and kitchen with about thirty other women.

Overcome in a deep depression, I had no inclination or energy to go back to work, visit friends, talk to anyone or even go out to bars. This truly was so out of my character suggesting that something was seriously wrong. My heart was so inconsolable and wounded that it took months of this isolation, depression, and agony before I could even pull myself up to go out. Totally withdrawn, no one could reach me. I just wanted to sleep my life away. These were the darkest, longest days of my life.

The Abortion Providers NEVER told me that abortion is **NOT safe**! They NEVER told me that it would leave deep emotional and physical scars! They NEVER told me that abortion actually kills a baby! They NEVER told me that abortion is a violent procedure! They NEVER gave me any alternatives or life options! They will NEVER tell you that abortion exploits women for their profit! The abortion counsellors use obscure terms such as "product of conception," "contents of the uterus," and "fetal tissue" to refer to your baby.

An old girlfriend Klofer came to visit me at the "Y". She encouraged me to get up, and go out, so I could try to fight this thing called depression. Slowly, hope began to germinate in my soul. After months of separation from everyone, I began to work again. Thank God, my employers were willing to take me back. It was extremely difficult, my self-esteem had deteriorated, and the emotional hurt and pain were so sensitive. Nevertheless, after a few months I was back into the bars again, trying to kill the pain and putting myself into vulnerable positions. Getting taken advantage of, I did not care anymore. I felt like a failure and was getting older too.

Within a year after my breakup with Benn, I was again pregnant, for the third time. This time I was not even sure who the father was. So ashamed at myself and caught in the predicament of being a single mother, I again resorted to having an abortion. Like multitudes of other women abortion had become another kind of birth control. This time I went to Women's College hospital and made them put me to sleep. I was a zombie.

You see, as diabolical as this procedure is, most women who have had one abortion will often have multiple abortions because they are not dealing with the reality of it. It is called "Denial." Some people have a seared conscience, like the Doctors and staff who promote and execute abortions. They know the truth about fetal development, so they must be either totally deceived, or just cold blooded assassins, motivated by money?

Drastically, most abortions are **not** done for "therapeutic" reasons at all! It is just a **violent form of ' birth control'** 97% of the time. Most women just want to "get rid of the problem." Having sex is okay, but with no responsibility. Most men shed their responsibility for this new life too. "I don't think I can afford it now, what about that new car? That job? That education? That vacation? Pride. Besides, it's only a clump of tissue." What lame excuses to slay the innocent. What deception, what beguilement!

Morgentaler and associates believe it is better to kill the "unwanted" than to let them live. Yet more than 300, 000 couples in Canada would love to have and care for those little 'unwanted' babies. In 1988 about 2.4 million couples were infertile in the USA, an increase from 500,000 in 1965! Aborting North America, is it Genocide, foeticide or suicide?

The Toronto Hospital News for January of 1990 read as a headline, **"Toronto abortions OUTNUMBER births!" There were 8,995 births and 13,185 abortions in the City of Toronto in 1988 according to a public health department report. That same month the Toronto Star newspaper reported the "Cash-for-'Babies' plan gets results in Quebec." Quebec families now get a $500.00 premium for the birth of a first child, $1,000.00 for a second baby, and a whopping**

$4,500.00 cheque for a third and each subsequent child! At least they give pregnancy some value!

We are actually an "endangered species." Yes, our birthrate has dropped to 1.7 for several years now. We are not even reproducing ourselves! Plus, we have an aging population...Think about it.

Today, it has become socially acceptable, and a woman's right to have her healthy baby killed. **Pro-choice? Some choice, the choice is to have your Preborn baby murdered for you by professionals.** Our Governments have legally sanctioned, and we pay for every abortion with our tax dollars. Blood money. A woman's right to kill her offspring? This is the most unnatural, barbaric act for a woman to commit.

Not one person in all three pregnancies ever encouraged me to let my babies live! Nor did anyone ever tell me the truth about fetal development. With the third pregnancy I asked the doctor what was actually developed. He grabbed a piece of paper and put an ink dot in the middle of the page. Then he exclaimed, "See here, it is just a little dot, a clump of tissue, it is nothing." The doctor totally lied to me!

Again I contemplated, *"Well if it is okay with the doctors, plus it's okay with all my friends, and it is legal, then it must be all right!"* I was at least eight weeks' pregnant this time! The truth of the matter is that she had a head, body, limbs, and a beating heart! Friends they are lying to women! No one ever told me about the impending physical, emotional, psychological and spiritual aftermaths of abortion. There was never an alternative given. Erroneously, women are not informed about the whole truth and risks involved with induced abortions.

If someone, anyone had warned me, I would have a 26-year-old daughter named Jennifer, a 16-year-old son named Daniel and a 15-year-old daughter named Rebecca. This knowledge rips my heart with grief, makes me sob and cry in remorse. It is like Rachel crying for her children that are no more. This was a prophetic word from Jeremiah, mentioned again in Mat. 2:13-18. *"They heard a voice in Ramah, wailing and loud lamentation, Rachel weeping for her children, she refused to be comforted, because they were no more."* This is in reference to when King Herod put to death all the male children two years old and under in Bethlehem.

He was seeking to murder Jesus, the Messiah. Our Government puts to death little children because of no restrictions or protection for them.

Do you know that there are **twenty-seven different physical complications** to the mother, that can arise out of these so called, 'safe' abortions? Some include infections which can lead to sterility! How about getting a lacerated or perforated uterus or cervix? Hemorrhages, Asherman's Syndrome, and punctures into other organs have occurred sometimes resulting in death. Scar tissue usually abounds.

They never once mentioned that I might regret this for the rest of my life! They never told me that I would be plagued with guilt, remorse, shame, depression and unbearable grief. Eventually the realization of abortion will hit the woman. One day they too will realize the severity of the act of having their own children killed. **Women must be informed on the devastating effects of these bloodcurdling procedures. The consequences to women and what really happens to the little babies must be publicized.**

Post Abortion Syndrome may not even manifest itself, due to denial, until many years later. Down the road, when they have met the 'perfect guy', settled down, and NOW they want to have their cute little cuddly babies to hug and to hold. Then whammy! Nothing is happening! I know first hand the pain of this kind of sorrow and grief.

Politicians, where are the Government Grants to do more research on the consequences of using years of synthetic birth control? What about comprehensive studies on the psychological, emotional and physical after-effects of abortion on women? What about more research on the links between breast cancer, cervical cancers and induced abortions?

According to Dr. Joel Brind who has done extensive research, he has concluded that having an abortion doubles your risk of getting breast cancer, compared to having the baby. There is definitely a connection. It makes common sense to me. We must take heed especially when they are doing abortions on more than **100,000 Canadian women every year**! Talk about "Reproductive Health?" There is absolutely nothing

Praying at the "Cemetery of the Innocents"

healthy or reproductive about a woman having her preborn baby killed. Abortion is not a treatment for pregnancy! Abortion is hazardous to women as well. It is a deadly solution to a social problem!

A mother's womb used to be the safest place in the world for a Preborn child. Today a mother's womb has become the most dangerous place in the world for a Preborn baby to be.

Hello, Government leaders! You should be outraged at such injustice to the tiniest, defenseless human beings. Where are the laws to protect EVERY human being from the moment of conception until natural death? Heinz, Pampers, Huggies, Luvs, General Mills, Quaker, all Department Stores, Teachers, Builders, Doctors, Dentists, Corporations, Insurance Companies ... where are your big donations to help fund the volunteer run Pro-Life organizations?

Can you imagine the boost to our economy if all those children were here, that should have been born? Right now abortion wipes out about 2,500 classrooms every year in Canada. There would be a demand for more teachers, diapers, clothes, baby furniture, housing, doctors, food etc. Corporations, your money and influence are needed to help educate and inform the public about fetal development, Post Abortion Syndrome and provide positive TV commercials to encourage chastity and single Moms to let their babies live.

As Christians my husband and I do not believe that it is God's will for us to use birth control. The Scriptures substantiate that it is God's will for us to "Multiply and be fruitful, and subdue the earth." Genesis 1:27 *"So God created man in his own image, in the image of God; male and female created He them.* Genesis 1:28 *And God blessed them, Be fruitful, and multiply, and replenish the earth, and subdue it: and have dominion over the fish of the sea, and over the fowl of the air, and over every living thing that moveth upon the earth."*

Again after the Great Flood God commanded his people to multiply and be fruitful. Many scriptures reaffirm His will, promising Abraham that he will be the father of many Nations ... confirms His will for us. The culmination is Deuteronomy. 30:15 *"See, I have set before thee this day, life and good, and death and evil;* Deuteronomy. 30:16 *"In that I command thee this day to love the LORD thy God, to walk in his ways, and to keep his commandments and his statutes and his judgments, that thou mayest live and multiply: and the LORD thy God shall bless thee in the land whither thou goest to possess it."* Verse 19 reads, *"Now choose life, so that you and your children may live."*

So now you are 33, 34, 35, 36, 37 ... the maternal clock is ticking. Time is running out. Your self-centred ego, tries to justify the barrenness, or sluff off the emotions to verify your independence and material wealth. Yet deep inside your heart there is a void, an emptiness, a vacuum, something is missing. This inability to now have children, at the snap of your fingers, affects your emotions, your marriage, your old age, and ultimately your life!

Yes, deep regret, remorse and pain grip your being for the past mistakes and selfish choices you ignorantly made, **but now it is too late!** The Hard Truth is that irreversible damage has been done. Your uterus may be full of scar tissue, your fallopian tubes probably look like they have been through a war-zone. There was a battle, or a number of them in that dark, warm, liquid place. Little human beings were killed there. Torn apart limb by limb, crushed and sucked through a tube, or scraped out. Now the evidence of those sharp weapons has left their marks in your body. Like a decrepit unmarked graveyard. Like mine.

But I thank God for His Mercy and Grace toward us, we can have hope, faith and trust in Him. Just ask God to forgive you of your sins. He does. It is phenomenal, the difficult part is to forgive yourself! Then work to save other lives! Romans 8:1 tells us that there is therefore now **no condemnation** to those who are in Christ Jesus and called according to his purpose and plans.

Sorry that I must describe such details, but this is so true for millions of women. According to the Alan Guttmacher Institute, who receives money from Planned Parenthood, (the largest abortion provider), millions of women around the world have had legal abortions. It is a thriving killing industry. This is reality! They are aborting the future. Women are choosing to have unlimited sex, and then choosing to have their offspring killed.

Only prayer and faith in a big God can help erase or ease the guilt. Perhaps God in His mercy and grace will provide a miracle and you will bear a child one day. It is the greatest joy and gift in life! My hope and prayer is that you will be blessed with children, despite your past. Be strong in the Lord, and the power of His might.

Perhaps you are expecting right now, or know someone who is, and are thinking about having an abortion. Please remember this. For whatever reason, God has allowed this conception to take place. There is now a unique little boy or girl growing inside you. He or she has a beating heart and is full of love. Get a book on fetal development or call the closest Pregnancy Counselling Centre, Birthright, or Right to Life group for help and advice. Most of all, let your baby live! You can do it. People will help you.

You may be feeling afraid and disappointed right now, but when you see and hold that precious child in your arms, you will sense complete joy, peace and love. There are Pregnancy Counselling Centres, Pro Life groups, Priests and Pastors that will help you practically, and emotionally. You are not alone! Your boyfriend may desert you at first, mainly due to shock. However, he will come around, especially when he sets eyes on that amazing little person. Perhaps you are courageous and unselfish enough to bless a couple who really want a child and cannot conceive themselves. There are open adoptions now where the birth mother chooses the adoptive parents and keeps in touch over the years.

FETAL DEVELOPMENT

The Pro-abortionists would like you to believe that the unborn child is just a mere "product of conception," "a clump of tissue", "a bunch of cells", "a fetus". This is deception! Guaranteed, they do not want you aware that it is a little baby who is fully human and fully alive.

If it is NOT a "BABY," then you are not pregnant! The word fetus means "the little one" in Latin. When a woman is with child she does not say, "Oh my fetus is kicking, " or my fetus is three months now, it is her "Baby!" You were once a fetus. It is just another stage in our human journey, like embryo, infant, toddler, adolescent, adult and senior.

The word for 'pregnant' means 'she became two souls' in ancient Ethiopia. There is no confusion there when a woman conceives. Many people will say that they are 'with child'. The real question is whether the child in the womb is a living member of the human race or not? The answer, undoubtedly determines that the deliberate act of abortion then kills a human being. Did you know that at the moment of conception, when one sperm out of millions, fertilizes that egg, it is like a computer micro chip? The whole genetic code is there. Whether this new person is male or female, colour of hair, skin, and if he or she will look like Mom or Dad? Inherent talents and giftings are all present right then.

Psalm 139:13-16 declares the wonder of life; *"For You did form my inward parts, You knit me together in my mother's womb. I will confess and praise You, for I am fearfully and wonderfully made... My frame was not hidden from You when I was made in secret... Your eyes saw my unformed substance, being yet unformed, and in Your book all the days of my life were written, before ever they took shape, when as yet there was none of them."* (Amplified)

 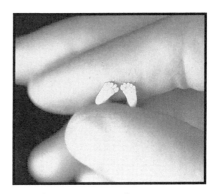

Each one of us was this tiny at one time! (6-7 weeks) Feet at ten weeks.

Science reveals that in the first month after conception, the greatest physical changes take place. We never again grow so quickly. **We are ten thousand times larger by the 4th week than we were at conception,** growing from one cell to millions. From head to foot, we were a quarter of an inch long, the size of a split pea. We already had **a head with primitive eyes, ears, mouth and brain, simple kidneys, a liver, digestive tract, a primitive umbilical cord and a big heart. This heart pumps sixty-five times a minute to circulate the newly-formed blood through a system of tubes that are completely separate from her mother's circulation.**

By a mere three weeks after conception, (before most women even realize that they are pregnant), the heart is actually beating! By 8 weeks there is a tiny human body, complete with head, arms and legs, perfect tiny fingers and toes, and all the vital organs are present. The only thing added now is time, and nourishment, nothing else is added. **He or she can squint, and close a fist if his/her palm is touched.**

By the 11th week, all internal organs are present and functioning. **He or she breathes, swallows, digests and urinates.** He or she is very sensitive to pain, can kick his/her legs, wave his/her arms and suck his/her thumb. From this time on nothing new develops or functions, only further growth and maturation.

Please note that most abortions take place from the 9th- 16th week and onward.

By the 12th week, or third month the heart is pumping up to six gallons of blood a day! He or she now gets food, oxygen and water from the placenta, which is the Latin word for cake. The awesome fact is that the placenta, membranes, cord and amniotic fluid are all formed from the original fertilized egg. The placenta is rooted in the lining of the womb. At four months it is a powerful organ which performs the functions of the adult lungs, kidneys, liver and bowels. As well as producing substances that will give the baby immunity to some infections. Wow!

The baby's blood flows into the placenta through the umbilical cord, but never meets her mother's blood (the mother can have a completely different blood type). Guess what? We do not stop growing once we are outside the womb either. The unique human genetic structure present in every cell makes this little one a **"human being with potential."** Not a potential human being like the abortion providers want you to believe.

The abortion providers would like us to believe that this little one is just a "product of conception". However, the TRUTH remains. Do not be deceived as I was. **It is a "Baby."** Sadly, today, like in Nazi Germany, they utilize the use of rhetoric and euphemisms to desensitize the personhood of innocent victims.

It is a miracle how quickly the baby develops. As medical science confirms, there is a unique individual growing and alive. Dr. Margaret White in her excellent book, "Two Million Silent Killings: The Truth About Abortion" exclaims,

> "Genetically, the foetus must be a member of the human race because of his twenty-three pairs of chromosomes in every cell nucleus; likewise he cannot be just a part of his mother or a part of his father, because these chromosomes are derived equally from both parents." It is extraordinary that, in spite of there being billions of people in this world, nowhere is it possible to find two 'identical' individuals. This remarkable fact, which shows the complete uniqueness of every human being, is due to

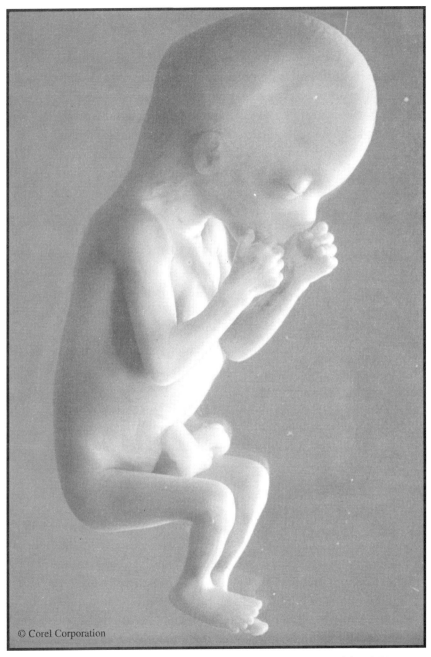

© Corel Corporation

This is an actual photograph of a 14 week old "fetus." Thousands of these babies are killed every year in Canada and the USA. How can we deny the inalienable rights of this little one?

the huge number of genes on the chromosomes and their remarkable diversity.

"Even 'identical' twins, which because they both come from the same egg and sperm are remarkably alike in many ways, are nevertheless not identical. They do not, for instance, have the same fingerprints. From the moment of conception the child is a dynamic, rapidly growing individual-over nine months the single fertilized egg will grow into trillions of cells in the new born child. Anyone who studies embryology knows that the egg and the sperm are alive. However, once they leave the ovary and testes their life span is limited unless they meet and fuse. Both the egg and sperm will have died a natural death within a week after sexual intercourse unless conception occurs. When this happens, a new person who may live for seventy years or so emerges if not murdered while still in the womb."

"Dr. White continues, another amazing fact is that the "combinations of chromosomes present at conception contain a library of genes with information from the past on the incredible helix of DNA. A single thread of DNA from a human cell contains information equivalent to over half a million pages. The stored knowledge at conception in the new individual's 'library' is fifty times more than that contained in the entire "Encyclopedia Britannica." Yet it is so minuscule."

We were just as human then, as we are now! The September 1970 issue *California Medicine* includes the sentence, "It is a scientific fact that human life begins at conception and continues intra or extra uterine till death". *Life* magazine, in a special issue, *The Drama of Life before Birth*, states "The birth of a human being really occurs at the moment one of the father's sperm cells fertilizes the mother's egg". In Chinese culture, a child is considered to be a year old, three months after birth. How can anyone who knows the truth about fetal development, deny the personhood of a Preborn child?

It especially bothers me and many others that some medical professionals, who call themselves "Doctors," have no conscience in taking the lives of these perfectly healthy little babies. Obviously, their God is the God of Mammon, the lust for money. The abortion industry is a multibillion dollar business. They prey on hurting vulnerable women.

What does medical history and the law reveal? Most religions condemn abortion as inherently evil, except satanic cults. The first mention of abortion in the Bible is in Exodus chapter 21:22: *"If men strive, and hurt a woman with child so that her fruit departs from her, and yet no mischief follows, he shall be surely punished."* Also, the Jewish moral code in 6 BC contains the phrase; 'Nor shall the woman destroy the embryonic child in her womb'. The earliest Christian reference to abortion comes in the second century AD in the *Didache* (also known as the *Instructions to the Apostles*). **"Thou shalt not kill; Thou shalt not commit adultery; Thou shalt not corrupt children; Thou shalt not commit fornication; Thou shalt not murder a child by abortion nor kill one after birth ..."** Under English law from which Canada's laws originated, abortion has always been a crime.

Hippocrates, the Father of medicine, knew that a doctor had to promise the best for his patients, and never to poison them. He taught them to know their limitations and to refer patients to specialists, cases they were not qualified to treat. He commanded them NOT to do abortions, but to lead a good life and never to commit adultery with a patient. His Oath included **"Neither will I administer a poison to anybody when asked to do so, nor will I suggest such a course. Similarly I will not give to a woman a pessary to cause abortion, but I will keep pure and holy both my life and my art."**

Long before Hitler came to power in Germany, Hegel had the fascist 'super-race' mentality. Hegel's philosophy was that if an action provides a solution for a practical problem, then it is morally justifiable. In other words it is okay to do evil, if you think the end result is good. In 1931, before Hitler came to power, psychiatrists in Bavaria discussed sterilization of the unfit and euthanasia for persons with chronic mental illness.

Dr. Ernest Ruedin, a professor of psychiatry in Munich, was able to get a law passed in 1933. This law allowed compulsory sterilization for eugenic reasons. It was the harbinger of the mass killings of mentally and physically disabled patients.

It is appalling how the Nazis tortured and murdered millions of innocent Jewish men, women and children. It is repulsive that they ended the lives of people of all ages who were disabled and deaf. They executed children who wet the bed, and all those who could not speak for themselves, in cold blood. **Abortion is Nazi ideology manifested today.** The "Kill the unwanted philosophy." Who will be the Next to go? The unwanted or inconvenient, sometimes include the disabled, the seniors, the poor, and the mentally ill.

After the Nuremberg Trials the whole world was shocked at the horrors of mass murder of the Jews. It all started in 1936 when the Supreme Court of Germany took away the rights of the Jews. It also became clear at the trials that even children with minor deformities or ones who wet their beds were experimented on and viciously slaughtered. Medical professionals in Europe decided that these atrocities must never happen again, and so in 1947 the World Medical Association was founded. They agreed that whatever the causes, they must never allow such crimes to recur. Research in medicine as well as its practice must never be separated from eternal moral values.

Margaret Sanger, a feminist who founded Planned Parenthood in America is the largest Abortion provider in the States. She had a motto that "More children from the fit, and less from the unfit." Sanger intentionally broke the law and provided birth control devices/methods in order to get a court case, thus, changing the law. Now abortion has become the birth control of choice.

Doctors must be quick to point out to their fellow members in society any policies that degrade or deny fundamental human rights. The **World Medical Association** recommended "**Affirmation of the aims and ethics of medicine in the spirit of the Hippocratic oath, should be published and applied in medical education and medical practice.**" It produced a detailed list of recommendations and an important declaration of medical ethics, called the declaration of Geneva to which all countries in the united nations assented. It included the promise. *"I will have the utmost respect for human life from the moment of conception. Even under threat I will not use my medical knowledge contrary to the laws of humanity."*

During the 1970's in Britain, Chloral, the sedative drug was used for extermination by the Nazis, and used later to kill disabled newborns. For centuries abortion was illegal in Canada and around the world. It is my observation that satan, the devil or whatever evil you want to call him, always goes after the weak and the young. The Bible states that he is out "to kill, steal and destroy."

Section 287 of the Criminal Code of Canada clearly states that abortion is a crime; Section 1 **"Everyone who, with intent to procure the miscarriage of a female person, whether or not she is pregnant, uses any means for the purpose of carrying out his intention is guilty of an indictable offence and liable to imprisonment for life."** It goes on to state that every female person who being pregnant with intent to procure her own miscarriage, uses any means or permits any means to be used for the purpose of carrying out her intention is guilty of an indictable offence and liable to imprisonment for a term not exceeding two years.

Notwithstanding, on January 28, 1988 the Supreme Court of Canada consisting of liberal minded judges, struck down the abortion law in the Morgentaler case on bureaucratic technicalities. These judges are appointed by politicians - not elected. Yet, they have the power to "strike down" our democratic moral laws!

Watching the late news that night, I cried aloud in disbelief that we had come so low in our society to allow the undaunted killing of innocent babies. Abortion on demand! Of course, the hard core feminists have had a lot to contribute to the "choice to kill" agenda. Their loud boisterous chanting, rhetoric, lies and intimidation have put doubtless fear and trembling into the hearts of weak Politicians.

It distresses me that people would really believe that if they again prohibited abortion on demand, thousands of women would begin to shove coat hangers up their vaginas. This fear mongering is outrageous! We would probably have another "Baby boom" resulting in a big boost to the economy. Hopefully, some women would courageously give their babies to childless couples and many women would practice chastity, mature and grow up. The philosophy that "Well, they're going to do it anyway" theory is ridiculous. Just because people are going to steal, kill and destroy does not mean that we should legalize those things, "Because they're going to do it anyway." Yes, there are absolute rights, and wrongs.

You are probably wondering how a young woman in this generation could be so careless about getting pregnant, while there are so many options and forms of birth control. Well, let me tell you. When I was sixteen, the doctor put me on birth control pills, however after trying several varieties, I began to get terrible side affects and had to stop taking them. Also, did you know that there are **many drugs that may cause the pill to become ineffective** such as ampicillin, analgesics, antihistamines, antacids, barbiturates, penicillin, tetracycline and many others. Also, they do not recommend the pill for women with any of the following: poor circulations, mononucleosis, blood clots, sickle cell anaemia, strokes, heart disease, alcoholism, retardation, hepatitis, psychiatric disorders, liver diseases, epilepsy, genital cancer, asthma, migraines, diabetes, etc. This is from the report on Oral Contraceptives, 1985 by the Committee on Reproductive Physiology to the Health Protection Branch, Health and Welfare Canada, September 1985.

The birth control pill puts an artificial lining in the uterus, which can prevent a fertilized egg (new life) from getting the nutrients he/she needs to survive, and it dies.

Intrauterine devices? No way, many Gynecologists do not recommend them at all. When I was about twenty-four years old, one hot summer weekend, I was attacked with intense abdominal pain. An IUD had been inserted into my womb about a week earlier. It had become totally infected which resulted in my getting 'Pelvic Inflammatory Disease.' Then unable to walk, and doubling over, my drinking buddies took me to the nearest Hospital. Although I had consumed many drinks and drugs, I could still feel the sharp pains. They rushed me to the emergency, where I was admitted and immediately given high doses of antibiotics intravenously.

Safe sex? That is a joke, especially since men hate to wear condoms or rarely will. There have been several studies that prove that latex condoms have natural voids or holes in them that are 50-500 TIMES larger than the HIV/AIDS virus.

To be really safe, just hang on to your hormones and your pants, and wait until you get married! Yes, the good old fashioned Godly way. It is the respectable way. It is a matter of life or death these days, for HIV/AIDS is out to kill you. It is primarily a sexually transmitted preventable disease, unless you unfortunately got tainted blood or an infected needle. The real curse of a sinful world is that there are always innocent/civilian casualties.

How many women from the 1960's on, let themselves go to such debauchery and hedonism, at the whim of every good-looking guy, loneliness or lust? I have not found one place in Bible scripture that exhorts women to use 'birth control'. God wants His people to multiply, be fruitful and subdue the earth. Children are the heritage of the Lord and they are a blessing, as stated in Psalm 127.

Peer pressure is bad in this generation of socially acceptable premarital sex. This does not imply that sex before marriage is right. It is absolutely wrong. I do not condone or approve of it now. Yet at the time I was stupid, ignorant, naive, and looking for love in all the wrong places. With no Godly morals, and always under the influence of alcohol, and/or other drugs, I was a fool.

Women must take having sex a lot more seriously than they do! This is when they should make the "CHOICE!"

Just check the local yellow pages under the heading **"Birth Control Services"** and you will find several abortion clinics listed. They are in my city. It is a multi billion-dollar industry. The abortion providers are blatant, and spending advertising dollars to rake in the dough from vulnerable, fearful young women. This is exploitation, preying on the emotions of women whose hormones are jumping with life. Isn't it logical then that abortion rates among teens in Calgary, Alberta has doubled while the birth rates have declined?

Statistics Canada reported that the number of pregnant teenagers increased from 39,340 in 1987 up to **46,753** in 1994. In 1974, 26 per cent of teen pregnancies ended in an abortion. But by 1995, 45 per cent ended in abortions. "**Teenagers have not only a high abortion rate, but also a high repeat abortion rate,**" a report by Surinder Wadhera and Wayne Millar. They concluded that teens apparently "have not fully benefited" from all the sex education and the wide availability of contraceptives. Duh!

In **Canada we are not even reproducing ourselves** and are at a negative birth rate. **Statistics Canada reported July 9, 1998 that fewer babies were born in 1996 than the year before. And fertility was at a near historic low with the average number of live births down to 1.59 for every woman.** The average age of mothers is now 29 years, and a higher proportion of births are out of wedlock. Do you think there is a correlation with the negative birth rates and abortion numbers? *Of course there is.* Statistics divulge that One in every Five babies conceived in Canada is killed. It is the leading cause of death. With more than 96,000 babies killed every year while in the sanctuary of their own mother's womb, we have become an 'endangered species.'

The economic loss of these children who should be here, and are not, is astounding. Canadian prosperity suffers. Our aging population will definitely feel the absence of the missing young. Instead these absent consumers cannot stimulate the economy, so businesses downsize, there are layoffs and bankruptcies occurring at record rates. Instead there is a curse on our health care system and economy, while millions of dollars are spent to exterminate babies. Multitudes of women undergo fertility treatments, while others need psychological and emotional help. It scares me that on one end of the hospital floor they try heroic deeds to save tiny premature babies, while down the hall they kill healthy babies in healthy mothers'. Women are seduced into the "choice" rhetoric and doctors falsely believe that they are doing women a favor by destroying their children!

The Politicians claim that "only medically necessary" abortions are done. Who determines what is medically necessary? The abortion providers! Don't you think that this would be considered a "CONFLICT OF INTEREST" since this is how these people make their money? There is obviously a bias here. Besides, they have NEVER denied one woman the request for an abortion. Not one, in hundreds of thousands!

Since more than 100,000 abortions are systematically done every year in Canada, **shouldn't we be sounding the alarm and blowing the trumpets, because there is an EPIDEMIC** in the land!

According to the research, Dr. F. Morcos and Dr. Ferri report that there is absolutely no evidence that induced abortions improve the outcomes of women with underlying psychiatric illness. In fact most studies suggest that 'therapeutic abortion is a risk factor in deterioration of pre-existing psychiatric or psychological problems, including psychosis, depression and suicidal risk. There are no reliable studies available assessing the long term psychological and social well-being of women after have induced abortions. Studies from Saskatchewan and Alberta suggest that a history of abortion was a marker for higher utilization of the health care system. The implication being that, if anything, the procedure had a negative, and not a therapeutic or beneficial effect on the health of these women.

Abortion is a procedure that disrupts a normal physiological process and carries a physical risk to the woman undergoing the procedure. In spite of the fact that over 23 million abortions have been performed in North America in the last 25 years, there are no reliable medical studies demonstrating its "therapeutic" benefit to women on either physical, psychiatric or psychological grounds! Therefore, it has no proven medical benefit, and cannot be defined as "medically necessary," in any context, other than political. The Provinces in this country have the legal authority to determine that abortions are not a basic health service and can opt to de-insure them. Especially, when the Health Care system is always crying for more money.

In 1986 Dr. Richard Kennedy then the President of the Alberta Medical Association stated: "Fewer than 5% of abortions were performed for medical emergencies due to serious health problems for women." Both he and the President elect of the AMA that year, Dr. Ruth Collins-Nakai called on the Government to de-insure abortions. Did you know that they do not require the abortionists to specify a medical reason for the abortions, when they submit their billings? There is clearly no accountability, just irresponsibility.

We pay for induced abortions that are supposed to be "medically necessary," because the pregnancy is a danger to women. Yet, the morgentaler/edmonton website advertises that only "any HEALTHY female may obtain an abortion at their clinic." See, these are healthy women, aborting healthy babies!

Tax-funded abortion in the last 25 years evidently does nothing to better women's lives, our families, business community or our society. We must stand up and be a voice for the voiceless and end the abortion holocaust.

While our population shrinks and ages, euthanasia and its rhetoric rise. An excellent book exposing the myth of "Over Population" is the **"Handbook on Population"** by Robert Sassone. He has gathered extensive research and statistics proving that there is more than enough food, land, space, water and air for billions of more people comfortably. He reports this perspective, "All the people in the world could stand without touching anyone in less than 200 square miles." He is very concerned about the negative birth rate in the US and Canada due to abortion, infertility and the effects on an aging economically poor, growth rate.

Another National Best Seller, is **"The Cost of Abortion,"** by Lawrence F. Roberge. He gives an analysis o f the social, economic, and demographic effects of abortion on the United States. Of course, if all those children were here, we would need more teachers, schools, clothes, housing etc.

Yet, countries that are experiencing an economic boom are those, like Hong Kong and Korea, whom many label as "overpopulated."

Planned Parenthood champions the personal "choice" of women to abort their babies on demand. Yet, incredibly they promote the China policy which institutes that women must abort their children, after the first. They are also forced to have IUD's inserted, and be sterilized after the second child. The women in China have absolutely no rights, and NO freedom of "choice" to let their babies live. This is okay with Planned Parenthood! What hypocrites! They peddle pills, condoms and abortions...Planned Parenthood has turned sexual promiscuity into a $167, 000,000 million dollar empire.

PSALM 94

God the Refuge of the Righteous

"O Lord God, to whom vengeance belongs-O God to whom vengeance belongs, Shine forth! Rise up, O Judge of the earth; Render punishment to the proud. Lord, how long will the wicked, How long will the wicked triumph?

They utter speech, and speak insolent things; All the workers of iniquity boast in themselves. They break in pieces Your people, O Lord, And afflict your heritage. *They slay the widow and the stranger,* **And murder the fatherless!** *Yet they say, "The Lord does not see, Nor does the God of Jacob understand." Understand, you senseless among the people; And you fools, when will you be wise? He who planted the ear, shall He not hear? He who formed the eye, shall He not see? He who instructs the nations, shall He not correct, He who teaches man knowledge? The Lord knows the thoughts of man, That they are futile.*

Blessed is the man whom you instruct, O lord, and teach out of your law, that you may give him rest from the days of adversity, until the pit is dug for the wicked. For the lord will not cast off his people, nor will he forsake his inheritance. But judgment will return to righteousness, and all the upright in heart will follow it.

Who will rise up for me against the evildoers? Who will stand up for me against the workers of iniquity? Unless the lord had been my help, my soul would soon have settled in silence. *If I say, "My foot slips," your mercy, O Lord, will hold me up. In the multitude of my anxieties within me, your comforts delight my soul.*

Shall the throne of iniquity, which devises evil by law, have fellowship with you? They gather together against the life of the righteous, and condemn innocent blood!"

Chapter 8

"Looking For Love ...
In All The Wrong Places"

My conscience had been seared since the age of thirteen when it came to drugs and men. The insurance business was profitable. When I put my mind and effort into it, I would excel in sales. I knew insurance was a necessity. My strong verbal skills influenced clients to buy.

Selling life and disability insurance got me thinking about our short time here on the earth. One question I always asked my clients was, "If you can tell me when you are going to die, then I can tell you exactly which type of Life insurance to get. If you are going to live a long life, buy permanent Whole life insurance. BUT if you are going to die accidentally or prematurely, then buy Term (temporary) insurance." This made us all think of our humanity and mortality.

Another hot summer day I was on the QEW highway, on my way to meet a girlfriend to go out for dinner and the disco. Again I had smoked up. Finding myself too close behind a car going up a ramp. Too quick to stop, her brake lights went on and I had to suddenly brake to avoid rear ending her. My front tire touched the gravel shoulder and my car began to fly out of control. All I could see was a huge concrete wall coming straight for me. So with all of my strength and perhaps the help of a guardian angel, managed to steer the wheels, turning the car so that the backside of the car hit the wall, instead of a head on collision. Wow! The adrenaline was really flowing now. The next thing you know, I am escalating down this enormous steep hill, all the way down to a huge mucky ditch. Thank God there were no trees, rocks, fences or other obstacles in my path. The car was a mess.

Now here I was all dressed up, in high heels getting out of my car, very angry and upset at this woman who slammed on her brakes right in front of me. It was all her fault! She caused me to lose control and land at the bottom of this huge ditch. Of course, at the time I didn't consider the fact that I was high on pot. The truth is; my perception was off. I was probably going too fast, and following too close. Isn't it true that we always have a tendency to shift the blame on others? As I began to proceed up the hill, I could hear a bunch of guys laughing their heads off. When I turned around, they were laughing at me, and heckling. "Hey, nice legs!" This was very humiliating, and I shouted at them, "Never mind!" I was irate.

The woman whom I had avoided rear-ending, pulled over to see how I was. Soon a policeman arrived to take a report, and a tow truck driver wanted the job. It appeared that I was fine, of course, but I was feeling no pain. The friendly tow truck driver rolled down the big embankment and hitched my big silver 1982 Chevy Malibu to the back of his truck. Then in a pleasant gesture, offered to drive me to my destination, the car in tow. It was another mystery how I survived that accident.

By now I was almost two hours late. I started to cry when Darlene opened the door. She quickly poured me a drink, and it was off to Mario's a Restaurant/Bar. It was one of those sheik places with lots of brass, mirrors, and fake plants. The music was contemporary and the young executive men frequented this spot. As we were waiting for the waitress, I began to feel very sore and extremely tired. I need another drink …

When my Fettuccine Alfredo arrived I couldn't even lift up my fork. All of my strength had dissipated. It seemed hilarious, at the time. I could hardly laugh, but it was true. It was as if every muscle in my body weighed 50 pounds. Darlene wanted us to move up to the bar-stools where all the guys were, but I could hardly sit up. Somehow, I persevered the bar scene. At last the bar closed, and she drove me home.

At around 5:30 in the morning I awoke in extreme pain and agony, every muscle in my body was screaming at me. Terribly frightened, I phoned my precious Mom crying in pain to come to my rescue. She drove me straight to the hospital. Fortunately again, there were no serious injuries, just strained and pulled muscles. Guardian Angels had again been working overtime to protect me. It would take a good week to recuperate.

One of my insurance clients, Barb, and I became friends. She had a big heart, was rather eccentric, drove a classy white Bentley, and was heavily into Tarot cards, New Age and the occult. Barb was about 10 years or so older than I, and we partied. She was very tall and skinny with fuzzy blondish long hair. She had divorced her rich husband a few years earlier, and their son about twelve lived with her. She had a nice renovated cabbage-town semi, with a crowded pool in the tiny backyard. Barb was accustomed to having nannies and lots of money. Yet it seemed to disappear so fast, for she was always liquidating one thing or another.

Barb was so dependent on her "fortune telling" cards that I would observe her do them repeatedly again, until she saw something that she wanted to see. She was very caught up in the occult, spirit guides and clairvoyants. The Bible asserts that mediums, witchcraft and the occult are an abomination to God.

Another woman whom I began to spend a lot of time with was my friend Grace. She became my best friend. She was also kind and generous. Grace was so classy. She looked like a model. I so respected and admired her.

Grace's boyfriend Dave, was blond, stunningly handsome, rich and definitely eccentric. He loved sports cars, boats and drugs. He had bought a big beautiful yacht which they named "Night Breeze." Grace began to manage a charter business for executive parties. This 65-foot motor yacht was first class. Grace had renovated it. She had exquisite taste in decorating.

She invited me to help her with bartending, and charter sales for cruises in the Toronto harbour. Our cruises would take us around scenic brightly lit Ontario Place. Daytime or night time cruises. This was the life. Fresh air, luxury, the high life, and good friends. However, there was an obscure side looming on the horizon.

My sales were slipping. Soon I became addicted to cocaine. One winter Grace organized an 'all girls' cruise. We flew down to Nassau to meet her on the most fabulous cruise ever, down in the Cayman Islands.

One afternoon we landed by Thunder Ball caves, where a 007 movie was shot. All five women dived into the unknown waters and headed for the outcropping of rocks and bushes in the midst of the sea. There were no other boats or people around. We had swum quite a way from the boat. We were all using goggles and snorkels to see the rich life and awesome colours of the world just beneath our bodies. We wandered through some narrow passages to get inside the big caves. My knee scraped along a sharp edge or some sea creature and it was bleeding a bit, and stinging, a plenty. More exhilarating was the fact that we were swimming in a gigantic aquarium, the Pacific. It was "Oceans Alive!"

As we started to head back toward the boat, it looked like it had drifted a mile away. Suddenly, Grace screamed, "Barracuda's!" I asked, "Really, where?" Mary yelled, "Hurry, let's get out of here!" Of course, the fact that I had cut my knee made me feel quite fearful of a shark attack. Hysteria seized us. We swam with great speed toward the yacht. The adrenaline was flowing our hearts were racing and fear struck our souls as our arms plummeted across the water. The boat seemed so far away. We had all seen one to many "Jaws" movies. Did we ever feel relieved after each of us boarded safely, feet and all?

It was a wondrous experience! Paradise, hot sunny weather, palm trees, sandy beaches, great food. This was so fabulous. However, one major problem, the fact that I was in bondage and a slave to cocaine.

I had to have it all the time. The stone really was not that great either. Sure you would be uppity up, and full of energy, like you had twelve cups of coffee at once. Then after only a few minutes you were down again, and needed more of the stuff. The sensation was so artificial.

After a while you were so numb mentally and physically, that you would become very edgy, and irritable. What a waste! My zeal for selling insurance had dwindled and I was more concerned about the flashy yacht life then meeting my quotas. The Sales manager started getting on my case. In time this deadly addictive drug took its toll physically. The consequences were lethal.

Strangely it was around this time that I began to SEEK God. Looking at the big picture, I began to *wonder. Who is God? Where is God? Why am I here? What is our purpose, and is there life after death?*

Dave and Grace decided to take the boat south to Florida. He decided to strip the boat and engine. He wanted to redo everything piece by piece. When he had his mind set on a thing, not even Grace could change his mind. One day he took off to get some parts on his motorbike. As she waited for his return, she kept busy trying to sort and tidy, and organize as best she could. He always had a reputation of being a fast crazy driver. Well this time he lost control, went flying and crashed head first into a telephone pole. He died instantly, on impact. What devastation. It was so hard to believe that he was gone. Poof, just like that, Dave was dead! This really took its toll on Grace. She had loved him so much.

God Is Love

Chapter 9

"What, Where & Who Is God?"

By this time friends were encouraging me to read Shirley MacLean's, "Out on a Limb" and various New Age and occult books. God knew that I was searching for the supernatural and seeking to find out the **truth**. The next thing I knew I was buying my own set of Tarot cards, I Ching set, Ruins and assorted paraphernalia. However, when it came right down to it, I would just keep on playing or shuffling until I got the results that I wanted to see. There was really absolutely nothing divine or truthful about those objects. One positive thing though, is that it did get me thinking on a more universal, celestial sphere. My whole paradigm on life was just beginning to alter and shift to a higher level. You know there is a verse that says "If you seek the Lord your God with all of our heart, and all of your soul, you will find him." Deuteronomy. 4:29

In 1985 at the age of twenty-eight, I was still drinking heavily and going out to bars. Deep down, there was a hunger in my soul to discover the truth about life. Curious, I started to read books and information about all the major world religions. It was very interesting to find out what their predominant beliefs and rituals were. Nevertheless, it astounded me that Moslems thought that it was okay for a man to have more than one wife. It is condoned in their holy book called the Koran. When I saw that, I thought *No way, this cannot be right. I would never want to share my husband with other women,* which would be like adultery, or worse polygamy.

When I noticed that Buddhists worshipped and revered statues made by men or machines, I perceived that was foolish. God couldn't be in a statue made by people. I couldn't even tolerate looking at the hundreds of ghastly looking gods that Sikhs and Hindus worship. This may offend some, but this is what I observed.

Further I came to the conclusion that not all religions can lead to the ONE HOLY true GOD, because they all have different ways of pleasing or obeying their gods. The main questions to consider are about sin, redemption, and reconciliation to God. The theory of 'reincarnation' is just foolishness to me, because mankind will sin. It doesn't make sense to come back as a frog with no conscience.

Recalling a sermon I once heard, I can give a good comparison to the differences. When we look at the tomb of Mohammed there is a dead Mohammed, when you look at the tomb of Budda, there is a dead Budda. But when you see the tomb of Jesus, it is empty, because He has risen from the grave and is alive. That is the real reason we celebrate Easter. For He overcame death for us so we could live eternally, if only we believe, and obey His commands. So I took a step in faith, and believed what men inspired by the Holy Spirit wrote thousands of years ago in the Holy Bible.

Now the search launched out to ascertain which church I should go to. First I went to a nearby Baptist church. It was a huge, beautiful old traditional church building, with the colourful stained glass windows and huge cathedral ceilings, you know the kind.

After filling out a visitor's card, the Assistant Pastor called me to come in for an appointment. He wanted to know a bit about me, then he asked me if I had been water baptized. I told him that they baptized me as a baby in a United church. He explained to me that there was no scripture in the Bible about baptizing babies. He then proceeded to show me verses where John the Baptist baptized Jesus when he was already thirty years old. John the Baptist said, "Repent, and be baptized for the remission of sins."

Therefore, since I was a baby when I got water baptized, how could I have repented of my sins. Repent means to feel bad about our sins, and CHANGE. The whole point of water baptism is that it is a public confession of our faith in Christ, and the water represents a cleansing, and washing of our sins. It is an outward symbol of the death of the old Denise. Then an inward cleansing with a new Denise coming out of the water washed, forgiven and redeemed through Christ Jesus. The infancy of a transformation from the old nature.

The aging Minister did give good sermons, we sang old hymns and they used an ancient pipe organ for the instrumental. It cost over $200,000 to refurbish that thing. This irritated me, as homeless - needy people roamed in the streets in front of this cathedral. Jesus said *"Do not lay up for yourselves treasures upon earth, where moth and rust destroy, and where thieves break in and steal. But lay up for yourselves, treasures in heaven, where neither moth nor rust destroys, and where thieves do not break in and steal; For where your treasure is, there will your heart be also."* Matthew 6:19-21. This Pastor would always close with prayer from the back of the church. It always brought shivers up my spine.

Though being water baptized, I still did not totally surrender my life to God at this time. My nights out in bars drinking, smoking and picking up guys continued. It was not long before I quit going to this church. There was no relationship with any of the people there. I felt so unclean, and polluted compared with the church members.

This would be a process of enlightenment. God had His hand on me. By the way, this is a TRUE story, the events actually took place and all the people, places and circumstances are real. Names have been changed for privacy, so as not to offend anyone! On the night of my 30th birthday, after an evening of dinner, dancing, drinking, and smoking drugs I was escorted home by a handsome man that I had just met. Suddenly in the middle of the night I consciously awoke, my brain was wide awake, my heart was pounding and I sensed that there was someone ELSE in the bedroom.

On opening my eyes I witnessed towering over us a huge masculine-shaped Angel. Fear paralysed me, but somehow I knew that he would not hurt me. The angel never said a word. Neither did I, but from that moment on, I had no more doubts about the fact that there were angels around.

In the next few days that followed, a Born-again Bell Telephone man came to service my phone. He noticed that I had a Bible in my small library case. So he began to ask me about the Bible and what I thought about it. "Oh, I think that it is just a bunch of fairy tales!", I retorted. Then he asked me, if I believed in the 'theory of evolution'? *'Well', I thought, 'That's what they taught me to believe in school.'* So I said "Of course I believe in evolution!" Then he reminded me of all of the missing links that the scientists could not find.

After he left, I began to ponder about that theory, and it came to me that yes, there were big gaps. Yes, there are missing links, between the plants and animals, and bigger gaps between animals and people. Where are all of the in between creatures of ape and man? What about the certainty that every living creature reproduces of its own kind? Whales have whales, giraffes have giraffes, gorillas' reproduce gorillas', and people have people, it is so OBVIOUS.

Then of course, God creates something like a caterpillar to evolve into a butterfly. Now that is evolution! Obe, the friendly Bell man would visit occasionally to go through some scriptures with me. He would give me the most profound answers for my philosophical questions. Obe encouraged me to start reading the Holy Bible and to check it out. However, I told him that I tried to read it when I was younger, but I just could not understand it, with all those "Thee's and thou's," it seemed too difficult and archaic. He just encouraged me to simply to pray in faith and ask God to help me understand His Word. Also Obe brought me a Bible in a more modern English version, the "New King James" version as I recall, that was a tremendous help too. The "Amplified" is my favourite now. It amplifies everything.

So my journey into the Bible began, the world's biggest selling book over the centuries. It dates back some 2,000 years. The Bible consists of sixty-six books or letters, written by thirty-three different authors. Some were Kings, one a doctor, shepherds, prophets, teachers, farmers, a former tax-collector and even fishermen. Interesting to read the words that men from many professions wrote. Yet from Genesis to Revelations it is the continuing saga about a magnificent, Holy and just CREATOR, GOD, who endeavours to reconcile sinful man to himself.

God does succeed in reconciling man to himself through sacrificing His son JESUS.

Since sin is what separates us from a Holy God, we needed someone who was sinless to give His life for us, to pay the price for the redemption of our sins. Similar to; if we were found guilty of a crime, and sentenced to prison, deserving the death penalty. Then someone else comes along and exchanges his life for ours. Because of God's great love for us, he gave His Son Jesus as a ransom, so we could go free, even though we don't deserve it. This is God's amazing grace. By faith, we ask for God's forgiveness of our sins, then believing in Jesus as Lord and Saviour. Thus wanting to serve and obey His commandments. He became my companion and boss.

You may think that you are a "good person," but we all still have sin in our lives. What about all those white lies, that cheating, that little thing you took, or the way you gossiped about others? What did you do when no one was looking? What about all those hurtful words you spoke? Etc. Sin is sin. We all have sinned, and fall short of the glory of God. We need to confess, repent and obey God's commands. But the most damaging to your own soul and spirit is to reject Jesus Christ as your personal Lord and Saviour, and end up in eternal hell. It seems to me that hell is like living in a nightmare where you never wake up. It is real. People who have had near death experiences, or who have died and came back often tell of their heaven and hell experiences.

Over the centuries, many people even gave their lives to preserve the Word of God, in the Bible. Many believers were martyred for Christ's sake. Even today, the Bible remains the most published, the most quoted, the most translated, and the most influential book in the HISTORY of mankind! The Bible is God's inspired word, and it requires prayerful, careful study. There's a great book called "What if Jesus had never been born?" by Dr. James Kennedy, revealing the great number of Christian inspired initiatives and works, such as schools, hospitals, and modern Governments. Christians also inaugurated the abolition of slavery, animal rights, common laws, women's rights, and rights for the Preborn etc.

As I began to read the Bible, I could hardly believe that most topics are covered in it. From adultery to murder, and stealing to hypocrisy it's all in there. Yet God is loving and just, and He will forgive us of all our sins.

One day Bernie, a Jewish friend dropped by. He wanted to smoke up with me. I told him that I had quit, that I was reading the Bible and started going to church. He just about flipped. He could not believe it, he had known me for a couple of years, and knew that I was a big partier. "Oh come on, Denise, just smoke this one joint, this is really good stuff." He smiled. Well, I tried to dissuade him for a long time then he lit it up anyway, and passed it to me with those big brown eyes of his. "Okay," reluctantly I took it and stated that "This is my last one!" So I took a puff. After a couple of minutes, I felt so guilty and awful, it made me paranoid. That was the last toke I ever had. Hallelujah!

My years of smoking pot had left oodles of scars and evidence of damage done to my lungs and mind. Not to mention all the smidgen holes in my car upholstery, and furniture. Such long term uses of marijuana, had left my short term memory brain cells the most destroyed. It was obvious that a lot of damage had been done since I was always forgetting things. Still, having a difficult time remembering some things from the past. Facts are marijuana is a terrible addicting drug full of THC and many poisonous chemicals out to destroy your lungs and throat with cancer too. Do not be deceived. If you open the door to alcohol, you will probably open the door to pot. When you open the door to addictive prescription drugs, cocaine and other substances, remember; those drugs are out to destroy your life and relationships. Think about it, every alcoholic or drug addict always started out just as a 'sociable drinker' or occasional drug user!

Back to the story. Obe had invited me to his church, but he felt that since the whole congregation was black, he figured that I would not feel as comfortable. It didn't bother me, but I took his advice and decided to go to a different church every Sunday, until I found one that I liked. Seeing the differences in each denomination was absolutely remarkable. Although each confessed Jesus Christ as Lord, they were all so profoundly different in ritual and tradition.

The Salvation Army does such great work with the poor and needy. Yet, they do not believe in water baptizing people, or in receiving Holy Communion, (partaking of the breaking of bread and grape juice, in remembrance of the Lord Jesus' body and shed blood for us). These acts are foundational to the Christian faith, according to what I read in the Bible. I thank God for all of the services they provide for single Moms, prisoners, the hospitals and all the social work they do.

Sadly, however, according to their policy statement, they believe that it's okay to abort a baby if the mother was raped, or if the baby has anomalies. This philosophy does not line up with scripture. Concerning the rape of the mother resulting in a pregnancy; "The fathers shall not be put to death (for the sins) of their children. **Neither shall the children be put to death for the fathers**; only for his own sin shall anyone be put to death." Deut. 24:16 Regarding anyone conceived with imperfection, *"And the Lord said to him; Who has made man's mouth? Or who makes the dumb, or deaf, or the seeing, or the blind? **Is it not I, the Lord?**"* Ex. 4:11

Many churches I visited were so dead. They were like walking into funeral parlours. They were cold. The people were frigid and suspicious. The majority were elderly and many seats were vacant. They had no evangelistic outreach into the community. They were ingrown, stagnant and complacent. Some have even bought into the world rhetoric and compromised the gospel of Christ to be men pleasers instead of God pleasers. Many want their ears tickled, rather than hear the truth.

Some, like in the book of Revelation tolerate that spirit of Jezebel. Rev. 3 spells this all out. Jesus said that there would be "Hot, cold and lukewarm churches." The lukewarm He will spit out of His mouth. They believe that living in sin, sex outside of marriage is okay. They think that sex and perversion is acceptable and unpunishable by God. Wrong, according to the Bible. By the way, love does not equal sex. They sanction practising homosexuals to be ordained as ministers and teachers of a Holy God. This is blasphemy! Love is not lustful sex acts. Obedience to God means to overcome our sins, including fornication. Satan has camouflaged churches of followers too. They promote self indulgence, self-centredness and hedonism, instead of self-discipline, a fruit of the Holy Spirit. *"For wide is the gate and broad is the way that leads to destruction and many are those who enter therein. But narrow is the way and strait which leads to life and few are they who find it."* Matt. 7:13,14. Jesus warned us of false teachers and preachers. Be careful of "Ear ticklers."

Some churches I visited appeared to be full of hypocrites. The people would get all dressed up, go to church on Sunday or just on special occasions. Then go home and get drunk, take pills, beat up their wives, or cheat on their income tax etc. They just went to church to be seen as righteous. It is a family tradition, and they like the rituals. God does not want us to have one foot in the church and one foot in the mire. He wants a personal relationship with His children, **not a form of godliness**. By the way there is no "perfect" church, but some come close.

Finally, I found the kind of church that I perceived Jesus was the head of. It was hot and ALIVE! The people were really friendly, they sang, clapped their hands like King David did in the Old Testament. They praised the Lord with their hearts, not just their lips. The preaching was inspiring and relevant to our lives today. They teach that Jesus was born of the virgin Mary. That he died on the cross for our sins, was beaten so we could be healed, rose on the third day, overcoming death so we could have eternal life. If we believe this, repent of our sins, and walk by faith, we will be saved.

He is off the cross now. He sent us His Holy Spirit so we would receive power to share His gospel and our testimonies. The Pentecostals believed and taught the WHOLE Bible, not just bits and pieces. They teach an uncompromising gospel, not wavering God's word just to please people. Here the folks I met were hungry to learn more about God's Word, who He was, how we could please Him.

In the Bible I discovered that they clapped their hands, shouted and sang unto the Lord in the book of Psalms. This became a whole new adventure as I totally surrendered my life to God. Asking Him to forgive me of all of my sins, and cleansing me from all unrighteousness. It was incredible how I went through so much grieving and pain as the old Denise, and her old ways had to die. This dying to the old self was necessary, to be born-again. This spiritual awakening, growing in the grace and knowledge of the living eternal God, creator of the universe and everything in it, is magnificent.

My favourite song is "Amazing Grace," how God saved a wretch like I was. This is a spiritual pilgrimage and God is not finished with me yet. We need to take it one day at a time. In my early journals I came across a great profound message that I would like to share with you. *"Watch your thoughts; they become words; Watch your words; they become actions; Watch your actions; They become habits; Watch your habits; they become character; Watch your character, For it becomes your Destiny!"*

As a baby Christian I came across an old buddy from my high school days up in Mapleville. I had decided to go and visit a local bar just to see who I would run into. Dan was there. When I told him that I was a Christian now and had quit doing drugs, right away he said that he was a Christian too. I asked him why he was drinking beer, and he said, "Oh I just have a couple, once in a while." As we spoke it seemed that he was pretty up on his Bible verses, and thus we had a lot in common. He is quite a big, burly, masculine type of guy and I found him very attractive. He asked me out, and the next thing you know, we were having an intimate relationship.

Since I had an apartment in Toronto, and he lived up north with his parents, he often came to see me. We were quite an item, he asked me for a key to my apartment, and he would stay over on weekends.

His parents lived on a farm, and his beautiful Godly mother was an inspiration to me. Her soft silver hair sparkled and her blue eyes glistened as she spoke. A woman of grace, wisdom and maturity. They had fostered mentally and physically disabled children for many years. Bryan who was about fifteen, tall, skinny, and had the maturity of a 4-year-old, loved to build little projects of wood and plastic materials. He showed me his little fort and some inventions he made in the back yard. Frank, sixteen, was short and stalky, he was so serious, and had difficulty handling his emotions.

Mary, Dan's Mom, was compassionate and ran the home like a good boot camp. Mary was always active, preparing dinner, doing laundry or housekeeping. Her husband was very quiet, and mostly kept to himself. Much like my own Dad.

Mary loved these boys and she taught them all about the love of God. She knew when to bridle her tongue, and when to speak a word in season. She never condemned our errors, but let the Holy Spirit deal with us. Her fervent prayers were being heard in heaven, as she steadfastly called on the name of the Lord for help and direction.

It astounds me now though, how she ever put up with our nonsense as young believers. What patience, what virtue, what endurance?

Anyway, the Holy Spirit began to convict me of our sin of fornication, (having sex outside of being married to each other). Soon I was telling Dan that we could not "fool around" any more. It was wrong, and I felt terrible about it. He would then reply, "Oh Denise, the spirit is willing, but the flesh is weak."

As a baby Christian, I just knew that I had to change my old lifestyle. It wasn't easy though. I had to quit doing drugs, and start saying no to booze. My flesh and soul had become so dependent on them. Stopping was demanding. With God's help, all things are possible, if you believe.

Undoubtedly, the hardest habit to break was smoking those cancer sticks. For seventeen years I had been a heavy smoker. One and a half to two packages were inhaled every day into my poor lungs. Holding a conversation, without having a cigarette in my mouth was unimaginable for me. Very addicted, proud and dumb, I had enjoyed smoking.

At first I tried to justify my smoking with God. I thought that *"Well, God created the tobacco, so I guess that smoking it is okay."* Then I heard a little voice inside say, *"Yes, but God created poison mushrooms that can kill you, does that mean you're supposed to eat them?"* *"Of course not"* I reasoned. Then I read the scripture in Corinthians that says, Our body is the temple of the Holy Spirit, and we are not to pollute it. That was enough evidence for me. *God is right, I have to quit smoking, besides it is much healthier not to indulge.*

Justifying our sins or habits is right from the pit of hell. Every thief, or murderer will always try to justify his or her crime, that does not excuse it. Besides, it would be a good example to my nieces and nephews, and hopefully it would encourage my Mom and the rest of the smokers in our family to quit. This would be a challenge.

This is how I quit smoking; maybe this will help you too or some-one you know. It worked! First I asked some faith filled Christians to pray for me. Then I cut down to ten cigarettes a day for one week. This gave me practice to resist smoking. Then with additional prayers I threw out my last pack. When the temptation came to have a cigarette, and it did, I would RESIST! Yes, every time I got the urge to smoke, I would just think to myself, *maybe later.* Then later when I got an urge to smoke, I would put it off and think *maybe later. Later, later, later ...* And guess what? Praise God, I have not had a puff in over twelve YEARS! Wow! I can hardly believe it. Freedom, health and fresh air! Now I find the stench totally repugnant.

Hope this assists and encourages you or a friend to quit. Remem-ber, that smoke and alcohol addictions are out to kill you, and destroy your loved ones too! Don't fool yourself or be enticed. We, who have overcome, know the waste of time, money, destruction of well-being and bondage that it truly is! Just read the labels on the very packages. It says it all. You teens out there, **"Be smart, don't start!"**

Dan and I went out for some months. He was very strong on a lot of theological points. He sternly warned me about all my involvement with I Ching, the ruins, tarot cards and the New Age philosophies. With my stubborn German pride, and self-centeredness I argued that this stuff was interesting and helpful. It wasn't until Dan showed me a few scrip-tures in the Bible that convinced me he was right. There is a higher truth, the Word of God. All these occult practices, were in reality forms of witchcraft and counterfeits to the power of God's Holy Spirit. I got rid of every trace of them. The day I threw all my old tapes, records, occult books and accessories in the garbage I could feel a weight lift off me.

Dan's dear mother invited me one weekend to a 'Women's Aglow' convention up in Beaverton. When we walked into the huge convention hall, you could sense a high regard for God in this place. We began to sing the most majestic life-giving songs. It truly was an experience of real praise and worship to God our heavenly Father. As I sang along, tears began rolling down my cheeks. I just sensed God's love, presence and comfort in that place. After an inspiring sermon by a woman on the fact that we consisted of Spirit, Soul, and Body, she emphasized the importance on having a relationship with God. Then she prayed and reverently asked if anyone wanted to come up for personal prayer. My heart was pounding. It felt like I should go up, but in front of all these people?

Then a voice from within, as clear as day, confirmed "**Denise, your virginity was stolen when you were raped at the age of thirteen.**" I had never told anyone that I had been raped, over the years. This revelation positively took a huge weight off me. Buckets of tears rolled down my face. So this was the root to all that promiscuity and all those bad relationships over the years. Simultaneously it all made sense. The devil had robbed me of my virginity, my integrity and self-worth. Through this pervert, satan stole my innocence, which in turn made me feel defiled, and indecent. Tears were now gushing down.

Head bowed and with great humility and anguish, I slowly made my way forward. Each step filled my soul with the most unbearable remorse and regret. It was then that I also began to mourn the deaths of my three children whom doctors had aborted. Until now, I had bottled up these emotions, never really dealing with or acknowledging the fact that these were indeed, little babies. The tiniest of humans who were perfectly alive, and then were killed at the hands of the abortionists. Barely able to see or walk because I was crying and sobbing so much. Doubled over, I took a step in faith and continued forward to the altar to confess these deviant sins.

A woman came up to pray for me. When she asked what I wanted prayer for. I blurted out in a loud voice, "Oh God please forgive me for murdering my own three children. I'm so sorry. I didn't know. I didn't realize … Oh God please forgive me …" I languished. A great gusher of pent up emotions trapped for years came forth. From the depths of my being, my inner soul I began to wail, like nothing I had ever heard or experienced before. Deep grieving and remorse belted out. It was incomprehensible. So much pain bottled up for so long.

The strange yet caring woman just cuddled me. She never said a word. Whoever you are, thank you for putting those loving arms around me. My nose flowed with mucous all over us and tears like a river flowed, yet we didn't mind. After using up almost a box of Tissue, it seemed like a very long time, I slowly maneuvered my way back to my seat. This confession and repentance although so difficult, changed the course of my life forever. For the better.

A peace that passed all understanding filled my soul. Love flowed over and through me. I could barely walk or talk. Pure tranquillity. It was then that I knew that God was so merciful and kind. To realize that God would even forgive me of these atrocities is so remarkable! Free from guilt, the weight of sin lifted off me. A new exonerated, decontaminated, consecrated woman!

Dan was getting exceedingly frustrated because now I made him sleep on the couch. Feeling a bit guilty that he was so put off, I went to bed and began to read my Bible. Just divinely turning to read 1 John where it says that if you know something is a sin, and you keep doing it anyway, it is wrong. It is also just lip service if you ask God to forgive you for something, then you just keep going back and doing the same things repeatedly.

So the Lord substantiated to me, that standing my ground with Dan was the right thing to do. Thoughts did come to me akin to *since we had already been intimate anyway, what was the difference, and what if he is going to be my husband anyway*. But no, I knew, that I knew, that I knew, having sex before marriage was wrong. On searching out all the scriptures that forbid fornication and getting the dictionary definition of it, I wrote them down for him to study. Then I prayed and asked that the Lord would give me a supernatural sign to show me if He really wanted me to marry Dan, or should we break up?

The very next morning was Sunday, and again we were running late, so I kept on him to hurry up. He was upset because he could not find the key he had to my apartment. "Come on!" I exclaimed. So off we went, he in his car, and I in mine. After the church service, I went up to the altar to pray for a woman. If someone was hurting, I could not just sit there, I had to go and comfort them. I prayed for her. Dan invited me out to lunch. At the restaurant we got into an argument over this woman's dilemma. The discussion heated, and he said, "Denise maybe we shouldn't see each other anymore." With a sense of relief, I agreed. We went our own ways.

When I returned to my apartment, lo and behold there was my apartment key. It was smack in the midst of the long, white shag carpet in the living room. The really bizarre thing was that the big round steel key ring had been totally pulled apart. It looked like an incredible hulk angel must have done it. Anyhow, this was a supernatural sign to me that God did not plan for Dan and me to be married to each other.

Involved and plugged into the corporate Bible studies and the young adult's group at church. I was hungry and thirsty to learn about God and His plans for my life. Literally, I dove into the Bible, totally surrendering my life to Him. It can be compared with my old life, living like a caterpillar. Eating the food of the world, vain philosophies, false theories, lies, deceptions, rhetoric, hedonism, sex, drugs and booze, etc. Then in opening the Bible, shutting myself off from the world, was like going into a cocoon.

Slowly as truth and light illuminated my soul, my character and ideologies began to transform into a lovely butterfly. This was a fresh new start in life. Now I was heaven-bound, instead of earthbound. What a freedom! A spiritual awakening had taken place in my Spirit, and now I was "Born-again." Just like Jesus explained to Nicodemus in John 3:1-8. Sure, part of me, my old selfish nature, still wanted to smoke and drink and indulge in sensual things. My perspective had changed. Now I wanted to please God, more than please myself. Fully committed to serving my Creator, and the Creator of the universe. Guess you could say, I was getting "brain washed!" We all need a brain washing, to get rid of the foul smut from the depths of Sheol that have crept into our consciences. God wants us to be obedient to what He has called us to.

My friend Elsie Underwood, a seasoned Christian says she took notice of me when I stood up in a College and Careers Bible study. Flashing a newspaper clipping that showed a woman with kids sleeping in a bus shelter because they had no place to go. "Can we do something? We have to help these people. Jesus said that we are to help the fatherless!" I exclaimed. Elsie and I teamed up and did street ministries together, and are friends for life. She is a fantastic water-colour artist. If you need any Canadiana paintings with Scripture inspirations on the back of each one, just write me for her address.

The Young Adults of the church were having a weekend Retreat up at Muskoka Woods. It was now the May long weekend of 1987. At the age of thirty, I had a clean slate and a new start on life. Never had I felt so good, before. By this time I had quit drugs, smoking, premarital sex, but still had the occasional drink. Thinking it was the sociable thing, I brought along a bottle of wine. Well, at the time I figured that if Jesus drank wine that it must be okay. However, as I matured in spiritual things and had done some extensive research I discovered that the Bible definitely forbids the consumption of alcoholic beverages.

It clearly admonishes in not five, but **75 Bible scriptures to abstain from alcoholic drinks**. It must be very important to God for His children not to drink alcohol for Him to have so many warnings and commandments not to indulge in the stuff! Drunkenness is a sin. This is what is says in 1 Corinthians 6:9-11. *"Do you not know that the unrighteous will not inherit the kingdom of God? Do not be deceived, neither the immoral, nor idolaters, nor adulterers, not those who practice in homosexuality, not cheats, thieves, greedy, nor drunkards, nor extortioners and robbers will inherit or have any share in the kingdom of God. And such were some of you."* So if drunkenness is a sin, like adultery, lying, stealing and murder, then when does it begin? Is it okay to steal a little? No. Is it okay to lie just once in a while? No. Is it okay to commit a little adultery with dinner, or just get drunk on holidays? Is it okay to be half drunk? Of course not.

Who has woe? Who has sorrow? Who has contentions? Who has complaints? Who has wounds without cause? Who has redness of eyes? Those who linger long at the wine, those who go in search of mixed wine. Do not look on the wine when it is red, when it sparkles in the cup, when it swirls around smoothly; at the last it bites like a serpent, and stings like a viper. Proverbs 23:29-32. What about the verse that says, *"Woe, (anguish, grief, sorrow, heartache) to him who gives his neighbour a drink."* Habakkuk 2:15. *Therefore be careful how you walk, not as unwise men, but as wise, making the most of your time, because the days are evil. So then do not be foolish, but understand what the will of the Lord is. And do not get drunk with wine, for that is dissipation, but be filled with the spirit.* Ephesians 5: 15-18.

The early translators made the grave mistake of translating eleven different words from the original Greek and Hebrew, all into the same

English word "wine." In the original contexts one can clearly see that when alcoholic beverages were forbidden to drink, the consequences were devastating. Although some scriptures encourage its consumption, these refer to the natural grape juice. Two thousand years ago they used to boil the grape juice into a thick syrup and use it for medicinal purposes if one had a stomach ache.

This misconception on the word "wine" in the Bible has caused the downfall of thousands of Priests and Ministers. Ruining not only their lives, but many innocent lives. Great Topic for another book? This modern day Goliath of booze is out to kill, steal and destroy your relationships, your family, your job, your life and the innocent lives of others.

Samuele Bacchiocchi wrote an excellent book entitled "Wine in the Bible, A Biblical Study on the Use of Alcoholic Beverages." In the USA, alcohol is costing more than $117 billion every year and claiming at least 100,000 deaths per year. This is twenty-five times as many as all the illegal drugs combined. The real human cost of alcohol in terms of retarded children, violence, accidents, child and spouse abuse, divorces, rapes, robberies, sickness, and death transcends statistical figures in dollars.

If you would like more information on this vital topic, write or call the **Woman's Christian Temperance Union**. Their head office for Canada is located at 4211 Yonge St. Ste. 318, Toronto, Ontario, M2P 2A9, or call (416) 960-8607. They have excellent brochures, resources and information on the harmful effects of alcohol and other drugs. They also sponsor an annual children's poster contest. Their American office is located in Evanston, Illinois. It is a world wide organization. An excellent help for overcoming addicts is the "Serenity-A Companion for Twelve Step Recovery" Bible complete with the New Testament, Psalms and Proverbs. If you could use a "Serenity Bible" they may be able to help you get one. The Lord opened doors for me to bring these self-help books into Prisons, detention centres and women's shelters. This has been quite an exciting adventure.

Chapter 10

"A Fresh Start"

As a young Christian I was so excited about my new straight, wholesome life as a believer. None of my old friends were interested in checking out church. They still wanted me to go out with them to the bars and dance clubs. Drinking, drugs and men had been the major purposes of our get-togethers.

Anne a mature Christian needed a ride up to the College and Careers Weekend Retreat, and she was brave enough to come with me, a baby Christian. She could not get over my wild driving habits and proceeded to pray a lot on the way. Anne was astonished to see a bottle of wine in my trunk. Pointing she said, "Denise, you won't be needing that this weekend." "Oh, okay" I responded. That was the end of drinking the world's old wine. I got into the new spiritual wine.

The first morning we had an excellent time of prayer and worship. The Holy Spirit was really ministering to me. Pastor Rod, an anointed man from Vancouver had what they call in the Bible, a "word of knowledge." He stated, "There is someone here who has been involved in Tarot cards."

At that statement, my heart just about jumped out, tears began to flow and I knew that he was referring to me. He then said, "Whoever it is, I just want you to come forward, the Lord has a word for you." Instantly the thoughts came to me, *Oh no, everyone will think you are into the occult, don't go up, everyone will look at you.* Pride and fear tried to keep me from going up. So I thought, *Well, if God wants me to go up, then I am going.* So with all the courage I could bolster, I slowly arose and went forward. Tears of remorse and repentance came.

The Pastor asked me to renounce everything dealing with the occult, tarot cards, Ouija, new age, I Ching, witchcraft etc. I did so willingly. He then gently placed his hand on my forehead, and I felt so light and peaceful that I began to fall backwards. Pastor Rod said, "The Holy Spirit is coming upon you now." Then my brain started to panic, thoughts of *Help, I'm falling echoed,* and I forced myself forward. Otherwise, I would have been flat on the ground. It was like a river of peace swept over me. I returned to my seat to discover that everyone else was now on their knees praying.

I too humbled myself and began to praise God and pray. To my astonishment, strange-baby-like syllables formed out of my lips. Anne sitting next to me said, "Hey, Denise you're praying in tongues!" " What is that? ," I exclaimed. She told me that she would show me all the verses in the Bible that speaks about the Baptism in the Holy Spirit with the evidence of speaking in other languages. Wow, I thought *this is interesting*. God is good! Feeling wonderful and full of joy, I rejoiced.

God was now bringing wonderful new friends into my life, like Elsie, Darla, Anne, Dee, Joanne, Julie, Darka and many more. We had so much fun without the crutches of cigarettes, booze, or other drugs, and NO more hangovers. Bonus.

It was about this time in the late spring that I moved to a pleasant high-rise apartment building where my parents were the superintendents. The sixth floor apartment had a spectacular view of bungalow roofs, and there was a big balcony. It was a good sized one bedroom. On the warm spring day that I moved in, I could hear this loud chirping noise. When looking up, I beheld the most beautiful grey and yellow bird with an array of feathers sticking up on top of her head. It turned out to be a cockatiel.

My first thought was WOW. This must be my housing-warming gift from God, the Father. At the time I had a little blue harlequin budgie. So I took some of her food, held out my hand to this bird on my balcony door, and called, "Here birdie, birdie." To my astonishment, she flew right over onto my hand. My heart leaped, quickly I brought her in and shut the door. She was a blessing.

Around June of 1987, back at the church I will never forget that Sunday when an older Missionary couple had shared some of their experiences out in the field. Then they had an altar call and asked if anyone would like to come up for prayer. They specifically wanted to pray for things like spiritual pride, unforgiveness toward others, bitterness, gossip, or any other sins. So recalling that I had been a bit proud lately, I went up.

Spring was in the air. God was bringing much inner healing into my spirit and soul. It was a time of total change, from a wild promiscuous bar fly, to a sanctified, renewed woman. The aging missionary woman came to pray for me first. She prayed in the spirit and then gently put her hand on my forehead. Again, I felt that peace flowing over me. This time I decided not to fight it, but just to let go and let God do whatever He needed to do in me.

The next thing I knew, whoosh, down I lay on the hardwood floor. "WOW!" Was the first thought that crossed my mind, "God, touched ME?" It felt like I had fallen backwards onto a soft bed, bouncing as if on a trampoline. It never hurt at all.

Facing the ceiling, eyes closed, a tear or two gently rolled down my temples. Suddenly worried that my dress might be up around my thighs, I tried to move to get up. Guess what? I could not even lift up my head, then it was if the Lord said, "Denise just relax, I want to minister to you." Apparently, I lay there for about ten minutes or so before I could get up. It was neat! My dress was fine.

Chapter 11

"You Have A Destiny!"

Proverb 14:25 affirms, "A true witness saves lives, but a deceitful witness speaks lies [and endangers lives]." Amp.

God has a purpose and a plan for each one of us. The Lord kept revealing scriptures confirming His will and plan for my life. The book of Ephesians says in 5:11 *"To have nothing to do with the fruitless deeds of darkness, but rather to expose it."*

In Isaiah chapter 43:9-11 the words leapt off the page declaring, "Let all the nations be gathered together, and let the people be assembled. Who among them can declare this, and show us former things? Let them bring forth their witnesses that they may be justified; or let them hear, and say, It is truth. You are my witnesses, says the Lord, and my servant whom I have chosen; that you may know and believe me, and understand that I am he; before me there was no god formed, neither shall there be after me."

Yes, I am a witness who must share the truth. God inspired me to write this book with the intention of making a documentary drama, made for TV. The object of revealing my horrible past is so that the wickedness, corruption, lies and deception to millions of people about

In 1990 Denise attended the Summit on abortion in Houston Texas this was called the "Cemetery of the Innocents" representing the thousands of children killed each day in America.

abortion, will be exposed. Ultimately, babies will be saved from murder and mothers healed emotionally, psychologically, and spiritually.

After numerous prophecies, (words of knowledge, wisdom and future directions from God through His anointed ministers) it was obvious that the Lord wanted me to go full time into this ministry. To publicly confess the shameful fact that I had three of my own children aborted. With the sanction of doctors, politicians, friends and even family, the truth of this diabolical procedure has to be proclaimed. With a sense of urgency, I am compelled to tell my story again and again.

It was not until January 28, 1988 while watching "The Journal," on CBC National news that I was impelled to come forward and fight the spirit of murder in our Nation. Henry Morgentaler's face appeared so smug, and proud because the Supreme Court of Canada had struck down our only abortion law. The ruling came on procedural grounds by a vote of 5-2 (Two of the justices did not hear the case.) The erosion of law began when they had amended it in 1969. This permitted abortions where the life or "health" of the mother was endangered, in the opinion of a committee of three doctors. Even this was just a mere smoke screen to allow abortion on demand.

I never had to go before any committee. They abused this protocol. It held no weight whatsoever. Besides not one abortion has ever been declined to our knowledge in more than a million pregnancies over the years. In 1988, the majority of the justices cited inequitable access and delays in access, as a tool for their decisions. Just bureaucratic technicalities! Since 1988, these unelected, liberal minded Supreme court justices set the precedent, to undemocratically make abortion available on demand, opening wide the floodgates to permit abortion to be used as a violent form of BIRTH CONTROL.

It was at this point, as I cried aloud, appalled at such a notorious decision that I was determined to do something to stop this killing. My own deep hurt, remorse and guilt reminded me of the tens of thousands of women who must also be bearing their own private pain from terminating their Offspring.

A mother's womb used to be the safest place in the world for a Preborn child. Tragically, since 1969 a mother's womb has become the most perilous space in the world for a Preborn baby to be.

Here I was a single woman, praying to meet my future husband but compelled to talk publicly about all of my dirty, blood stained laundry. Can you imagine how embarrassing this was? This had to be God. In the natural it was such a horrible experience to relate. God gave me the courage and determination to speak out despite my own pride and selfish desires. There was a greater purpose at stake. The pro-choice jargon and rhetoric are capitalizing and deceiving women.

The very first time that I stood up to share my testimony, I could barely talk. Overwhelming floods of emotion poured out. The room was packed with young adults mostly singles who gathered weekly for prayer, singing, Bible study and fellowship. At this Pentecostal church, you could really sense the love of God, and the genuine love for people. The scripture teaching was accurate, in context and inspiring. Knowing that God forgave me is consoling. Forgiving oneself is the most difficult! The pain of contrition, the regrets, disgrace, and the humiliation to confess such a sinister act as abortion for convenience lingered upon me.

Yet, resolved to expose the truth about abortion, I had to go on. My mission is to expose the cover-up of what abortion really is; the slaughter of tiny babies, and the exploitation of women.

There are always **two victims with every abortion** -One dead, and One wounded! There is a fire in my bones, and I am out to fight this goliath of murder, by faith.

The cost of humiliation and shame is a small price to pay for the lives that will be saved due to the whole TRUTH being broadcast.

I offered my life to God, as a living sacrifice. Forgiven, because of His shed blood on the cross, even as a procurer to three murders. Acceptable by faith and by His righteousness, not mine.

GOD Begins to Open Supernatural Doors...

Coincidence, I think not? On January 29, 1988, I glanced outside my window while sitting at my desk. There was a big crowd of people standing across the street. My insurance office was in downtown Toronto on Bloor Street near Sherbourne. Being the inquisitive type, I wanted a closer view of the picket signs being displayed. Quickly throwing on my coat, I jogged across the street to find out what was happening. As I got closer and began to read the signs, I asked a demonstrator what they were doing? She replied, "This is about Constable David Packer, the police officer who refused to guard the Morgentaler abortion clinic. They ordered him to resign, or be fired."

My heart went out to him with compassion. Just then he walked outside. I just felt to give him a hug and encourage him not to give up. I remember saying "Thanks. You're doing the right thing." It so happened that just then a photographer snapped our picture and we were on a quarter page of the Toronto Star, January 31, 1988.

Prolifers encourage Constable David Packer during his tribunal. January, 1988

David Packer had recently been cited for a heroic rescue of a child from a fire, a few weeks earlier. Yet, management threatened to fire him for not guarding the abortion mill! What a brave man to stand up for his convictions, even though it meant great financial loss to his family and his whole career. He was right, how could he "defend" a business whose sole purpose is to destroy and rip little babies out of their mother's womb and then get paid for it? As a trained police officer wanting to uphold the law and protect life, how could he stand by and let them kill innocent human beings? What a courageous and gallant man, I prayed that God would bless him and his family abundantly for this sacrifice.

As an insurance agent, I felt that it was important for me to seek the Scriptures and find out if Christians should have life insurance. Quickly I discovered that yes, indeed there were references that exhorted believers to provide for his own family. Further, it is our duty to look after the widows and the orphans. So it was in the March/April 1988 Pentecostal Assemblies of Canada leaders "Resource" magazine where I had my very first article published. "A plea for the Widows - Is life insurance Christian?" Praise the Lord! The Pentecostal Testimony published my testimony called, What the Pro-Choicers Don't Tell You!" They also published "Massacre of the Innocents," an article I wrote.

The very first time I heard Bev Hadland speak, joy and awe filled my being. Here was a woman overflowing with enthusiasm and energy. Her vitality is used to speak to teens. She promotes chastity and secondary virginity. Bev felt a calling to warn our Nation's youth about the consequences of premarital sex. She has lots of statistics on the facts of Sexually Transmitted Diseases, birth control malfunctions, deceptions and myths about love. Bev also has a powerful message on self-esteem, resisting peer pressure and promoting total abstinence until marriage. An exuberant speaker. She wrote a fantastic book entitled, "Hang onto your Hormones!"

Bev and I met and hit it off great. She let me know that she was working on a video, titled "CHASTITY, A QUESTION OF CHOICE," and asked me to share my story. Willingly, I consented and headed to the studio.

It just so happened that the very same morning they scheduled me to tape with Bev, The Toronto Star published part of my story of abortion. They were doing a feature article in the "LIFE" section about "The Dilemma of unwanted pregnancy." I was just one of five women they used. My story revealed the true pain and remorse of a woman who had made the greatest mistakes of her life, and in humility was willing to admit it. Most of the other women were still in denial.

My friend, Anne, happened to co-host 'Food for Life,' a Christian Television program. She invited me to come and share my testimony on that program. This was in May of 1988. It aired all across Canada. Truly God was opening doors for me to proclaim the truth in hope that women listening would hear of my horrible experiences and let their babies LIVE! This was the hope that we had. If one woman expecting, changed her mind and let her baby continue to live it was worth it. All the pain, shame and humiliation would be worth every second of it!

On making myself available to speak, it was decided that I should make up a Biographical sketch and send it to the churches. Disappointedly it became evident that some of the churches that claimed to be Christian, believed in abortion on demand. This totally shocked me at first. Yet, Jesus did warn us that many would come in His name, but would not be of Him. They have bought into the deception, and ungodly ways.

Some Christian organizations, newspapers, magazines and churches avoid or ignore the topic. They are afraid to offend anyone. Jesus said; Matthew 18:10, 14 *"Take heed that you do not despise one of these little children"* *"It is not the will of your Father in heaven that any of these little ones should perish."* They preach a happy, men-pleasing gospel with no suffering or tribulation involved. Let us not shine too bright or be too salty! Jesus said in Matthew 5:13 *"You are the salt (preservative) of the earth; but if the salt looses its flavor, how shall it be seasoned? It is then good for nothing but to be thrown out and trampled underfoot by men."*

This is what God thinks about the act of abortion. The Bible is full of scriptures that denounce the shedding of innocent blood and respect for life. Isaiah 44:24 states *"Thus says the Lord, your Redeemer, and the one who formed you in the womb, I the Lord, am the maker of all things."*

Psalm 139 proclaims ***"Truly you have formed my inmost being; you knit me together in my mother's womb ... "*** And in Jeremiah 1:5 God declares, *"Before I formed you in the womb I knew you; before you were born I sanctified you; I ordained you a prophet to the nations."* God has a purpose and a plan for each one of us. He created us in His image (Genesis 1:27) and He loves us. Psalm 127:3 affirms that ***"Behold, children are a gift of the Lord; the fruit of the womb is a reward."***

One of God's great commandments is **"Thou shall not murder."** Also, in Exodus 20:1,13 and Jeremiah 7:6, we are not to shed innocent blood.

According to the Torah, which is the Old Testament, Is man permitted by God to take a life before birth? No way! "If men who are fighting hit a **pregnant woman** and she gives birth prematurely, but there is no serious injury, the offender must (still) be fined whatever the woman's husband demands and the court allows. But if there is serious injury, you are to take life for life, eye for eye, tooth for tooth, hand for hand, foot for foot, burn for burn, wound for wound, bruise for bruise." (Exodus. 21:22-25) Also in the book of Amos 1:3 it records, "Thus says the Lord: For three transgressions of the people of Ammon, and for four,

I will not turn away its punishment, **Because they ripped open the pregnant women** in Gilead … " In Matthew 18:14 Jesus said, *"Even so it is not the will of your Father who is in heaven that one of these little ones should perish."*

Should a child conceived as a result of rape or incest be aborted? Though this rarely happens. No way! "Fathers shall not be put to death for their children, **nor shall children be put to death for their fathers; a person shall be put to death for his own sin."** (Deuteronomy. 24:16) Besides, should the crime or behaviour of the father, justify killing the baby? Why add murder to the charge?

Should a child who might be born disabled or mentally handicapped be aborted? No way! *"So the Lord said to him, Who has made man's mouth? Or who makes the mute, the deaf, the seeing or the blind?* **Have not I, the Lord?"** Exodus. 4:11, Isaiah. 45:9-11, Romans. 9:20,21

As I began to study the ancient Bible on the subject of abortion, I came across many affirming scriptures. These scriptures encouraged me to go on and not to be afraid, not even for my life. Jesus commands us to love the sinner, but **hate** the sin.

Another set of scriptures from the Old Testament was etched in my heart and that was from the book of Ezekiel, chapter 3: 17-21 **Ezekiel is a Watchman:**

> *"Son of man, I have made you a watchman for the house of Israel; therefore hear a word from My mouth, and give them warning from Me:* **"When I say to the wicked, 'You shall surely die,' and you give him no warning, nor speak to warn the wicked from his wicked way, to save his life, that same wicked man shall die in his iniquity; but his blood I will require at your hand.** *Yet, if you warn the wicked, and he does not turn from his wickedness, nor from his wicked way, he shall die in his iniquity; but you have delivered your soul. Again, when a righteous man turns from his righteousness and commits iniquity, and I lay a stumbling block before him, he shall die; because you did not give him warning, he shall die in his sin, and his righteousness which he has done shall not be remembered; but his blood I will require at your hand. Nevertheless if you warn the righteous man that the righ-*

Denise picketing in front of the old Morgentaler abortion morgue in Toronto.

teous should not sin, and he does not sin, he shall surely live because he took warning; also, you will have delivered your soul."

Chapter 33:1-11 *"Again the word of the Lord came to me, saying, 'Son of man, speak to the children of your people, and say to them; When I bring the sword upon a land, and the people of the land take a man from their territory and make him their watchman, when he sees the sword coming upon the land, if he blows the trumpet and warns the people, when whoever hears the sound of the trumpet and does not take warning, if the sword comes and takes him away, his blood shall be on his own head. He heard the sound of the trumpet, but did not take warning; his blood shall be upon himself. But he who takes warning will save his life."*

"But if the watchman sees the sword coming and does not blow the trumpet and the people are not warned, and the sword comes and takes any person from among them, he is taken away in his iniquity; **but his blood I will require at the watchman's hand.** So you son of man; I have made you a watchman for the house of Israel; therefore you shall hear a word from My mouth and warn them for Me. When I say to the wicked, 'O wicked man, you shall surely die!' And **you do not speak to warn the wicked from his way, that wicked man shall die in his iniquity; but his blood I will require at your hand.**"

"Nevertheless if you warn the wicked to turn from his way, and he does not turn from his way, he shall die in his iniquity; but you have delivered your soul. Therefore you, O son of man, say to the house of Israel: 'Thus you say, "If our transgressions and our sins lie upon us, and we waste away in them, how can we then live?" "Say to them; 'As I live,' says the Lord God, I have no pleasure in the death of the wicked, but that the wicked turn from his way and live. Turn, turn from your evil ways! For why should you die, O house of Israel?"

Continuing steadfastly with the Lord, I developed a personal relationship with the King of kings and the Lord of lords. Jesus Christ became my boss, friend and intercessor. Jack Chamberlin the producer of 'Nite Lite', a Christian phone-in TV Talk Show that aired live from two a.m. to five a.m. called to invite me to be a co-host once in a while. What an honour. God was really moving and He was opening doors of opportunity for me to expose the truth about abortion over the air waves. It was jittery, yet exciting to be on TV. We received many calls from hurting people seeking prayer and Godly advice. The Lord had me speak in more than fifty churches that year. And more than forty the next. We

September 17, 1988 Christians for Life held the largest Pro Life Rally in Canadian history to date.

must remember that *"Righteousness exalts a Nation but sin is a reproach to any people."* Proverbs. 14:34

One day I saw a flyer about a National Rally for Life and telephoned Ian Speirs the Coordinator, in Quebec. He felt called of God to organize the largest Canadian Pro Life, Pro Family Rally in Canadian History thus far. After sharing a bit of my story with him, and offering to help, he asked me if I would assist them in promoting the Rally. He requested that I organize the people in the Toronto area. Also he said that another speaker had cancelled and asked if I would share my abortion experience on Parliament Hill in Ottawa. Without hesitation I accepted. We started Christians for Life-Toronto, a nonprofit, charitable group of prayer warriors.

Through my contacts and new friends at church we had about 12-16 people meeting Thursday nights for prayer, fasting and plans to fight the goliath of abortion in our land. We held our first major rally in Toronto on September 8, 1988 at the Toronto City Hall. Dynamic speakers like Rev. Ken Campbell, and Bev Hadland, singers Rick Dees, who wrote an awesome song entitled, "September," and Randy Dyer attended. Randy tried to intervene to save the life of his own child, when his girlfriend decided to have an abortion. He unfairly lost the case, and they destroyed his son. Randy has gone on to cut his first CD. His heart and music reveal the pain he has endured as a biological father unable to protect his own tiny child from slaughter.

This first Rally in Toronto brought hundreds of people together in agreement to stand against abortion. We were welcoming the Life Line runners. Tom Anthony reported for 100 Huntley Street, he interviewed me and the clip aired on the 700 Club in the United States and also across the Canadian broadcast. We always sent out media releases in advance but No other media showed up! The media has proven to be biased when it comes to the topic of abortion.

There were people walking across Canada from the West Coast and from the East Coast to meet at the Parliament Buildings in Ottawa on Sept. 17, 1988. Excitement mounted as we got together to orchestrate the rally on the hill. Ian spearheaded it as the President of Christians for Life-National.

NATIONAL RALLY FOR LIFE

"The issue of abortion became the unifying link between Evangelical Protestants and Roman Catholics, and even French and English-speaking Canadians." Tom Anthony of 100 Huntley Street reported on TV. The police estimated that more than 25,000 people were present. The exhilaration mounted as news that Mother Teresa, a Nobel Peace Prize winner, was going to speak to this large Canadian crowd. She was a living saint who loved and knew Jesus. God had called her to work in Calcutta, India to help those living in extreme poverty.

Our Christians for Life executive Board had prayed earnestly that she would come to address the issue of abortion from a humanitarian point of view. We knew that she was well respected and known for her diligent and compassionate work. Praise the Lord, she accepted our invitation! Mother Teresa felt called of God to come to our Rally and be a voice for the voiceless. She had rarely made public appearances.

Mother Teresa was modest, very short and aging, yet full of God's love and goodwill. She announced to the huge crowd gathered, "Every abortion kills two ... the child and the conscience of the mother ... If you do not want the child, give it to me! In destroying the child, we destroy the image of God." In an interview with reporter Mike Duffy she stated again emphatically, "I know only that people are hungry for God, and it is for us, to all help each other to grow in holiness. That is why Christ has died on the cross, to show us how to love. And then He has made himself the bread of LIFE to give us LIFE. To give us life. And he loves us now. That is why it is important that we, all of us, take the trouble to have that one on one relationship, to be alone with Him. Receive His tender love, and give our love to Him. God is love."

Duffy then asked her, "What is the role of women in the church?" She replied, "Be a good woman, a good mother, a good wife. That is much greater than anything else. He then asked her, "What is your message to Canadians regarding the issue of abortion?" With certainty she replied, "We must remember that, every one of us, and **every unborn child, has been created for the greater glory of God, and has been**

created for greater things, to love and to be loved. So if we remember that ... there will be more love, more tenderness, more concern for that gift of God-the Child." He then asked her if there was any room for compromise? She responded, "No! They must decide before the conception."

Pro Life groups pondered how we could save Preborn children heading toward the slaughterhouse, in a peaceful, nonviolent way.

I knew that the public, especially women needed to hear the truth about what really goes on behind clinic doors and be warned of the consequences. It came to me that God uses ink, so I began to write.

The Barrie Examiner published my testimony entitled, "Telling the world; Relating her experiences helps woman fight abortion 'deceit'." Beth Ryan of 'NOW' magazine, published an interview that I had with her also.

Randell Terry brought Operation Rescue to Canada. This is a peaceful, nonviolent demonstration dedicated to saving babies scheduled to die on death rows. He is a man determined to do everything he can to try and stop the murder of the innocent. The Biblical basis being Proverbs. 24:11,12 *"Rescue those being unjustly sentenced to death, do not stand back and let them die. Do not disclaim responsibility by saying you never knew about it. For God who knows all hearts, knows yours, and He knows that you know, and He will reward everyone according to their deeds."*

The truth of the whole matter is that we now have a society where doctors have become the paid assassins. Surveys show that the silent majority do not believe in abortion on demand, yet they remain devilishly quiet. Durante once said, "The lowest place in the pit of hell is reserved for all those complacent ones who said or did nothing." The Bible also heralds in Revelation 3 that those who are lukewarm in their Christianity, He will spit out. One of my favourite sayings is by Edmonde Burke an English writer who wrote, *"All that is necessary for the triumph of evil, is that good men do nothing."* If we really believe that abortion is murder, why don't we act like it is? How can we keep silent?

Nobel Peace Prize winner, Mother Teresa said, "It is a poverty to decide that a child must die, so that you may live as you wish."

Joe Scheidler author of "CLOSED-99 Ways to Stop abortion" and Denise

Chapter 12

"Operation Rescue ..."

The alarm buzzed at 6:00 a.m. to wake me up. *Oh, that is too early for me.* Forcing to drag myself out of the warm comfort of my bed, I arose. Soon I began to pray and ask God for His guidance and direction. There was an eerie silence and it was totally black outside, very still. When I walked into my apartment living room and glanced into Chuckies' bird cage, I sadly discovered that he lay motionless, dead on the bottom of his cage. *Oh no,* my heart jumped, but I didn't panic. Quickly I went and wrapped some paper towel around him and unhappily put him away.

Today was October 29th, 1988. It was a brisk cold morning, and about 75-100 people gathered to lay down their lives for a peaceful demonstration outside Morgentalor's notorious abortion chambers. Pro Lifer's are weary and discouraged after repeatedly sending letter after letter. Over twenty years of writing the Political Parties in office to no avail. We have signed multitudes of petitions over the years, and it all seems to get ignored. We know that we know, that we know, that they are killing innocent little babies, with the Government's approval. Finally we were going to really do something practical, to save at least a few lives. If we really believe that abortion is murder, then why aren't we responding like it is? We should be outraged at the injustice.

The landmark decision from five unelected, morally void, liberal judges under pressure from the pro-abortion and feminist forces, struck down our abortion law. These left-wing death promoters had the money to hire expensive lawyers, and won on technicalities and bureaucratic rhetoric.

Denise speaking out to warn women, save babies, and educate the public.

It was an "access to medically necessary services issue" they argued, never defining what deemed to be "medically necessary." The real issue is a woman's right to have her own child killed. What victimization! It isn't a choice, it's a child! A healthy woman, aborting a healthy baby is not a medical necessity. **Pregnancy is NOT a disease or sickness.** The Preborn are not gobs of tissue, cancers or tumours, but tiny little human beings. We all began our life in the warmth of our mother's womb.

How could we as "Christians" disobey the civil authority and "trespass" onto the front and back steps of the abortion clinic? Simple, in Acts 5:29 the scriptures consistently teach that when "man's law" and God's law conflict, we must obey God rather than men." Read also Exodus.

6:5-10, Acts 4:15-20. This too was the Biblical basis for the actions of **Corrie ten Boom**, who hid and protected the Jews during the Nazi holocaust. **Maximilian Kolbe** and many other brave Christians ran the underground railway, smuggling lawful slaves to freedom in Canada. Even a secular society, once they get all the facts, acknowledges that they must not obey a law that sanctions a great evil. This is an opportunity to unmask the evil of abortion and save lives!

Peaceful Civil disobedience is the only alternative when every other means of communication has failed to bring about justice for the youngest and weakest in our society, the Preborn. It is like when you know that a paid assassin is given little children to drown in his backyard swimming pool, and no one will stop the slaughter. The procurer shouts "It is my choice, it is my kid". The assassin screams "It is my property, it is my business, get lost!" Sometimes trespassing is necessary, to save the lives of innocent victims scheduled for extermination.

This was the first International US and Canadian Rescue. The purpose was to unveil the evil of abortion, and confront it, head on.

The video cameras rolled as Catholics and Protestants were united together and praying for the salvation of babies. We also prayed for God's help, courage and humility. Most of all we prayed that women would let their children live. We prayed that the abortionists and all their staff would be convicted by the Holy Spirit of their sins, stop and see the light!

Joan Andrews a US heroine, had just been released from prison. She had served a long 2.5 year prison sentence because she walked into an unoccupied room at a Pensacola, Florida abortion centre and attempted to just unplug an abortion baby suction machine. That was it! The judge, William Anderson actually sentenced her to **five years in jail**! It is ridiculous that on the very same day the same judge sentenced two men convicted of being accessories to murder, only four year sentences!

For years Joan Andrews Bell has been defending the Preborn in practical ways, just to end up thrown in jail for peaceful protest. Here is her affidavit in part: Joan Andrews Bell, of full age, upon her oath, says:

"I am the named defendant ... This is my statement of conscience. This is why I cannot accept probation."

Human life begins at the moment of conception. This is an undisputed fact of medical science. It is confirmed in every human biology and physiology book. It is confirmed in the field of embryology and fetology. Dr. Jerome Lejeune, Dr. Liley, and all the experts of medical science I have read, confirm this fact. **The research does not need further defence. It stands on its own uncontested merit.**

Even the 'Supreme' Court in Roe and Doe could not refute this fact. The court acting in a cowardly manner, pretended the fact did not exist by refusing to address it. The court lied by claiming that it is unknown when human life begins. The court ignored documentation in legal briefs, which contained undisputed scientific and medical proof that life begins at conception. The court preferred, instead, to enshrine social reasons as the "**impeccable**" basis for launching a brutal holocaust against the most defenseless in our society, the Preborn. All proponents of abortion maintain the same intellectually **dishonest position that recites hollow rhetoric that Preborn children are "blobs of tissue," and that this "developing tissue" must be destroyed for social reasons.**

Nevertheless, the Scientific fact is that "Human" life begins at conception, and has inalienable rights, yet are those deprived of their lives, is ignored. Not surprising. **Every holocaust in history has stood on the same corrupt and faulty premise which claims that certain categories of people must die under the guise of social necessity, proclaimed emotionally in an effort to mislead.**

In my 24 years in this sorrowful struggle, I have never met an abortionist yet, nor any proponents of the "**choice to kill**" position, who when willing to discuss the facts instead of spouting falsehoods, did not admit that **abortion is the act of killing a human child.** However, the facade gone, they maintain that killing is necessary for social reasons. It's a sham. Truth and reason have been rejected and **Truth** has been stomped underfoot. Distorted logic is maintained through an act of the will.

We in America **(and in Canada) know we are killing children!** God help us, we are a people who condone or ignore the brutal destruction of human life for a myriad of shallow and baseless reasons. We have made destruction of children our one, true god. It comes down to a matter of false values, convenience and Birth control. Do we value human life or do we uphold falsehood and personal selfishness?

Indeed, the **"choice people"** have manufactured their own private laws dependant on neither a morally based legal tradition nor moral norms of human conduct and moral behaviour. **Tragically and shamefully, government power and legal sanction has been given to this slaughter of the innocent, thus corrupting and undermining our whole system of law and order.** The courts of our land have unleashed anarchy against its most vulnerable members. North America now stands under judgement of history, and the just hand of God.

It is not surprising that after World War II, not only were the doctors of Nazi Germany held accountable for the murder of the innocent, but also the Judges who had followed laws of a corrupt legislature which legislated Jews to be "nonperson" and "enemies of the State." We mock justice today and show ourselves to be the greatest hypocrites.

God is Truth. Because God is Truth, all correct knowledge, judgement, understanding, wisdom, and science come from God and have their sole validity in the relationship they have to eternal laws of Truth, proceeding from the Universal law-giver, the **Creator of the Universe**.

Human life is sacred because mankind is made in the image and likeness of God. **Abortion is not only a crime against humanity, in that individual human beings are denied due process of law, but it is a crime against God!** Without measure or limitation, all human life is sacred because we belong to God, and we shall one day return to Him. By our merits and choice, we will either gain eternal happiness with God or lose God forever.

To declare that certain human life is not sacred, is to declare that no human life is sacred, that no one is to be universally cherished and protected. In essence, it is to say there is No God, and all reality is anarchy, that truth is meaningless, justice is nonexistent, and love is outlawed … It is my humble privilege to follow my conscience and my Catholic faith in defence of the innocent and the just. **I will not cooperate with immoral, unjust laws corruptly and cowardly imposed on the American people for the sake of pretending to solve social and economic problems by murdering innocent children.** I will not accept probation. **To accept probation would be to accept the lie that I harmed society by trying to peacefully, prayerfully, and nonviolently save children from a brutal death by abortion, and that I therefore intended to be rehabilitated.** To accept probation demands that I sign my name to a paper which says I will obey unjust laws. Indeed, I will not obey unjust laws nor consent to cooperate with the murder of the sacred lives of God's precious children. I could no more adhere to the unjust laws of this land, or in any way give credence to evil enshrined in law than deny God Himself. **With God's help, I will with trem-**

bling and shame for my own sins and weaknesses, accept and defend the Laws of God.

Finally, the United States, like all of Western Civilization, has a legal and moral tradition that accepts the fact that abortion is a crime against human life. The great evil was illegal up until the U.N.-Supreme Court decided to reject the facts of science and the legal and moral traditions of this country. **Against all moral norms, the Judiciary falsely "legalized" child killing.**

Abraham Lincoln said, in response to the argument that Blacks were not fully human because slavery was legal, "It is never right to do wrong, even when sanctioned by the law."...

Thomas Jefferson wrote that the first and most basic duty of government and of law is the protection of human life, NOT its destruction. He maintained that if government violates this most basic right, which is its primary purpose for existing, then it forfeits its authority to rule ... Recognizing that in America today, so-called "unwanted" Preborn children do not have protection under the law, it is only fitting that those of us who love them, and align ourselves with them, be denied freedom, and be condemned to jails and prisons. Preborn children, denied legal protection, often find the womb, a tomb. We, the born, who struggle on behalf of these abandoned children, can find our tomb of reparation in a jail cell or prison dungeon. And yet, the deepest and darkest tomb and dungeon of all is the human heart in a nation gone murderous. **When a child can be coldly dismembered, while alive, in utero, with national approval, and the brutal sanction of law,** there is no hope for such a nation without Divine Intervention. My only prayer is for God's will to be done in all things, and may repentance come so that no immortal soul is lost.

In summary, there are three platforms to my continued decision to serve God and refuse to cooperate with the Abortion Holocaust in America: 1) Science. The undisputed medical, scientific fact that human life begins at conception … privilege to suffer imprisonment for the love of God and for the sake of innocent children. I surely have enough sins of my own to warrant long hard reparation behind bars, but I pray God will use any time of separation from my family to also atone for the sin of abortion, even in the smallest way … As this holocaust of the Culture of Death has shown time and again, this whole struggle goes far beyond unjust laws and a government gone bad; it is a war between good and evil. That is why the Court is not putting me in jail to serve a fixed sentence. Instead, there may be an effort to coerce me to violate my conscience under cruel pressure of jail and the suffering caused to my family by an indeterminate incarceration. With God's grace, I will die in jail before I place even my family before God. If anyone puts God first, can he ever doubt God's protection for his family? No, never! **Regardless of what happens, my husband and children are in God's hands** … Thank you, dear, sweet **Jesus,** for this opportunity to draw closer to You!

Signed: Joan Andrews Bell, Sworn to and subscribed 22nd Day of Dec. 1997

At 8:42 a.m. I had volunteered to be a 'sidewalk counsellor' offering women help, and alternatives from abortion. *Frequently with tears in my eyes, I would say, "I have had an abortion in a clinic, you are wide awake during the whole procedure."* *"Right now your baby has a beating heart. He or she is ALIVE!"* *"We can help you with baby furniture, clothes whatever, it's not too late."* Holding a tiny plastic replica of a Preborn baby in the palm of my hand, I would show them what a baby really looks like at ten weeks.

Joan Andrews and Denise in Houston, Texas

If I had time, *I would warn them of the 27 possible physical complications that abortion can have on them.* They could get an infection, lacerations or cuts on the cervix, etc. leading to permanent sterility or having plenty of trouble bearing children later on.

With both entrances to the Morgentaler abortuary secured with Pro-Lifer's peacefully sitting in front of the doors. We could see the Pro-abortion forces gradually increasing, as more University students arrived. You could easily distinguish them because of their feminist grimaces and chanting. Finally, the police arrived. At around 12:45 p.m. I approached the Police Chief, and said, "The feminists are going to harass us, I hope that you are going to protect us. *We are here peacefully, protecting Pre-born babies from being killed, and they are here to disturb the peace."* He never replied.

At the front door and at the back door, the Pro-Lifer's were gently and sincerely singing the "Hallelujah" chorus. The extremist pro-abortionists brazenly began to chant. Using a large megaphone, they blared, "Not the church, and not the state, women must control their fate!"

125

Repeatedly. Then they started to bellow, "1-2-3-4, open up the clinic door!" These chants, so misleading and rebellious reminded me of a Jezebel, Absalom type of spirit.

Unawares, one of the Pro-abortionists suddenly jumped up and started to climb on top of the heads of the praying Pro-lifers. The Pro abortionists began pushing, shoving and kicking the pro-lifers ... They endured the persecution. Meantime, we Pro Lifers continued to sing that ancient familiar tune ... "Jesus loves the little children, all the children in the WOMB, red and yellow, black and white, they are precious in His sight, Jesus loves the little children in the womb." We repeated that chorus over and over, often with trembling. The opposition sure did not like that song. They detested us.

We had song sheets with us that really helped us to focus and keep calm amid the raging storm. The tension was extremely high. We could sense great demonic oppression, and fear would try to grip us, but in Jesus Name and trusting in Him we endured till the end. Martin Luther King used peaceful picketing, marches and nonviolent sit-ins, as methods to stop the racist segregation that was rampant in the United States in his day. It worked! It is much more difficult to raise up Christians against the spirit of murder.

Around 1:30 p.m. the police officers started to drag away the limp bodies of the Pro-lifers. I began to cry as one by one, they hauled them off into the paddy wagons. Referring to what goes on in the abortuary, I entreated; "It is the shedding of innocent blood. Those babies are alive. You were once in your mother's womb."

Those poor officers were caught in the middle of a spiritual and moral war zone. We sang from the depths of our hearts to the Abortionists inside the abortuary and to the ones standing against us. This was a tune from an old Beatle song ... "All we are saying ... is give life a chance ... All we are saying is give life a chance ... all we are saying ... is give life a chance ... "

As they dragged the last few rescuers into the paddy wagon, you could hear Natalie, a dedicated mother of three, and registered nurse entreating the police. "Please be on our side-It's a baby, not a bunch of cells," she cried out in a loud voice. "It is a BABY!" echoed, as the officer slammed the paddy wagon door. They drove off, leaving the Pro-abortionists cheering in ecstasy and now blocking the front door of the abortuary themselves. They were thrilled and haughty to see us go. The abortionist was "back in business".

On this eventful day in Canada, more than 11,000 rescuers shut down forty-two abortion centres, effectively and peacefully, from coast to coast. There were 4,663 people who were willing to lay down their lives and risk arrest. A total of 258 clergy from various denominations and 2,644 ordinary citizens were arrested that same day. In Toronto, more than eighty rescuers participated in this first rescue. In less than one hour we peacefully blockaded the infamous Morgentaler slaughterhouse.

Did we win, or did we lose? We are confident that some women who had scheduled abortions for that day, changed their hearts and minds and let their babies live. **If it made the difference to even ONE CHILD, it was worth all the suffering and pain we endured.** This works! At this first Operation Rescue, forty-one were arrested and charged with breach of the peace and released.

Of course the left-wing liberal media portrayed us as the fanatical dangerous demonstrators. While showing clips of the pro-abortion feminists and neo-Nazi's who were chanting and angry with us, they reported that this was the "anti-choice," instead of Pro Life demonstration. It appeared like we were the pro-abortionists on TV.

If it had been Greenpeace, Animal Activists, Mahatma Ghandi, or Martin Luther King Jr. the media would call it Passive Resistance or Civil Disobedience. In any event, when Pro-lifers have a peaceful sit in, they call us radical, violent, and outrageous. The power of liberal left-wing media.

When picketing our posters always express the **TRUTH**, such as: **"TWO VICTIMS TO EVERY ABORTION-ONE DEAD & ONE WOUNDED; ABORTION STOPS A BEATING HEART!; LIVE AND LET LIVE,"** and now one of my favourites, **"EVERYONE DESERVES A BIRTH DAY!"**

Other slogans read, "If it is **NOT** a baby ... then You are not **pregnant! Preborn babies are people too! It is a CHILD, not a choice!**

PEACE in the womb, stop abortion violence! Adoption is the loving OPTION, Abortion Hurts Women, and Abortion Kills Children." There are laws in Canada to protect Eagle eggs, Spotted Owls and other endangered species. However, there is nothing to protect **baby humans!** Do you realize that we Canadians are an "endangered species?" The environmentalists declare an "endangered species" when it's birth rate drops to 1.7. The Canadian birth rate has been at a mere 1.7 for several years now. We are not even reproducing ourselves!

DECEPTION REVEALED

The abortion providers call it "Reproductive Rights" Excuse me? *The right to reproduce came when the woman made the choice to have sex with a man. There is nothing right, or reproductive about killing a newly formed human being.*

They call it a "Termination of pregnancy." *Every pregnancy will naturally terminate at nine months. Abortion is really the EXTERMINATION of tiny individual human beings.*

For the record, neither I nor any Pro-Lifer I have ever met, condones the shooting of abortionists. *Apparently, the notorious shooter is a disgruntled father whose baby an abortionist killed?* Also, having a clinic blown up surely is much more advantageous for the abortionist side. This way they win public sympathy. Morgentaler received millions of dollars to start a brand new killing centre. Besides, Pro-Lifer's believe that, **"Two wrongs do not make a right."** Jesus teaches that we are not to render evil for evil.

The next thing you know I get a call from Campaign Life Coalition that I am the first named defendant in a $1,000,000. (that's a one million-dollar) civil lawsuit, by Henry Morgentaler. He had a strategy when he launched this lawsuit. It was used as a catalyst to get the interlocutory injunction. His purpose is to scare and intimidate us from peaceful protest. We are bad for his business he claims. Any babies who live, because their mothers changed their minds don't think so!

Because Henry is a rich abortionist and can afford lawyers, and we cannot, we must reluctantly give in to the judgement without the cost of a trial. Thus, injustice prevails for lack of funds! Where are the millionaire evangelists and prosperity teachers when you really need them? I have contacted a number of them for help - with no response. They hoard up luxury and treasures for themselves while satan slaughters the innocent. 1 John 3: 1-18 *"By this we know love, because he laid down his life for us. And we also ought to lay down our lives for the brethren; But whoever has this world's goods, and sees his brother in need, and shuts up his heart from him, how does the love of God abide in him? My little children, let us not love in word, or in tongue, but in deed and in truth."*

This case sets a terrible precedent in history. Where is the jurisprudence now? The fact that this injunction is so broad, and interferes with our basic HUMAN RIGHTS of Freedom of Religion, Freedom of Speech, and Freedom of Expression is irrelevant to the abortion providers. Talk about censorship! Where is the Human Rights Commission to defend "Pro Life" issues? No "choice" for us.

Any trade-union body would flip if they got an injunction prohibiting them from peaceful constitutional picketing on public property! We were simply doing peaceful picketing on public sidewalks, educating and warning women about the dangers of abortion, and offering alternative solutions. Today, through this injunction, we are not even permitted to hold a picket sign proclaiming the fact that "Abortion stops a beating heart," or allowed to pray on the public sidewalk! It could affect the abortion business, and save babies from execution.

On September 14, 1999, The Toronto Free Press published a report that in the year 1997-98 that alone, the Ontario taxpayers paid a whopping $567,325.00 to fund abortions. Ontario taxpayers in the last several years have handed over $2,611,828.00 towards Morgentalers death camp. It also states that his rent costs which we pay for, will exceed $5,000,000. The approximate cost to Canadians for killing 100,000 babies in the year 1992-93 was an enormous $55,964,593.00 Health care dollars wasted and used to kill, instead of helping and treating our people. Hello, anybody there?

"Denise and single Mom, with baby who did not get aborted!

Do you realize that right now in Canada it is legal for a woman to go topless in public in Ontario? It is okay for men to parade down main streets practically naked promoting homosexuality. And Recently, a British Columbia Supreme court judge struck down the CHILDREN'S pornography law! But whatever you do, don't stand on a public sidewalk with your clothes ON, and pray or hold a sign of truth. Because if it is in front of an abortion clinic the police will come and throw you in JAIL! It has happened often to Linda Gibbons, a grandmother who knows the reality of abortion.

What about the Human Rights Commission or the Canadian Charter of Rights protecting the Preborns? They quickly stand up for the homosexuals and lesbians. Doesn't it state that **"EVERYONE has the right to life, liberty and freedom," and we are "NOT to discriminate against anyone because of their AGE, or mental or physical disability?"**

Thanks to liberal-minded judges, it was okay for Henry Morgentaler to break the law in the fall of 1984 and commit illegal abortions. He had obliterated the tiny lives of about 18,000 healthy, innocent babies in the sanctuary of their mother's wombs, even while abortion was still against the law according to the Criminal Code of Canada. The Criminal Code correctly makes provisions to protect the humanity of the Preborn from the hands of abortionists. However, that jury selection must have been subverted, since all twelve jurors voted to let him go and continue the exterminations.

Aren't our judges and Government leaders discriminating against the weakest in our civilization when they allow abortion on demand on the youngest, most defenseless in our society? Recently there have been cases where they have charged pregnant women for sniffing destructive solvents that were harming their unborn children. Thank God, and Bravo, for the Edmonton police who had the courage and common sense to intervene to protect the health and safety of that unborn child, July 22, 1998.

Upon hearing the tragedy of 12 students shot and killed in cold blood in Littleton, Colorado, I was inspired to write this poem.

"Students are told there is No God"

We evolved from apes,
You are just a fluke,
No heaven or hell,
Just party till ya puke,
They say "Freedom of Choice"
to kill the babies.
Kill the disabled and kill the ladies.
Kung fu fighting, I'm so cool",
Violence breeds a deadly pool. No censorship,
Anything goes...
Nudity, homosexuality,
a condom with holes!
Booze, drugs - escape reality
wars - divorce
It's the "No God" mentality!

How many more will perish by the spirit of "Antichrist"?

Deeply involved and committed to Pro Life work, I resigned in 1989 from my seven-year insurance career. It was another step in faith as there was no salary in Pro Life work. My parents thought I was crazy to give up that good, secure job selling insurance. But my heart was just not in it anymore, I was now on a mission from God.

Chantal's Baby

After hearing about the horrible dilemma of Jean-Guy Tremblay on the news, I was prompted to help him save his baby's life, somehow. He was the father of a child conceived and growing in his fiancé's womb. She was adamant to end this baby's life. He took her to a Quebec Court and fought for the right to life for their child, and WON. He got an injunction prohibiting Chantal from cancelling the life of their child. She then decided with the help of the abortion providers to take the case to the Supreme Court of Canada, to get the right to kill this baby.

During this ordeal, the Lord gave me a vision to have a big Baby Shower for this woman with child. We would hold it in front of the Supreme Court of Canada, in Ottawa, our Nation's capital. This is the arena where the fight for life takes place. Jean-Guy had won the case in the Quebec court. Nevertheless, this woman and her feminist Pro abortion entourage were determined to use her rights to destroy the life of this perfectly healthy baby. They had absolutely no regard for the rights of the biological father to protect his baby from being executed. Nor did they consider right to life for the Preborn baby. This little baby was now more than twenty-one weeks old, viable and helpless against any abortionists' weaponry.

We rallied about 150 people together, and organized three bus loads of dedicated Christians from the Pentecostal and Catholic churches primarily. It was a five-hour journey from Toronto to Parliament Hill in Ottawa.

We asked everyone to bring a Baby Shower gift for Chantal. We wanted to let her know that we cared about her, and the baby. The bus cargo holds were crammed full of baby-gifts. The baby was still alive. If she would not receive the gifts, we would donate them to local pregnancy care centres, to help and bless other single Moms. The Lord had revealed to me in His word that we are to overcome evil with good. We remained positive with prayers and hope that Chantal would let this baby live. We prayed.

On August 1, 1989, we appeared at the Supreme Court of Canada with a huge playpen. It was filled with big stuffed toys including an elephant, a huge giraffe, and lots of dolls. Practical items also, like diapers, a swing-o-matic and about fifty gift-wrapped presents addressed to Chantal and her baby. It was fantastic! Danielle, a young woman who had been through a horrifying second trimester abortion was beside me.

Before the court case was completed, they announced that she fled across the border to the US. Rebelliously, she had her five and a half month old baby aborted anyway. Case closed, another baby dead. We had tried to intervene. Before God we proclaimed that her baby was indeed a little person with humanity, and that we wanted to help her in practical and loving ways. The blood is on her and the abortionist's hands now. God gives us a free choice and he will never override our will. However, His judgement will come, unless we ask for forgiveness and change our ways.

Another Baby Killed

The night before Chantal's Baby Shower, I had a speaking engagement in Quebec. Ian Speirs the National Director of Christians for Life had arranged for me to share my abortion experience to a group of people there. Most times when I share, I relive the remorse, pain and the shame of my experiences. Often tears cascade down as I look back at the atrocity. Sometimes it is very difficult even to speak, or keep going on. Nevertheless, I must, so I persist. After my talk, I gave an invitation to any woman who had an abortion, or was thinking of having one, please to come and talk to me, so I could pray for them. Knowing that they can receive God's forgiveness and inner healing, is vital to their recovery.

Head down, tears streaming, Danielle, a slender, petit woman approached me. In a soft, gentle voice she wept and said, "I really need to talk to you, can you come over to my place afterwards?" "Sure," I replied. Danielle lived with her Mom, and her four-year-old son. She had him when she was eighteen years old. This frail young woman proceeded to tell me her story. She and her son had been living with this guy Steve for about a year, when she found out that she was pregnant.

Steve was furious and upset. He did not want to have another kid. He had demanded that she go have an abortion. She resisted. Deep in her heart she knew that it was wrong. She thought that with time, Steve would adjust to the fact that she was carrying his child. Wrong! He kept pressuring, condemning and threatening to ship the kid to Trinidad with his Mother if she had it. This frightened her.

Danielle had been stalling. By now she was more than five months along. To get Steve off her back, she made an appointment for an abortion at the Toronto General Hospital. She figured that the doctors would say, "You are too far along, it is too late, go home and wait to have the baby." She expected that they would give her a list of organizations that could help her.

Dead wrong! They did not say anything like that at all. Instead they just reiterated what the boyfriend was saying. They convinced her that if she carried through with this pregnancy the boyfriend would leave her and she would end up on welfare! "They told me that this was the best thing. It was no big deal." She went on to charge how they had ensnared her. She was very reluctant. Yet they persisted, casually persuading her until she gave in. The counsellor said, "We'll just inject saline in your belly, you'll have a few cramps and an early delivery, and it will all be over." Scared, but trusting them, she grudgingly went ahead with the procedure. They made it sound so simple and easy. If it's okay with the doctors, then it must be alright, she thought.

First they doped her up with Tylenol 3 and codeine, then later with Valium, a strong pain killer, that made her quite groggy and took away her wits. All alone, with no one by her side, a doctor proceeded to insert

Chantal Daigle "Baby Shower" August 1, 1989 in front of the Supreme Court of Canada

a 6-inch needle into her rounded bulging belly. The pain was indescribable, she lamented. First they withdrew quite a bit of fluid from the growing bulge in her belly. They then injected a high concentrated salt solution and poison mixture into the amniotic fluid. "At that moment I felt my baby move, but in no other way I had felt her move before. I fought back the tears as the smiling Doctor, assured me that it would all be over soon," she recalled. (This poison burns the baby's skin. The premature baby is then forced to swallow the poison which then burns his/her throat and lungs.) No choice here! (Dr. Paul Ranalli a neurologist, confirms that babies do feel pain.)

They also injected a Prostaglandin drug to force labour. They drew the hospital curtains around her bed. She began to get contractions. She had felt the little one thrashing around frantically, fighting for her life for about an hour, and then the kicking stopped. With the realization that her baby was now dead, she understood that she had betrayed and killed her own child. Danielle wanted to die herself! Later they injected her with Demerol. She was in hard labour for thirteen long hours, twice worse than normal birth pains. This was NOT what she had expected. During this time she cried, screamed, vomited and fainted. This was NOT how they described it would be!

The next morning will haunt her for the rest of her life. The girl across from her gave birth to her dead baby hysterically screaming, "Euhh, that is gross! It is a baby!" While a nurse came to take out the other girls baby, Danielle terrified, was trying to hold her legs together, "My baby is coming!" She quickly buzzed for the nurse as she screamed. But Danielle didn't want to let the baby go. She thought, *Oh Baby, I am so sorry, I want you to be alive again!* Her bed was a mess, water, placenta and a tiny little girl, fully complete. She had perfect little arms, and legs, delicate tiny fingers and toes, she was beautiful. Nevertheless, Danielle now had a totally dead corpse, yet still warm, leaning against her right thigh. Quiet, and motionless. "I wanted so badly to hold her, to go back just 14 hours, and change my mind, but now it was too late." Blood all over. "Oh, my God" she wailed, "What have I done?" Deep remorse and guilt flooded her soul. The nurse looked in, and smiled "Oh, I have to get a pan, I'll be right back," and left her to mourn the death of this baby. The nurse then returned to dump the baby into a cold steel bed pan like a stinky piece of meat! Danielle continued, "I had killed a perfect baby girl, so beautiful and pure, defenseless, like a lamb led to the slaughter. She was killed because of inconvenience and selfishness. Maybe Steve's idea to send her to Trinidad wasn't so bad after all. At least she would be alive today!" The nurses left Danielle in the same bloody bed sheets for three days after that! She got a high fever, an infection and had to stay an extra few days on intravenous. What is safe about that? She felt that she deserved to die now.

Danielle was in shock. This was too much to bear. How could they do this to such a perfect harmless baby? The boyfriend kept telling her while she grieved, that she could always have another kid. However she knew that no child will ever replace the one that was killed. They soon broke up and she moved in with her loving Mom, who comforted and consoled her. She confided in me that since this abortion ordeal, she has had many nightmares, has suffered deep depression and sleepless nights. With both of us crying and grieving the loss of this child, and the horrid experience of this procedure, I led her in a prayer.

First we thanked God for His mercy, grace, and forgiveness. Then I had Danielle repeat a prayer after me. Sobbing she repeated these words, "Heavenly Father, please forgive me for having premarital sex, forgive me for having the abortion, and please forgive me for all my other sins?" She genuinely repented. I asked God to bring healing and restoration to her tormented soul. And prayed for God's blessings on her.

FORGIVEN

The Bible records in Psalm 103:10-12, "He has not dealt with us according to our sins, Nor Punished us according to our iniquities. For as the heavens are high above the earth, So great is His mercy toward those who fear Him; As far as the east is from the west, So far has he removed our transgressions from us ... " James 5:16 says, "Confess your faults' one to another, that you may be healed." In 1 John 1:9 it proclaims, "If we confess our sins, He (God) is faithful and just to forgive us our sins and to cleanse us from all unrighteousness." Read also Psalm 32:5,

Roman's 10:9 and Rev. 3:5. We must also forgive the abortionists and ourselves. Jesus said *"Your heavenly father will forgive you, if you forgive those who sin against you, but if you refuse to forgive them, He will not forgive you."* Matt. 6:14,15 Then they are in God's hands to deal with, not ours. The Lord still wants us to be the salt & light of the earth though. Mark 11:25,26

After rededicating her life back to Jesus Christ, I encouraged Danielle to read her Bible every day, pray, pray, pray, and find a good alive church. I explained that little Sarah, (whom she had named) was with the Lord in heaven, and that one day she would be with her. The Pentecostals are quite good, I suggested. She seemed relieved, and peaceful. We hugged, and I asked her to join me for the Chantal Daigle Baby Shower the following day. "Don't worry, I'll be there, we must try to save the life of her baby!" She did not want any woman to have to go through that horrible procedure. Over the years I have spoken to hundreds of women - devastated and crushed after coming to the realization that they had actually killed their baby.

Chapter 13

"Are We Really In The Last Days?"

Days, months and many years have come and gone, while attempting to finish this work. You may be quite sceptical, and agnostic, like I once was. Therefore, I urge you to take a deep breath. Open your heart, open your mind and take a step in faith to discover your own purpose and journey in this life. It is an exciting adventure. It is a challenge to maturation and about our priorities in this life. Think about it. In one hundred years from now, will it really matter how much money was in your bank account; what you wore; what type of place you lived in; or what kind of car you drove?

What will matter, is if you were important in the eyes of a child. Did you help the fatherless, the poor, or those in a crisis? Were you as Dr. Laura Schlesinger puts it, "Your kids' Mom, or Dad?" Were you a light in this dark world? Or did everything centre around your selfish desires, and your will? Were you an example of God's love to your family, friends and enemies, praying that they would all come to know the way, the truth and the life?

For the sake of our civilization, and for the future of our children, **We can make a difference,** if we humble ourselves, change for the better, pray, and let God have His way in our lives.

Were we conceived for such a time as this? Look at the facts, use your common sense. As we draw near to the end of this millennium, and the year 2,000 approaches, we clearly see the fulfillment of ancient biblical prophecies unfolding before our very eyes. It was recorded thousands of years ago that the regathering of Jews to Israel is a clear sign in both the Old and New Testaments that our age is just about over. The incredible fact that **Israel became a nation in 1948** amid such hostile adversaries is remarkable. On June 6, 1967, for the first time since 586 BC, when Nebuchadnezzar captured the Jewish people, they took back control of the entire city of Jerusalem, thus, signalling the approaching end of Gentile world power.

Jesus warned his followers in the book of Matthew chapter 24, *"**Take heed that no one deceives you.** For many will come in My name, saying, I am the 'Deliverer', and will deceive many. And you will hear of wars and rumours of wars. See that you are not troubled, for all these things must come to pass, but the end is not yet. For nation will rise against nation, and kingdom against kingdom. And there will be famines, pestilence, and earthquakes in various places. All these are the beginning of sorrows.*

*Then they will deliver you up to tribulation and kill you, and you will be hated by all nations for My name's sake. And then many will be offended, will betray one another, and will hate one another. Then many false prophets will rise up and deceive many. And because **lawlessness will abound**, the love of many will grow cold. **But he who endures to the end shall be saved. And this gospel of the kingdom will be preached in all the world as a witness to all the nations, and then the end will come."***

In addition, Luke recorded Jesus' warnings of the signs of the times and the end of age, that His believers **should not** be deceived. They should not be terrified of wars and commotions. He then said, *"And there will be great earthquakes in various places, and famines and pestilence; and there will be fearful sights and great signs from heaven. But before all these things, they will lay their hands on you and persecute you, delivering you up to the synagogues and prisons.* ***You will be brought before kings and rulers for My name's sake. But it will turn out for you as an occasion for testimony."***

Also, the book of Thessalonians, chapter two confirms that there will be an **increase of lawlessness** and anarchy in our land. This will empower the spirit of Antichrist to dominate the attitudes of many people. Strong feminist lobbying to the United Nations, and pressuring the legislatures to include that "all women around the world will have the right to reproductive health" is frightening. In other words this means that all women around the world must have the right to have their babies assassinated, while in the sanctuary of the womb. This is not healthy for the Preborns or for women, as you will see. This kind of ratification will then open the door to more persecution of Pro-Lifers who want to protect the Preborn and possible victims of Euthanasia. Read the book of Revelations chapter 17. See the connection?

Do you recognize the signs of the times? According to the ancient word of God, first there will be a "falling away" an apostasy of fundamental Christian teachings. There are a few denominations already who have publicly announced policies they have changed, which are totally contrary to the Biblical teachings. They have gone the way of the world compromising the word of God, to be 'Politically' correct. Examples are with a couple of denominations who are now ordaining practising homosexuals as Ministers, and sanctioning abortion on demand. This proves the end is near.

Then the lawless one shall appear; according to the visions of Daniel 7:25; *"He shall speak pompous words against the Most High, Shall persecute the saints of the Most High, <u>And shall intend to change the times and the law.</u>"* 8:32-39 says, *"Those who do wickedly against the covenant he shall corrupt with flattery; but the people who know their God shall be strong, and carry out great exploits. And those of the people who understand shall instruct many; yet for many days they shall fall by sword and flame, by captivity and plundering. Now when they fall, they shall be aided with a little help; but many shall join with them by intrigue. And some of those of understanding shall fall, to refine them, purify them, and make them white, until the time of the end; because it is still for the appointed time."*

Then this ruler of lawlessness shall; *"Do according to his own will; he shall exalt and magnify himself above every god, shall speak blasphemies against the God of gods, and shall prosper till the wrath has been accomplished; for what has been determined shall be done. He shall regard neither the God of his fathers, nor the desire of women, nor regard any god; for he shall exalt himself above them all ... Thus he shall act against the strongest fortresses with a foreign god, which he shall acknowledge, and advance its glory; and he shall cause them to rule over many, and divide the land for profit."*

Pat Robertson [1] of the 700 Club wrote, "For an Antichrist figure to come into the modern world, there must be a breakdown of the world system as we know it now. There would have to be breakdowns in currency, in law and order, and in the power structures of national states. A financial panic could help pave the way for him, so could a nuclear war, or chemical war. Such disasters could leave people crying out for a man of peace, who will be Satan's counterfeit to Jesus Christ. This man will seem to be like Jesus, until he is ready to show his true self. He will probably quote scripture. Then he will be incredibly cruel.

The Antichrist will be the most hideous example of dictatorial power that the world has ever known. Remember that the Antichrist spirit is in anybody who tries to draw people away from Jesus, saying, "Come worship (idolize) me." Systems, curriculums currently being taught in our schools, media, and intellectual circles are often much like that, which will ultimately lead people to the Antichrist, because he will be the consummate figure of humanism."

Francis Frangipane wrote in his book, "The Three Battlegrounds" about Spiritual Warfare: in the Mind, the Church and the Heavenly places; "The other churches in our cities are not our enemies! We must learn to war against the illusions and strife, the fears and jealousies that are sent from hell to divide us. If Jesus is eternally praying for our 'oneness' (John 17:20-23), then we must recognize that Satan is continually fighting against it. The devil knows that when we become one with Christ and, through Him, one with each other, it is only a matter of time before this Jesus-built Church will destroy the empire of hell!" Jesus said in the book of Matthew that the church that He is going to build - the gates of hell shall not prevail against it!

Friends, we have much work to do, the harvest is plentiful, but the labourers are few. Don't hide, don't be afraid, we need your help!

Moral Decline?

The Human Rights Commission fined the Mayor of London, Ontario $10,000.00 because she refused to grant permission for a Homosexuals parade. Most of her constituents supported her refusal to give them a permit. Now even child pornography which sexually exploits vulnerable children is legal! How repulsive! Isn't it schizophrenic when at one end of the hospital doctors and nurses are doing everything to save premature babies, while down the hall they are killing them? Why aren't they called premature fetuses? How can life or death be determined just by whether someone is "wanted" by someone or not?

Predictions abound about the chaos and pandemonium that will strike the Corporate and Government structures around the world when many of the computers may zap out at the year 2,000. Traffic lights, utility companies, main frames and technology will collapse, they charge. Observe the events and attitudes of Todays' generation, the "We're here for a good time, not a long time," viewpoint.

With pornography outlets at almost every corner to seduce and exploit youth and our men. With all of the vulgar language, nudity and violence so blatantly shown on Television. With more violent crimes among youth, and so much liberal media, we are obviously fulfilling words echoed two thousand years ago.

The renowned Prophet Isaiah records in chapter 5:20 *"Woe to those who call evil good, and good evil; Who put darkness for light, and light for darkness;* Who put bitter for sweet, and sweet for bitter," ...on it goes, such revelation of our times. Have you noticed the youth of today calling things they really like, "wicked?"

President Clinton, an adulterous, unfaithful man who deceived his wife and country to cover-up his affair should have resigned. This affair progressed while he was on the job, and repeatedly over a couple of years. Not to mention all the other women he had relationships with. What kind of example is he to the men, children and teenagers of that Nation and the world? If it is okay for him to get away with it, as the leader, this could incite more immorality in the nations.

Is he really any better than Saddam Hussein or Slobadan Milosovec? **Clinton refuses to ban "Partial Birth" abortions in the USA.** This is more repulsive than his sexual exploits. This hideous procedure involves taking the lives of viable, or healthy **Full-Term Babies.** They are just inches from their head being totally delivered out of their mothers' womb alive when they are viciously killed.

Warning: the following is a graphic and true account.

Brenda Pratt Shafer, a Registered Nurse from the United States, writes her eyewitness account of her conversion **from "Pro-Choice" Nurse to Pro-Life work.**

She has worked as a Registered Nurse since 1982. In 1993 Brenda accepted an assignment at an Ohio abortion clinic. Here is her account of what happened.

> "*I stood at the doctor's side as he performed the partial-birth abortion procedure. What I saw is branded forever on my mind. During the first two days we inserted laminaria to dilate the cervixes of women who were being prepared for the abortions.* **These women were past the 20-week point, or five months along.** There were seven of these women in all.
>
> On the third day the doctor asked me to observe as he performed several partial-birth abortions. I was present for three of these procedures. I'll describe the first one in detail.
>
> **The mother was six months pregnant** (23 weeks and the baby can survive outside the womb)! A doctor told her that the baby had Down Syndrome and she decided to have an abortion. She came in the first two days to have the laminaria inserted and changed, and she cried the whole time. On the third day she came in to receive the partial-birth procedure.
>
> The doctor brought the ultrasound in and hooked it up so that he could see the baby. I could clearly see the baby's heart beat on the ultrasound screen. The doctor

went in with forceps and grabbed the baby's legs and pulled them down into the birth canal. Then he delivered the baby's body and the arms-everything but the head. He kept the baby's head just inside the uterus.

The baby's little fingers were clasping and unclasping, and his feet were kicking. Then he stuck the scissors through the back of his head, and the baby's arms jerked out in a flinch, a startle reaction, like a baby does when he thinks that he might fall.

The doctor opened up the scissors, stuck a high-powered suction tube into the opening and sucked the baby's brains out. Now the baby went completely limp.

I was totally unprepared for what I was seeing. I almost threw up as I watched the doctor do things.

He delivered the baby's head. He cut the umbilical cord and delivered the placenta. He threw that baby in a pan, along with the placenta and the instruments he had used. I saw the baby move in the pan. I asked another nurse about it and she said it was just "reflexes."

I have been a nurse for a long time and I have seen a lot of death, people maimed in auto accidents, gunshot wounds, you name it. I have seen surgical procedures of every sort. But in all my professional years, I had never witnessed anything like this!

That baby boy had the most perfect angelic face I have ever seen. I was present in the room during two more such procedures that day, which involved healthy mothers with healthy babies. After I left that day, I never went back."

Published by Easton Publishing Company, Inc. Box 1064, Jefferson City, M0, USA, 65102 for copies and a catalogue of Pro Life Literature, write them.

This is really happening folks! Human butchers! 1990's and about 5,000 of these viable little babies are diabolically killed in cold blood annually in the United States. Primarily it is healthy women of healthy fetuses having this done. Abortion advocates want it allowed in Canada as well, and it probably is being done, since there is no law to ban abortions at any stage in this country anyway. It is a matter between a woman and the surgeon who kills the baby. "God keep our land glorious and free?" He may not.

Wake up, church. This is not a social issue, but a demonic stronghold to bring God's wrath and judgment! *"Cursed be he who takes a bribe to slay an innocent person." Deuteronomy.* 27:25, 2 King 24:4, Psalm 10, *"Yes, they sacrificed their sons and their daughters to demons,* {2 Kings 16:3} *And shed innocent blood, even the blood of their sons and of their daughters, whom they sacrificed to the idols; and the land was polluted with blood."* Psalm 106:37-39, Proverbs. 6:17 declares that God hates the hands that shed innocent blood. Isaiah chapter 1, condemns the shedding of innocent blood and God proclaims **"Learn to do right; seek justice, relieve the oppressed and correct the oppressor; defend the fatherless ... "** Please read chapter 59 also! Jeremiah. 7:6; 22:3, Joel 3:19 records the consequences of shedding innocent blood in your land, *"Egypt shall be a desolation, and Edom shall be a desolate wilderness, for their violence against the children of Judah,* **because they have shed innocent blood in their land."**

How is it that **abortion**, which for centuries was a criminal act of murder, today is considered a "right?" It has become a violent form of "Birth Control for the "woman with child?" Now the death culture is working toward legalizing **euthanasia. Who will be the NeXT to go?** At this rate the elderly, the disabled, and the poor will be the NeXT to go, if you do nothing to stop it.

The Drug Culture

What about the **drug culture?** Dependents, users and liberal minded doctors who want to legalize heroin, marijuana and other narcotics? Don't be deceived by drug users who want to legitimize their habits for "medicinal" purposes. This is preposterous. The pharmaceutical companies would love to harvest new markets. The tobacco giants love people to get addicted to their products - even if it kills them. Smoking marijuana is harmful to one's lungs, throat and brain cells. There are multitudes of pain killers and other drugs that can relieve pain effectively. It is an excuse. Next they will want to legalize cocaine and acid for so-called medicinal purposes. It is more rhetoric! We already have seen the damage, abuse and epidemics caused when giving out free needles and allowing drug addicts the freedom to possess and use heroin with no restrictions. As was the case with the experiment in Zurich, Switzerland.

The outcome resulted in an increase in the number of addicts. More people got infected with **HIV/AIDS, and there were many more reported overdoses.** The value of properties declined in this drug infested park area. Garbage, used needles and drug paraphernalia littered the ground. There was also great concern for safety of children in the area. They had to halt the program. **It was a complete failure!** Crack and speed are quickly escalating as the most damaging and addicting drugs on the streets. Why? The "No God" mentality.

My street experience revealed that there are so many emotionally damaged people. The majority are hurting because of family breakdown. A combination of neglect, having alcoholic, or materialistic parents is a primary cause. The fact that most have been sexually abused, or are fatherless is tantamount to drug abuse. Sometimes, the addicts are just simply spoiled, lazy and self-indulgent.

Many secular "professionals" want to refer to alcoholics and drug addicts as having a "disease," thus removing all responsibility for the addict to quit, and negating all accountability. My dictionary defines a disease as a "morbid condition of the body, or of some organ or part; illness ... any deranged or depraved condition of the mind.". It is not a deranged or depraved mind, but an act of the "will" to purchase and consume the liquor which causes drunkenness. Please think about it. Cancer is a disease. **Alcoholism is an addiction.** There is a big difference. However, alcoholism and drug abuse will cause diseases to form in the liver, heart, kidneys, lungs and wherever else it spreads. One can use self control, with God's help, to prevent and stop alcoholism and other addictions, but one cannot stop a disease from manifesting or spreading by self-control. The disease is inflicted upon them, whereas drugs are voluntarily bought and inserted into the body for temporary pleasure. Nevertheless, I know and believe in the power of prayer in Jesus' name to heal all sickness and disease, and to set the captives free. He has freed me and countless other believers.

Our Governments spend billions of dollars every year on alcohol and other drug addiction treatments, counselling and care. They pour vast amounts of money into the welfare system. Special Treatment Centres, extra Police enforcement costs for related crimes, Health Care and Mental Health Care ... Yet, they never get to the root of the problems, still forever trying to keep up with the demands for assistance. Sadly, at great taxpayers' expense, with little or no positive results. Government statistics suggest only a 3-7% success rate on getting people off the cycle of addiction.

On the other hand, there is good news! Non profit, non Government programs like Alcoholics Anonymous, Narcotics Anonymous, Teen Challenge, New Life Girls' Home and Turning Point for Women boast excellent recovery rates. Teen Challenge for example, has an **86% success rate on total recovery**, and that is **after a five year follow up!** They must be doing something right. They are!

Teen Challenge for men, New Life Girls' Home and Turning Point for Women are Christ-centred programs aimed at getting to the root of the addictions. They focus on bringing inner healing to the souls of hurting men and women, by introducing them to Jesus Christ and His plan of salvation. They learn to forgive those that have hurt and marred them. Then they ask God to forgive them for the mistakes and bad deeds they have done. They are encouraged and challenged to a disciplined life, resisting temptation and controlling themselves. **It works!** With God's help ALL things are possible. So why aren't our Politicians endorsing, supporting and expanding these vital programs?

The rampant use of alcoholic beverages has become America's number one drug problem. Costing more than $117 billion a year and claiming at least 100,000 lives every year, 25 times as many as all the illegal drugs combined. The substantial human tragedies are the multitudes that are maimed, injured, born retarded, victims of divorce, crimes, violence, sickness and death. This transcends the statistical figures in dollars and death. Drinking "moderately" has led more than 18 million Americans to become heavy drinkers. There are not two or three, but **75 Bible references condemning the drinking of alcohol beverages.** [2]

Sodomy

It is clear in both the Old and New Testaments that **homosexuality, and lesbianism are an abomination to God.** He wants them to repent and live eternally. **Roman's 1:18-32** *"Therefore God also gave them up to uncleanness, in the lusts of their hearts, to dishonour their bodies among themselves, who exchanged the truth of God for the lie, and worshipped and served the creature, rather than the Creator, who* *is blessed forever, Amen. For this reason God gave them up to vile passions. For even their women exchanged the natural use for what is against nature. Likewise also the men, leaving the natural use of the woman, burned in their lust for one another, men with men committing what is shameful, and receiving in themselves the penalty of their error which was due."* Also, read Leviticus 20:13

They also condemned these perverted, lewd acts as criminal offences a few years ago. According to "Martin's Annual Criminal Code-1989 in the text of the Criminal Code, ... " It states in Section 159. (1) **"Every person who engages in an act of anal intercourse is guilty of an indictable offence and is liable to imprisonment for a term not exceeding ten years or is guilty of an offence punishable on summary conviction.** Does not apply to any act engaged in, private between a husband and wife, or any two persons, each of whom is eighteen years of age or more, both of whom consent to the act, **unless** it is done in a public place or if more than two persons take part, or are present ... " Shouldn't this make homosexual porno-flicks illegal?

Our tax dollars are funding Military soldiers to have sex-change operations costing thousands of dollars, because these guys are having identity problems and want to dress up like women and have sex with other men. Not being able to have sex with a woman is unnatural for a man.

While they deny straight folks, necessary medical health care. Many people are forced to wait months for heart surgery, cancer treatments etc. because of insufficient funds.

Already, in cities like Toronto and Vancouver, where homosexuals are gathered in greater numbers, they shout the loudest. By doing so they have influenced liberal, secular Boards of Education, Politicians, and the media.

Tomorrow will our appointed liberal-minded judges endorse, and thereby actuate bigamy, or paedophilia, or beastiality? Politicians are not listening to the majority of Canadians who do not want Homosexuality propagated in the schools. Nor do they condone the fostering and adoption of innocent straight children by homosexuals and lesbians.

Currently the Government is changing the definition of spouse to allow homosexuals the "right" to adopt straight children. Recently, the Canadian Minister of Justice announced that she wants to lower the age of consent for Homosexual sex with youth. Where is the body and mind of Christ here to defend the rights of the innocent and naive?

Whom do children most imitate and use as their role models? Of course, their parents or caregivers are the primary role models for children. The Bible stipulates in Proverbs. 22:6 *"Train up a child in the way he should go, and when he is old he will not depart from it."* Indications in studies are that children who are raised by lesbians or homosexual couples will likely become homosexuals also.

Recently books have been filtering into schools in Ontario and British Columbia to influence the Primary grade children that Homosexuality (acts of sodomy and buggery) is an acceptable and normal life style. They want to desensitize children into believing that same sex couples are natural, and that it is appropriate behaviour. This is wrong, wrong, wrong!

Good-looking homosexuals are visiting some High School Classrooms in Toronto as "Role" models to promote Homosexuality as an alternative lifestyle. Then if any of the teens disagree with the morality of their sexual preferences' they then stigmatize them as" homophobic or bigot" and told to get counselling. The left-wing media powers are forever shifting each fight for traditional family values on the rhetoric of deception and lies.

Homosexuals demand our tolerance. Are they tolerant to anyone who doesn't condone their behaviour? No! Following is their real agenda according to Michael Swift, a Homosexual activist, "They are going to sodomize our children in the schools, public arenas, sports clubs, bathrooms" and wherever they can get a hold on them. They want their sexual behaviour to be deemed normal. They want to be recognized as "married" and be permitted to adopt and foster straight children. They are already in some places. We must be aware of their tactics and stop the infiltration and propagation of homosexuality to our children.

There is absolutely no proven scientific evidence that people are born as homosexuals or lesbians. They propagate this theory so they can win acceptance and an excuse to continue these perverted sex acts. This does not give them the right to shove their sexual behaviour into the faces of our children. Documentaries reveal that the majority of homosexuals and lesbians have had traumatic childhood experiences such as sexual abuse, neglect and being fatherless. They need compassionate counselling and deliverance from sodomy.

A Priest once told me in a conversation about the Vriend case here in Alberta that we shouldn't try to interfere with the rights of gays. He gave the example of Jesus addressing the woman caught in adultery, stating that we shouldn't throw stones. My rebuttal to his analogy is this: First of all we are not throwing stones at homosexuals or lesbians. This punishment was literally meant to kill the person caught in a crime against God. They caught the woman in the very act of adultery.

Furthermore, after the accusers left, Jesus then instructed the woman to "**Go, and SIN NO MORE.**" In other words, do not continue with this relationship, don't do it again, repent and change. Notice that this sin dealt with sex, outside of marriage. Fornication is a sin. 1 Corinthians also confirm God's will, and commands, in chapter 6 verse 9,10 *"Do you not know that the unrighteous will not inherit the kingdom of God? Do not be deceived. Neither fornicators, nor idolaters, nor adulterers, nor homosexuals, nor sodomites, nor thieves, nor covetous, nor drunkards, nor revilers, nor extortioners will inherit the kingdom of God."* The good news is that we can change our ways. The next verse goes on … **"And such WERE some of you. But you were washed, you were sanctified, you were justified in the name of the Lord Jesus and by the Spirit of our God."**

This happens when we ask God to forgive us of our sins, and repent, resist the temptation and by faith ask Jesus to take control of our lives. My favourite song is "Amazing Grace." It is awesome that our God would forgive a wretch, like I once was. And He is not finished with me yet. It is a process. First He deals with the surface stuff, like our addictions, sexual sins, and outward problems. Then He has us deal with the inner sins like: selfishness, pride, stubbornness, anger, unforgiveness, selfish ambition, gossip, slander etc.

We, believers in Christ, want homosexuals to have jobs, as long as it is not promoting their sexual practices to our children. We do not want them fostering or adopting children. We hope that they will see the error of their way, change their lifestyles and live without the threat of AIDS or other STD's.

Homosexuals in fact, are the main carriers and spreaders of the HIV/AIDS disease. Statistics Canada reported for 1995 that 59,241 people died from cancer, another 62,600 died from heart diseases. While 1,165 men got AIDS and 101 women got this deadly disease. The Federal Government indiscriminately pumps millions of dollars into AIDS research, prevention, distribution of condoms, graphic explicit materials on how to have so called "safe" sex, complete with phone-in hotlines. Condoms leak! The HIV virus is .1 micron in size. Naturally occurring defects in condoms are 5 microns. 50 times larger than the AIDS/HIV virus.[3] Meanwhile the escalating death toll affecting the majority of Canadians every year is cancer and heart disease. Those organizations struggle every year to get funding. We should be pumping money into vitamin and mineral supplements which help prevent degenerative diseases.

If one wants to have loving commitment and sex, a man should find a good wife and a woman find a good husband. It can be wonderful with God's help. This is the way God intended. Unless of course you want to stay single and be celibate. Besides, God did not create Adam and Steve, but Adam and Eve.

Today there are many Ministries dedicated to helping homosexuals and lesbians get free from that lifestyle, such as "Exodus" and "Another Chance Ministries," in British Columbia. These individuals who really want to change can make that decision, receive inner healing and live happy, healthy lives. Read "The Journal of Human Sexuality," 1996 which includes very informative articles such as "The Gay Gene?" by Dr. Jeffrey Satinover, M.D., "Gender Identity Disorder" by Dr. G. Rekers, Ph.D., "Kinsey and the Homosexual Revolution" by Dr. J. Reisman, Ph.D., "The Gay Youth Suicide Myth" by Peter LaBarbera and other interesting studies. Also, "Homosexuality- A Report for the Government of Canada" by Chad Van Dixhoorn, 1994, it is most credible and well documented.

First the Bad News…

Twisting and editing out the truth, they shout cries for the spirit of Antichrist, hedonism and rebellion. Chanting, screeching discrimination, and professing to be wise, they become fools. Violence on TV desensitizes and then encourages our children to act out this violence fuelling rebellion and disrespect of elders. News reports are full of the increasing horror. The power of TV disperses hidden corrupt philosophies and demonic agendas. Is there no shame or humility when they blanket evening programs with foul language and nudity exploiting women and children? How many more innocent teenagers will be gunned down or mutilated in cold blood? As I was writing this book, another fourteen year old shot two students at a school in Taber, Alberta. Violent movies. Violent minds.

Whatever happened to the enforcement of Section 163 of the Criminal Code of Canada which condemns the corruption of morals, including selling, exposing, possessing, printing, publishing, or circulating **obscene** material? Despite these laws, the pornography business is making billions of dollars through exploitation and prostitution.

Numerous television programs displaying fornication and adultery as acceptable conduct has influenced our young adults to believe that promiscuity is a 'cool thing'. There are no repercussions, "If it feels good, do it", is the attitude. They are not aware that the *"wages of sin is death."* The ramifications are inevitably, heart break, STD's, and thousands of aborted babies.

Studies prove that Sexually Transmitted Diseases, that kill or maim, are spreading among our youth and young adults at unprecedented rates. "Oh, but let us not censor what graphics go over the airwaves, that would infringe on the art culture." Nonsense! There is a difference between pornography and art. So-called artists have gone so far now as to display lewd homosexual pornographic explicitness and another so-called artist displayed a crucifix submerged in urine as a piece of "art." This is atrocious, and funded by taxpayers. Can you imagine the outcry if he submerged a Star of David, or defiled a Moslem symbol or relic? Nudity should be kept for privacy, not publicity.

Why aren't they enforcing the laws when it comes to NUDITY or OBSCENITY? Do you know that legislatures elected by the people created these laws and yet they are not enforced? Section 174 of the Criminal Code of Canada states;"Everyone who, without lawful excuse, is nude in a public place ... " To me a public place must include broadcasts on Television, Homosexual Parades, and nude beaches etc. How about you?

It was upsetting for many Canadians to comprehend the rationale behind the CRTC (Canadian Radio and Television Corporation) decision made in 1997. They totally rejected four Christian, Pro-Family, Pro-decency programmers. They claimed that "balance" was the problem. Insisting that Christian programmers must include eight hours of multi faith (anti-Christian) programs before they could get a licence. Unbelievably, on that same day the CRTC gave a license for a 24-hour nudity "Playboy" channel to operate in Canada. How ludicrous! Lots of balance there?

Does the "Golfing" channel have any balance? The CRTC does not require them to also program football, fishing or cooking? Or what about the History channel having to program current events shows, or the news channels having to show fiction cartoons, where is their "balanced" programming? **The only two Countries in the whole world who would not permit a Christian television station were Cuba and Canada!**

Since 1969 'Planned Parenthood' began instilling their philosophies into our schools, complete with dildos and detailed instructions on how to use condoms:

More and younger adolescents are sexually active, and are dependent on birth control.

Sexually Transmitted Diseases have increased to epidemic proportions.

About 46,000 Canadian teens become pregnant annually.

More than 15,000 have abortions each year.

Higher rates of cervical cancer.

Increased infertility in otherwise healthy young women ...[4]

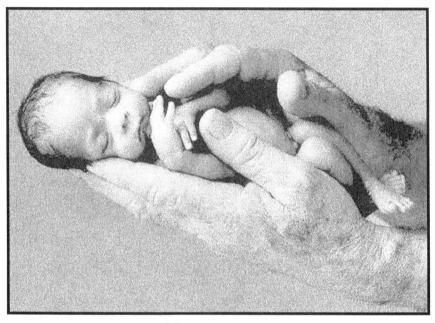

Every life is precious

Has all this knowledge about sex "How to" classes, slowed, or hindered the staggering amount of young women getting pregnant or people suffering with Sexually Transmitted Disease's (STD's)? Of course not, teen pregnancies and STD's are skyrocketing. They should be encouraging abstinence to teenagers.

This is what Rocky Mountain Planned Parenthood said in 1977 on teenage sexual activity: There are only two basic kinds of sex: Sex with victims and sex without. Sex with victims is always wrong. Sex without is always right." Also, "If this is a girl you've just met and she agrees (to have sex), you're in the clear provided that she's old enough to have some sense." They also claim that "The fetus becomes a baby at birth" in How To Talk With Your Teen About The Facts Of Life, PPFA, 1995. This is what they tell teenagers about babies. "Babies are NOT sweet little things. They wet and dirty themselves, they get sick, they're very expensive to take care of." PPFA 1974. In a Minnesota, South Dakota newspaper ad, October 16, 1996 they wrote "BABIES ARE LOUD, SMELLY AND EXPENSIVE, unless you want one."

Robert D. Crist, M.D. (who had three women die shortly after he committed abortions on them) is "one of the most skilled and competent and committed physicians performing abortions." President of Planned Parenthood in the Kansas City Star, April 27, 1997.

Dr Pulver (charged with a "bungled abortion") has an outstanding record of service with thousands of women" The Niagara Gazette, October 2, 1997.

The current Health Minister for Alberta states "The Alberta government policy is to **only fund abortions which are 'medically' necessary.**" Most Provinces make the same rhetorical statements when accused of permitting abortion on request. The truth is, abortion is a form of birth control. The abortionists even blatantly advertise in the yellow pages right under the "**Birth Control Services**" section! And although Health Care funding is forever getting cut, there are waiting lists and shortages of beds for really sick people with cancer, heart disease, etc. needing surgery or treatment. They are denied access.

Meanwhile, not one woman has ever been denied or delayed the "right to have her Preborn baby killed." Yes "killed," because if he or she was not alive, you would not have to kill him or her. That is the sole purpose of an abortion! It is always done for any reason, at the snap of a finger, to healthy babies in healthy women, and we pay for them all! The morgentaler clinic-Edmonton website blatenly declares, "Who can obtain a clinic abortion?" Their answer, "ANY HEALTHY FEMALE from five to eighteen weeks pregnant can get an abortion at the Morgentaler clinic..." Oh, do they say any **healthy female?** Yes! So where is the "medical necessity? How pathetic! As Rev. Ken Campbell from Choose Life Canada puts it, "It is just kill the unwanted philosophy." Abortion is not a medical treatment for a pregnancy, it only hurts women and takes an innocent life.

For decades the people have protested abortion to the politicians. The politicians say it's between the doctor and the woman. The women go to the abortionist whose job is to kill the baby. In 1993 the Ministry of Health in Ontario revealed that in that year alone in Ontario "26,061" babies nine weeks old or less were massacred at the hands of abortionists. Please note that in gestational weeks we need to give or take a week or two for miscalculating the exact age. In that same year "14,391" tiny human babies who were **ten to thirteen weeks old** were slaughtered in their mothers' womb.

There were 240 babies silently executed at the age of 18 weeks. Another 330 babies were viciously dismembered at nineteen weeks old. Another 372 babies poisoned and burned to death at five months or twenty weeks old. Still another 103 babies were inhumanely murdered inside the womb, from 21 weeks up to 37 weeks. Do you really want to know how? This is a FULL TERM BABY! These statistics are only for the Province of Ontario, and this only represents the year of 1993. Every Province and Territory has its own horrific stats every year we permit this holocaust to continue!

In 1993 the Province of Alberta reported that doctors annihilated the innocent lives of **2,586 babies** at the tender age of **nine weeks gestation.** Doctors assassinated **5,665 babies between the ages of 9-12 weeks.** There were **619 babies butchered in the womb from the ages of 13-16 weeks,** which is in the second trimester. They massacred **another 193 little babies between the ages of 17 to 20 weeks** gestation which is a five-month-old "Baby!" Please note that babies can survive at this age outside the womb! There are even eleven reported cases of babies slaughtered through the diabolical procedure of induced abortions after the 20th week or five month period! This is happening all across Canada every year. The babies feel extreme pain too.

The April 12, 1999-edition of the Alberta Report has a story about some nurses in the Calgary Foothills Hospital who are forced to participate in late term abortions. Just in this hospital alone they performed forty late term abortions in 1998. One nurse recounts the fact that a **30-week-old baby,** (almost full term) survived the execution. She was miraculously born ALIVE! Distraught nurses were forced to let her die. They were given strict orders not to save her! She helplessly died twelve hours later! They are discriminating and practising eugenics because babies are sometimes not "perfect." Isn't this really genocide, feticide or infanticide?

Over the years thousands of people have sent thousands of letters to all of the following, pleading with them to stop permitting abortions. Listen to the rhetoric and euphemisms here:

The Canadian Medical Association goes on to state in their policy summary on "Induced Abortions" dated December 15, 1988 that: "An Induced abortion is the active termination of a pregnancy before the fetus can survive independently of the maternal environment. According to current medical knowledge viability is dependent on fetal weight, degree of development and length of gestation; **extrauterine viability may be possible if the fetus weighs over 500g or is past 20 weeks' gestation,** or both." (Gestation begins at conception) *So why on earth are they allowing thousands of abortions past the 18 to 19 week ages?*

The Canadian Medical Association's policy statement also specifies: "It must be remembered that when the fetus has reached the stage where it is capable of an independent existence, **termination of pregnancy may result in the delivery of a viable fetus.**" "Elective termination of pregnancy after fetal viability may be indicated under exceptional circumstances." In other words; The choice to kill a baby who is old enough and strong enough to survive outside his/her mother's womb, can still be executed under certain circumstances!

Their Policy Summary continues … "**Induced abortion should not be used as an alternative to contraception**" … So why are our Governments permitting abortionists to do just that? Check your yellow pages lately? In most major cities, right under "Birth Control Services," are the abortionist's advertisements. By the way, the number of women having more than one induced abortion continues to rise.

Statistics Canada show that repeat induced abortions increased from 20% in 1985 to 30% in 1995.

How, and Who are enforcing the CMA guidelines? There are thousands of babies assassinated from 18 to 37 weeks gestation every year in Canada! How can we allow life or death to be determined by whether or not someone is "wanted" by his or her mother? This is outrageous! Why isn't the media scrambling to get these details made public? Why don't they interview the pathologists?

The only two counties in the whole world that force women to, or allow abortion on demand at any stage in pregnancy are China and Canada!

Abortion. What does this really mean? Just try to explain it to any child. It is so simple, so plain, so satanic. It is taking the life of a perfect tiny human being, while growing in the shelter of his mother's womb. A mother's womb used to be the safest place in the world for a Preborn baby. Today it has become the most dangerous place in the world for a baby to be! Not only for the Preborn child, who is killed, but it is also violent for the women who undergo the procedure. Eventually women will suffer mentally, emotionally and physically, Life is the natural choice! Women are naturally caregiver's and protectors of their children.

The most common type of abortion is the "**Suction Curettage.**" They forcibly dilate the vagina and cervix. Then abortionists inserts a razor sharp cutting instrument that is attached to a high-powered vacuum. With this device he dismembers the Preborn child.

Dr. Bernard Nathanson an ex-abortionist produced a video showing a 12-week-old baby sucking his thumb, and kicking his perfect little feet on Ultra Sound. A violent intrusion enters the baby's space when the abortionists' cold sharp suction instrument begins to threaten his life. The baby's heartbeat races, until he is viciously dismembered. You can clearly see his tiny mouth open in terror. It is called the "Silent Scream." The exterminator then goes in with another instrument to crush his head and bring it out. Thank God that a number of ex-abortionists have seen the light, like Carol Everett, and others who are now strong Pro Life advocates.

They also destroy babies using a D & C or "**Dilation and Curettage**" This is similar to the above, but without the suction. They just rip the young one apart, crush his/her head and then scrape it out into a bucket. There is a lot of blood and bigger body parts.

Then a D & E or "**Dilation and Evacuation**" are done on babies who are three to five months old. This is revolting since the baby is bigger still. Usually they insert dilators or 'tents' the night before to force the cervix to open. Then an instrument like a sharp pair of pliers is

These real tiny body parts were found in a garbage bag behind an abortion clinic. How can anyone see the evidence, and deny the fact that these were little children created in the image of God?

inserted into the womb. Because the baby's bones are harder, the pliers are more effective in dismembering his/her body parts. They then pull out the limbs. They crush the head because it is too large and too firm to be pulled out intact. *This is really happening to fully human, and fully alive babies!*

The Second Victim

There are twenty-seven possible Physical complications to the woman from induced abortion. Including lacerated cervixes, perforated bowels, infections, bladder damage, ruptures, vomiting, complications to future pregnancies, Asherman's Syndrome, and sterility many of these problems can lead to death … Some women may never again conceive, or have their own children down the road, due to an induced abortion. Some women have even died, in so called "safe clinics." Yet the abortion providers advertise that these are "safe abortions." **Safe for** whom? What exploitation! David Reardon's book entitled "Aborted Women-Silent No More" discloses a "Systematic cover up" when it comes to reporting physical complications from abortion.

The nine most common "major" complications to the woman resulting from vacuum abortions are: infection, excessive bleeding, embolism, ripping or perforation of the uterus, convulsions, hemorrhage, cervical injury, and endotoxic shock. Taken from Ann Saltenberger's book, **"What Every Woman Should Know About Legal Abortions."**

Dr. Vincent M. Rue,Ph.D, developed the diagnostic criteria for Post Abortion Syndrome, a "post traumatic stress disorder," from the American Psychiatric Association Diagnostic and Statistical Manual of Mental Disorders-Revised, (DSMIII-R:309.89). Washington, D.C. American Psychiatric Press, 1987, page 250.

A. **Stressor**: The abortion experience, ie., the intentional destruction of one's unborn child, is sufficiently traumatic and beyond the range of usual human experience so as to cause significant symptoms of re-experience, avoidance and impacted grieving.

B. **Re-experience:** Recurrent intrusive distressing recollections of the abortion experience, recurrent distressing dreams of the abortion or of the unborn child, reliving the experience, flashbacks, intense psychological distress at exposure to events that symbolize or resemble the abortion experience, anniversary reactions of intense grieving and/or depression or on the projected due date of the aborted child.

C. **Avoidance:** Persistent avoidance of stimuli associated with the abortion trauma...

D. **Associated Features:** Persistent symptoms (not present before the abortion) as indicated by at least two of the following: 1. difficulty falling or staying asleep 2. irritability or outbursts of anger 3. difficulty concentrating 4. hypervigilence 5. exaggerated startle response to intrusive recollections or re-experiencing of the abortion trauma 6. reactions to exposure to events or situations that symbolize or resemble an aspect of the abortion (e.g.,breaking out in a profuse sweat upon a pelvic examination, or hearing vacuum pump sounds) 7. depression and suicidal ideation 8. guilt about surviving, when one's unborn child did not. 9.

self devaluation and/or an inability to forgive one's self 10. secondary substance abuse...

E. **Course:** The duration of the disturbance, of more than one month's duration, or onset may be delayed (greater than six months after the abortion)...

Psychological complications to women after having persuaded abortions include: Depression, grief, anguish, numbness, regret, shock, trauma, nightmares, flashbacks, abuse in future children etc. Another must read for statistics and education on the subject of abortion is Dr. & Mrs. Wilke's book, "Abortion, Questions and Answers" Why aren't these books listed in our public libraries? Women who have been victimized by the pro-death culture need God's forgiveness. They ultimately need inner healing, love and compassion too.

On the other hand, some people are born with great physical abnormalities, diseases and impediments. However, that does not give us the right to murder them. Robert Latimer is a recent example of a man who murdered his disabled daughter because she became a burden and inconvenience to them. In the court documents they revealed that Tracy Latimer had a personality, she had feelings too. The disabled need our support, love and compassion, not murder. There is no justification.

We as a society must love and cherish every person, whatever **the physique, mental status, ages,** sex etc. Hey, it is even in the Canadian Charter of Rights and Freedoms. It also states that "Every **individual** has the right to life." Guess what? From the moment of conception each one of us became an individual!

What days are we in? 2 Timothy chapter 3 reports; *"But know this, that in the last days stressful times will come: For men will be lovers of themselves, lovers of money, boasters, proud, blasphemers, disobedient to parents, unthankful, unholy, unloving, unforgiving, slanderers, without self-control, brutal, despisers of good, traitors, headstrong, haughty, lovers of pleasure rather than lovers of God. Having a form of godliness but denying its power. And from such people turn away!"*

So don't be surprised when so called "Ministers and Priests" advocate abortion, homosexuality and same sex marriages. Mat 7:15 *"Be-*

ware of false teachers who come disguised as harmless sheep, but are wolves and will tear you apart." The Bible is clear about what sin is. God wants us to repent, and that the wages of sin is death, if you don't. John 10:11-13.

Jesus did warn us about the "Hirelings" men and women who would be in a position of a Minister or Priest. They put in time, get a pay cheque but are following another doctrine or gospel. Cults thrive on a little bit of this passage and a little bit of that. They like to make you feel good, proclaiming that you are god and you have the power to control everything. That is new age thinking and it is blasphemous.

Jesus did say that the one thing that would herald his return is the proclamation of the gospel. Thus the computer/Internet age, has opened the door for the gospel to be preached around this globe. Unfortunately it is also broadcasting degrading, evil material. We must discern the times.

We were born for such a time as this. Listen to the evidence, have ears to hear what God is saying in these last days, and "Choose life, so that you and your children may live." Deuteronomy. 30:19. Men and women must come to the true knowledge of and respect for all human life. As **Mother Teresa once said, "World peace must begin in the womb!"**.

Chapter 14

"What Do We Do Now?"

"Do not grow weary in well doing, for in due season you shall reap a harvest, if you faint not." Gal. 6:9,10.

In September of 1989 inspired by the Lord and what Danielle had told me about her saline abortions, we decided to start picketing Hospitals. There is something terribly wrong when hospitals permit abortion on demand. It is obnoxious to believe that just because a baby is not wanted by its mother that he/she should be killed! If they don't want their baby give it to me.

There are more than 300,000 couples in Canada who would love to have a baby and cannot. There is an eight to ten year waiting list to adopt a baby, and it is growing. Surely, many of these women aborting, will be devastated down the road, when they "want" to have children and cannot. They will recoil at the loss due to their abortions. The consequences of induced abortions are devastating. It is real. I know this pain! Hospitals should be places where we save and preserve lives, not destroy and discard lives in the human waste disposal. **Shame** on the Pathology lab technicians who silently examine these little dead bodies, and never speak out! **Shame** on the Abortionists, Gynecologists, and the staff who support and work for them. **Shame** on the Colleges of Physicians and Surgeons who do not protect the rights of the Preborn, and distribute licenses to the abortionists! **Shame** on all the Ministers of Health and Justice over the years in our Federal Governments who have not upheld the law, and constitutional rights of the Preborn. **Shame** on the Ministers of Health and Justice in the Provinces that permit abortion on request, and use our tax dollars to pay the assassins. **Shame** on the Canadian Medical Association, (CMA) which letterhead states "Leadership for Physicians … Health for Canadians" who help facilitate the slaughter of innocents. Hypocrites!

Nevertheless, these policies on abortion are in total opposition to the Hippocrates Oath, and the Medical code of Ethics. Ask any Neonatologist or Fetologist about whom their patients are? They will inform you that the unborn child is the second patient. Today, operations are being done to help and save those fortunate babies whose mothers actually **want** them. The 20/20 TV program did a fantastic documentary on a woman whose baby girl "fetus" had a tumour on her lung that was killing her. Doctors first suggested that they either just do an abortion, let her die naturally, or try the new surgery.

The mother prayed, and without hesitation decided to go along with the fetal surgery to save the baby's life. The baby was about five months old or 21 weeks when they did a C-Section. The doctors gently pulled a tiny perfect little arm and hand out, exposing the arm, shoulder and upper back of the baby from the womb. They anaesthetized and then operated on the baby, removing the deadly tumour. Quickly they closed up the womb as best they could. It was a dangerous, but successful operation. The beautiful little girl was born only two weeks later. Again she survived, the premature birth, with the help of doctors and technology. She is a walking miracle girl and survivor. So cute, and so alive.

Dr. Paul Ranalli, a neurologist at the University of Toronto, Ontario gave a presentation called "Pain, Fetal Development, and Partial-birth abortion" on June 27, 1997 to the House Judiciary Committee of the State of Ohio. He concluded that the "spinothalamic" system is fully developed at about 12 to 14 weeks of gestation. This is the system that conveys pain signals from pain receptors throughout the body to the

ALLIANCE FOR LIFE • ALLIANCE POUR LA VIE

ALLIANCE FOR LIFE APPALLED AT BABIES LEFT TO DIE AT FOOTHILLS HOSPITAL, AB, FOLLOWING "GENETIC" ABORTIONS.

FREEDOM OF CONSCIENCE, FREEDOM OF SPEECH TRAMPLED

We are appalled at the forced participation of nurses at Foothills Hospital in Calgary in "genetic terminations" of late term babies. These babies are being born alive following abortion and simply left to die. "Is this not infanticide?" asks Anna Desilets, acting general manager of Alliance For Life. "Nurses who are devoted to caring for pregnant mothers and new babies are obligated to take part. "not participating in terminations is not an option," says a Feb1999 memo to Maternity Care Centre staff.

Shocking too is the report that the publishers of the weekly magazine *Alberta Report* have been served papers and are scheduled to appear before a provincial court for exposing and reporting on this practice of genetic cleansing at Foothills. "Where is freedom of the press to report events and the impact of these events?"

Alliance makes the following recommendations respecting these events.

- According to the Criminal Code, babies born alive are owed care to sustain life. Those babies, whether perfect or not, are owed the dignity of a birth certificate and the necessities of life. Where they are not fed and cared for, charges of infanticide should be laid.

- Freedom of the press must be assured so that all of us can freely seek the truth and utter our opinions. We call on Civil Rights leaders to take up the cause of the *Alberta Report* publishers.

- Conscience clauses, such as those recently negotiated with nurses at Markham Stouffville Hospital in Ontario, must be activated across Canada to maintain the human rights of nurses.

- Genetic cleansing of those deemed to be imperfect must cease. This is an attack not only on the individual but on all who suffer disabilities.

- 30 -

For more information contact
Anna Desilets at 204-942-4772

PROVIDING NATIONAL LEADERSHIP IN PROLIFE EDUCATION

B1-90 Garry Street Winnipeg Manitoba R3C 4H1   Telephone: (204) 942-4772 Fax #: 943-9283 thalamus. To support this belief that a fetus in the second trimester can feel pain, he cites three signs: * a fetus will "withdraw from painful stimulation" * two types of stress hormones which are detected in adults who are feeling pain are also found in a fetus from when a blood sample is withdrawn. He quotes Nicholas Fisk of London, England, who observed this reaction as early as 19 weeks and J. Partch of Kiel, Germany, who observed it at 16 weeks.

In summary, a 20-30 week old fetus actually will feel more pain than an adult. It appears that a fetus may feel pain as early as six weeks old. The evidence that the fetus feels pain is anatomical, physiological/ Hormonal, by his/her behaviour of withdrawing from the pain source and changes in his/her vital signs.

Remember, there are always two victims to every abortion, -one dead, and one wounded. Abortionists are definitely not considering the well-being of their tiniest patients. Many of us who know the truth are praying that again the politicians will declare protection for the Preborn. Hopefully, before God's judgment and anger manifests on the earth.

Toronto General and Women's College Hospital were first on our list to expose these diabolical procedures. In Sept. of 1989 we sent letters to the Hospital Boards warning them that abortion is a 'deadly solution to a social, economic or a birth control problem'. We implored them to stop permitting it, encouraging them to save lives, not destroy them. They never replied. Shame, shame on the men and women, who call themselves doctors and take innocent lives by their own hands! How repugnant. Yes, they do hide behind their surgical masks. Masks of rhetoric, lies and deception.

On Saturday Sept. 16, 1989 we held the "Come mourn for the Preborn" rally at Nathan Phillips Square, Toronto City Hall. At this Pro Life Rally we wanted to commemorate all the babies whom they had aborted in Canada. We wanted to first recognize them as tiny human beings, with a spirit and soul. We wanted to give them a decent funeral procession. Showing them and God that we did care, and that we do see their humanity. No matter how tiny their bodies were, and however short their lives were.

A Christian funeral director donated a tiny little white coffin, and about thirty baskets of beautiful fresh flowers. Red and white carnations, yellow daffodils, long stemmed huge white and red mums. The smells and colours were vibrant. It was a cool, damp and cloudy day. Someone had brought three white crosses. We displayed colourful stuffed animals that surrounded the small white casket.

Behind the display Pastor Rick D'Arazio, Rev. Hudson Hilsden, Politicians, Bev Daw and other women who were victims of the abortion industry spoke out. Stretched along the glass windows at the far back was a huge 20 foot white banner, with a big red heart to one side stating, "Abortion STOPS a beating heart."

As organizer, I wanted to present "The Way Inn," (an outreach of help, love and hope for pregnant women) in recognition of the life saving roles they have played next door to Morgentaler's pro-death clinic. They were forced to relocate because of the injunction. On behalf of Christians for Life I presented Joanne Dilemann the Director of The Way Inn, a plaque. It had been established by Rev. Ken Campbell, of Choose Life Canada. They provide education, homes, furniture and practical assistance to unwed mothers. My good friend, Rick Dees, sang a song he wrote, entitled "September," while a young teenager demonstrated through drama the dilemma of abortion, and the heart-cry of the unborn child. There was not a dry eye in the place. About 400 people attended this event at Toronto City Hall. We have discovered and studies support the fact, that the majority of media persons are biased "Pro choice." Another excellent book to read is "Pro Life Answers to Pro choice arguments" by Randy Alcorn.

There is so much bias and rhetoric in the media that the majority of Canadians are not seeing the whole, true picture on this issue. Studies also prove that the majority of Canadians do not condone abortion as a form of birth control which it has become. I hope that you will wake up to the urgency to expose this diabolical procedure and stop the holocaust.

We can make a difference by voting for Politicians who are Pro Life. We need to continually picket hospitals and abortion clinics that kill Preborn babies. We must continue to write letters, give financial support to Pro Life and Family Action groups who lobby Government officials and keep praying! In humble obedience to the word of God we all must

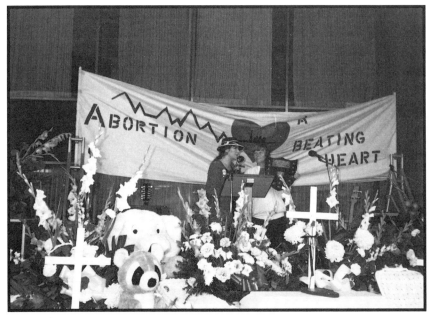

September 16, 1989 "Come Mourn for the Preborn" memorial service at Toronto City Hall

stand for the sanctity of life and Justice for the Preborn. Proverbs 31:8 commands us to "Speak for those who cannot speak for themselves, for the rights of all who are defenseless, and unjustly sentenced to death."

Walk by Faith

Friday night I received a phone call from the Pro Life action line. They informed me that Morgentaler was having a conference on "abortion techniques." They were planning a sidewalk picket in front of the glamourous Harbour Castle Hotel. This prestigious hotel is situated in downtown Toronto by the waterfront of Lake Ontario. The woman on the phone asked if I could be there for the next morning. Without hesitation I replied, "Sure, I'll be there," just knowing that I had to be there.

The next morning I arose so early, that it was still dark outside. Feeling a bit apprehensive for some unknown reason, I began to seek God and pray fervently for his direction and guidance for the day ahead. First asking for His forgiveness and mercy upon me for all my sins and shortcomings. Then thanking Him for his goodness, provisions and grace toward me.

After putting on the full armour of God as stated in Ephesians 6, the Helmet of Salvation, the Breastplate of Righteousness, the Belt of Truth, the Shield of Faith, the Sword of the Spirit-which is the word of God. Having my feet ready to go where He wanted me to go, I continued. "Lord, I give my life to you today as a living sacrifice, holy and acceptable and pleasing unto you, which is my reasonable service. I pray a wall of fire and a hedge of thorns of protection around me, and plead the blood of Jesus over me and the other pro lifers. I love you Lord, and help me to hear your voice, and obey your commands today, in Jesus Name, Amen."

Then as I began to sip my coffee and look for some blue jeans to put on, I abruptly heard, "No, get dressed up!". "What?" I said aloud. Then I heard, "Get dressed up in a nice outfit." It was just like a big debate that I had with the Holy Spirit. *But, running shoes and jeans would be so much more comfortable.* But He persisted, and so finally I said, "Okay, I'll get dressed up." Reluctantly, I chose my modest navy blue skirt-suit, new panty hose and high heels. Grabbing my purse and a plastic bag full of Pro-Life pamphlets and literature, I headed down the hallway and to my car in the underground garage. Feeling a bit anxious, I started to pray and sing praises all the way downtown. Arriving at the scene, I drove across the street to the closest parking lot. With hardly any money I told the parking lot attendant that I was with those picketers and explained to him the horrors of abortion. "Well," he paused, "Go park over there, it is on me." "Praise the Lord," I gladly shouted. With the purse swung over my shoulder, and convinced that I must take the plastic bag, I proceeded across the street. My fellow Pro-Lifers were slowly walking back and forth in long strides with big bold signs. *I had absolutely no idea of what God had in store for me to do. No idea of what was about to happen, just all dressed up and praying for direction.*

After greeting a few of them, the Lord said, "Keep going, go into the Harbour Castle." So by faith, taking it one step at a time, I proceeded into the Harbour Castle. It had been quite a while since I had visited this place. It was familiar since I had been to insurance conferences and drinking bouts there before. This time I was sober.

Walking into the huge Hollywood style front Lobby without a clue where I was going, I asked someone at the front desk where the Morgentaler conference was. They told me that it was upstairs in a Dungeon Room. I mean Conference room. So off I went, up the escalator and down the hall.

There I was in front of the doors about to walk in, when a man standing at the door asked me if I had registered yet? "Oh, no, how much is it?" I asked. "Well, it was $650.00 for the weekend, but they've reduced it to $350.00." He answered. "Oh, is that all?", I exclaimed. Glancing around, I noticed two tables out front. One had a sign that said "Media," and the other was full of literature.

The Lord quickly reminded me that I was now a freelance writer. It was just a couple of weeks ago that I had my very first article published in a Christian magazine. *This is getting exciting, I thought.* "Oh, well, actually I am a freelance writer, -did I miss much? I'm late." I non-chalantly responded, and began casually to move forward. He quickly moved aside, pointed his finger and said, "All of the media are over there against this wall." "Great, thanks a lot." I replied, and headed in.

It was a very cold, big dark room. Flood lights hit a raised platform where Morgentaler was giving a speech. He was arrogant about having this conference and how pleased he was to have so many doctors there. *Yuch, how disgusting! Now what, Lord?* I spotted an empty seat. It seemed peculiar that all the tables were just two seaters. Quickly, I sat next to a man in a suit. They were all in suits, I think. Only one or two women present, I noticed. There were a lot of photographers taking pictures of Henry. After his introduction speech, he thanked the media and they all left. Except me. It was as if I were somehow glued to this chair. It was not time for me to go, not yet.

Soon after all the reporters left, an extremely handsome, well dressed, tall gentleman went up on the stage. He began to describe the details of the different abortion tools and instruments that they used. Of course to me it was more like a huge arsenal of weapons of mass destruction ...

After a few moments of listening to him describe how these weapons of war worked to terminate the lives of little babies nestled in the sanctuary of their mother's womb. I started to become quite nauseous. Sweat began to roll down my forehead.

It was becoming very difficult for me to contain myself. Horrid flashbacks began to seize my mind. Pictures and feelings from that abortion while I was wide awake, almost made me vomit. It was like reliving all those emotions and pain all over again. I began to pray in my heart, *"Lord, please help me, What do you want me to do? What am I doing here? Lord, I cannot take this much longer, or I'll be sick, or burst out crying or something!"* Help!

He said, "Look in your bag." Slowly, I reached into the bag and quietly shuffled the Pamphlets on Fetal Development and Complications of Abortions. I passed several to the man sitting beside me, a doctor, I presumed. He slightly raised them to take a peek, then he quickly put them down in front of him. Never making eye contact with him, I kept busy with what was in the bag.

There was dead silence in that huge room, except for the speaker. It was chilly, cold and dark, not surprising. The arsenal weapon's sales agent kept referring to the woman, as "the patient." I felt very uncomfortable listening to all that. Then I felt the smooth bumper sticker in the bag. Instantly, I turned to look at the wall beside me, and was amazed and startled!

What, this is the Harbour Castle? For on the wall right beside me were big sections of ugly plywood full of staples and bits of paper. *Oh, Okay Lord, now I got it.*

When the time came that I just could not take it any longer, spiritual boldness rose up in me. I stood up, and in a very loud, clear voice exclaimed, "**I was a patient!**" With a thump, thump smoothing down each end, I stuck the white bumper sticker on the plywood. It had a red heart on the right side, and a bold black heart monitor line zigzagging across it. It read, in large bold print, "**ABORTION STOPS A BEATING HEART.**" Without a sound, the whole place was shaken. I just turned around, grabbed by purse and bag, and non-chalantly walked out of there, down the escalator, and straight out the door. My heart was pounding.

Incredibly relieved to be out of that den of vipers, I prayed, "Lord Jesus, convict them of the sin of murder. I prayed that the fear of God would come upon them so they would get the revelation that abortion always has two victims.

Hopefully the truth that abortion stops a beating heart, and that it hurts women also penetrated into their souls. One day they will each have to stand before God's judgment seat and answer why they continued to kill the innocent. Then be condemned to eternal hell for the shedding of innocent blood. It is awful to hear about how ancient tribes and heathen cultures sacrificed their babies to false gods. Yet, today, this legal, ultimate, rampant child abuse takes place in the womb.

Women need to make their choices before having sex. If they choose sex, then they must regard and respect the result of that choice,-another life. Daily, news records the horrors of child abuse. We heard about the woman who strapped her two little boys in the back seat of her car and then pushed it down a hill. She stood and watched for about nine minutes as they sank deep into a miry lake. Drowning these precious children because her boyfriend did not want kids!

Not too long ago in Toronto a man tied many books to the backs of his two little boys, and then threw them in the frigid cold waters of Lake Ontario to drown. The younger brother died. One son miraculously survived the vicious attack of his own father. A witness came to the rescue! Mothers and fathers neglecting, beating and killing their own children. Why? It is the "Kill the unwanted," death culture.

Dr. Philip Ney, has done a thesis and antithesis on the relationship between abortion and child abuse. He states, "For over a decade those who wanted abortions on request argued that it was necessary for every child to be a wanted child. However, there are reasons to believe abortion on request not only has not solved the problem of unwanted, neglected or battered children, but it has worsened the problem."

In Dr. Ney's Report he shows evidence that 1. Death to Canadian children from social causes rapidly increased after early abortion became available on demand in 1969-70. 2. British Columbia and Ontario with the highest rates of abortion are also the provinces with the highest rates of child abuse. Newfoundland, Prince Edward Island, and New Brunswick with low rates of abortion, have low rates of child abuse. 3. In the United States it is estimated that in the next decade there will be 1.5 million battered children, resulting in 50,000 deaths, and 300,000 permanently injured children.

The most common cause of death in American children aged 12 months to six years old is murder by their own parents!

4. More than 90 percent of the battered children are from 'wanted pregnancies'. 5. To abort was not considered any more frequently by child battering parents than by the controls. 6. Abuse is not more common among defective or retarded children. 7. Adopted children are more frequently abused.

He also reports that there is a pyschopathogenesis linking abortion and battering. "Rather than preventing child abuse, abortion on request may be a cause of the increase in battered and murdered children."

Dr. Ney concludes in his extensive report that "Although permissive abortion has been advocated on the grounds that it will reduce the prevalence of child abuse and infanticide, **there is NO evidence to prove it has**. There is a growing concern that it may have contributed to the problem. This article outlines eight possible methods whereby an increasing rate of abortion will lead to an increasing rate of child abuse ... If the hypothesis is correct, medicine by endorsing abortion on request may be jeopardizing the safety and care of a large number of children."

If the tiniest of human beings have no protection, and at a whim can be murdered, sanctioned by Government and conducted by "Doctors," then why not hurt, maim or kill them outside the womb? Not much of a difference, is there?

It all begins with "**Personhood**," or lack of it. Back in 1857, people of colour were not considered" persons." They had NO RIGHTS or freedoms. Slavery was the free labour of the southern USA. These individuals were treated worse than animals. They could be bought, sold, beaten or killed without questions. Who were the puritans to tell slave owners what they could or could not do with these black slaves who were their property? Coloured folks were the ownership of the slave owners to do with as they wished. "This slave is my property! He is my business! It is my right, I bought him, I can do what I want with him. It is between a slave owner and his slave!" "My body, my rights, my choice." Sound familiar?

It was a long hard fight for the rights of slaves, and then segregation meant continued discrimination. The book "Uncle Tom's Cabin" exposed the truth about the horrid treatment of slaves and their plight for freedom, humanity and a little dignity. When Dr. Martin Luther King, called of God, preached the accuracy of God's word, he knew that God was no respecter of persons. He declared his dream, stood against the Goliaths of racism and accomplished great deeds for coloured people.

In 1936 the Supreme Court of Germany made an amendment to its constitution, stripping Jews of all of their rights. Abruptly, Jewish people had no rights, and were no longer considered "persons," thus opening the door of murder to millions of innocent men, women and children, who were "unwanted" by the Nazi's. They were starved, poisoned, tortured and systematically executed. They also massacred the disabled and elderly (eugenics). Nothing has really changed, except the age of the victims.

Today, Preborn children are not considered "persons" by the Supreme Court of Canada, even though they are discriminating against the youngest of human beings. Babies who are unwanted by their mothers and others become human garbage or used for fetal experimentation.

Women,-children are a blessing, not a curse! Believe me, multitudes of women would not start shoving coat hangers up their vaginas to kill their babies if abortion again became illegal. The abortion providers want people to believe this to keep themselves in business.

Thank God for the honourable **"Canadian Physicians for Life,"** who are appalled at the destruction of human life at the hands of others, in their profession. They have about 2,800 associates and are growing. They hold reverence for every human life from the moment of conception until natural death.

This is their statement outline on the topic of "Therapeutic Abortions" "Since 1969, more than 500,000 pregnancies have been terminated by induced abortions. The medical profession has been an essential element in this process. **The Canadian Physicians for Life urge the Canadian Medical Association to reverse its support of abortion for the following reasons: 1) Abortions are performed for** "social reasons, **NOT FOR MEDICAL PROBLEMS...**" 2) "The outcome of a psychiatric illness is not adversely affected by the continuation of a pregnancy..." 3) "The long term consequences of abortion to the mother are likely to be more serious than we at present recognize..." 4) "The development of fetal medicine has dramatized the status of the unborn child as a Patient, and therefore, the responsibility of the attending physician..." 5) "Abortion, like suicide, does not allow for any second thoughts or regrets..."**

Their statement continues, "In 1948, in reaction to the Nazi Holocaust, the World Medical Association framed the Declaration of Geneva to prevent, ever again, the erosion of the respect for human life. It affirms: 'The health of my patient will be my first consideration. I will **maintain the upmost respect for human life from the time of con-**

ception; even under threat. I will not use my medical knowledge contrary to the law of humanity.' We are now faced with a new holocaust. The medical profession still has the respect of the public so that its voice, on behalf of the unborn, their patients, can help change the thinking of society. We urge the Canadian Medical Association to act now!" They have not.

Power In PRAYER

For years I had been praying for my husband-to-be, whoever he was, and wherever he was. Specifically, I would pray that the Lord send labourers across his path that were Born-Again and Spirit Filled. That God would fill him with His Holy Spirit, power, love and a sound mind.

While I was praying for this husband of mine to-be, without even knowing him, he met a guy at work, who was a 'Born-Again' Christian. He gave him a brochure on how to get 'saved' and go to heaven. He invited Paul to church. After hearing a powerful sermon, Paul asked Jesus to come into his heart and change his life. He wanted to know God.

My friends and I would pray for our future husbands with fervency. I recall praying, that if there was any other woman in his life, I commanded that she get out of it in 'Jesus' name. (He had been living common-law with a woman and they broke up soon after his conversion to Christ!) Prayer is truly a powerful tool, in the name of Jesus.

We met at Paul's church, and he pursued me. We had no hanky-panky until our wedding night. That was a miracle! On March 9, 1991, we got married, and flew to picturesque Cartagena, Columbia for our honeymoon. By mid April our precious son Shawn, was conceived. Thank you Lord! An ultrasound at just fifteen weeks showed him waving a perfect little hand. You can also see his cute little toes in the photo. Now, knowing the truth and wonder of life, I loved being pregnant.

The labour pain was not nearly as severe as I had anticipated it would be. I was a bit irritable though. Paul could not do anything right. I'd ask him to hold my hand, then complain that he was not holding it

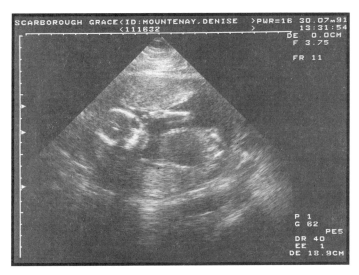

Ultra sound of Shawn Paul at 15 weeks old, see him waving?

tight enough. You know? After 21 hours in labour, my cervix had only dilated three centimetres. It totally malfunctioned!

The baby started to go into distress! Doctors insisted that I had to have an emergency C-section. Well this was out of the question. I had not read anything about C-sections. When devouring all of the Pregnancy and Childbirth books I would just skip the C-sections. I thought *"No way. I'll never have to have that operation."* But, here I was. In fifteen minutes they had me prepared and ready for surgery. He made it!

What amazing love and happiness to behold my very own child! Yes, Shawn Paul Mountenay was a survivor. He was the only child to remain alive in my womb. Thank you Lord God, for opening my eyes. For taking off the blinders and blessing us with the greatest gift on earth, a child! A baby to hold, to love, to cuddle, to teach, to show and get to know. Nursing was a challenge at first. I was sore and tender. The wonderful nurse I had encouraged me to hang in there, glad I did. Breast feeding is the most convenient, easiest, healthiest thing for a baby, and the cheapest too.

A child to nurture, protect and grow. Crawling, walking, talking, so many adventures. Camping, rides, slides and zoos. Time to hug, time to know, time to go to school. Discipline early is a good rule. Giving, sharing, caring and play, play, play in the pool. My son, my pal, my lovey! Oh thank you God for your mercy and grace. Women who choose to kill their sons and daughters will lose. Children have so much love to give and behold. How wonderful to have a child!

In February of 1993 we were thrilled to discover I was pregnant with our second child. However, complications came. Around the beginning of April, I started spotting blood and tiny blood clots were appearing. Sensing something was terribly wrong, I went to see Dr. Robson, a Christian Doctor, and he immediately booked an appointment for me to go and have an Ultra Sound. On April 16 the ultrasound technician could not pick up a heart beat for the baby. It had been about 12 weeks since my last period. Words cannot express the fear and anxiety that I felt with this news.

They could see the gestational sac and baby. However, the size did not correspond with how big the baby should have been according to the dates. He measured only about 7-8 weeks old, not 10-12 weeks. The heart had stopped beating for some unknown reason. The Diagnostic technicians' report read in capitals "NO FETAL HEARTBEAT IS DETECTED, and gestational sac quite large with respect to fetal pole. Findings suggest fetal demise and missed abortion."

Doctor Robson suggested that since I wasn't going into labour to deliver this baby prematurely, and since it was evident that for whatever reason this baby had died. I had to consider having a D & C (dilation and curettage).

This procedure just plagued me. Here I was again having to go through this procedure. Tears and torrents of fear attacked me. How can I go through another horrible procedure like that again? Flashbacks, dread, anxiety assailed me.

While getting prepared for the surgery, Pastor Rob and his wife came to visit. They were so precious and comforting to me, as I wept in remorse and grief. We hugged, we talked, we prayed. I felt the peace of God surround me, and I knew that this baby's spirit was with the Lord. Now I could relate to other women the hurt of having a natural miscarriage. What the devil meant for evil to hurt and destroy me, God turns it around for good. One day I will also see this child in heaven.

Therefore, I have come to trust totally in His will for my life, and that includes how many children we will have. Generally speaking, there has been a lot of propaganda over the years to suggest that we are over populating the earth, and it will be catastrophic. This is totally untrue. The truth is, there is enough space and food to feed everyone and many, many more. The real problems are monetary control, greed, power, selfishness, and distribution. Especially with today's high technology and scientific advances, not one person should have lack. Besides, God always provides for His people.

We would love to have more children, and we never use any birth control, however, the gynocologists have discovered that my uterus is so scarred and damaged from the abortions, that they cannot believe that I was able to carry Shawn. Furthermore, my cervix is so badly scarred that it is incompetent. The cause of abortions! Perhaps, God will grant another miracle child before my maternal clock stops ticking, or perhaps we will foster or adopt children?

Tragedy In The Courthouse

The potency of prayer became evident the day I witnessed my only brother, Tommy, viciously attacked with a knife from behind. He had grown up to be a courageous police officer and family man. This is the short version.

In 1996, Tom and his partner were chasing two thieves at 3:00 a.m., who were driving a stolen jeep. There was a Canada-wide warrant out for their arrests. They were wanted for two armed robberies, home invasions and questioning. When they came to a cul de sac, the jeep stopped. Tom and his partner ordered the suspects to stop, and get out of the jeep. Instead, the driver decided to accelerate on the gas and hit Tom, who was standing in front of the jeep with his gun extended. On the jeep's impact, he simultaneously fired the one shot. It hit the teenager, who was driving, and he died instantly. Although Tom never discussed the case with us, we knew that he was just endeavouring to do his job.

Toronto Star Headlines read "Charge Officer in Slaying, Slain Teen's Mom Urges." She was quoted by reporters that the police officer who shot her son "should be charged with murder". Clayton Ruby who represented Henry Morgentaler against me, on the one million dollar lawsuit, also happened to represent this woman. (Coincidence?) She was suing for millions of dollars.

Nevertheless, after pressure, the S.I.U. actually charged Tom with 'manslaughter.' We were quite concerned about his safety and future.

On the first day of the preliminary hearing, my mother and I watched in terror as Tom stood inches away. Right out of the blue, a guy jumped him from behind with a homemade knife. *Tommy did not have a chance!* We watched in horror, shocked, as this guy swiftly stabbed Tommy four times in the back and once in the neck! *Tommy was helpless.* He collapsed, falling to the floor. Blood was squirting out of his neck from a gapping wound. It was the most vile scene. I beckoned a man to put pressure on his neck, as I knelt beside Tom, trying to comfort him. There was a big commotion behind me as others fought with the attacker to obtain the weapon and hold him down. Another officer was slashed in the arm as he tried to subdue the maniac! Getting up, I kept yelling for someone to call 911. It had happened so fast, yet it seemed to commence in slow motion. It was surreal.

Sharon, Tom's wife, rushed to console him. Tommy was at death's door. His head was swelling, he was stark white, and was losing a lot of blood. His oldest daughter, a teenager, was wanting to come and see, but a number of people kept her away. Meanwhile, two men dragged my Mom across the huge foyer to the other side. Frantically, I ran to and fro, asking where the ambulance was. Running to our Mother, I grabbed her hands and declared, "Let's pray." With the most impassioned prayer, I pleaded for God's mercy and grace for Tom, and proclaimed in faith, that he shall live, and not die, in Jesus' Name. It seemed forever for the ambulance to arrive. Another ambulance came to take Mom who could barely breathe - my dad and I travelled in her ambulance.

A few months later we actually had to go back to the same court, and continue the preliminary hearing. This time there were dozens of police officers all around, protecting us-some in army fatigues, some in plain clothes, and some in uniform. The hearing was extremely interesting. The whole truth came out. All the angles were exposed, many witness came forth. This would make another great book! After hearing all the evidence, the judge declared, "Case dismissed." Tom was free to go. We just cried! All that agony, and near death experience for nothing. Tom was innocent, he was just trying to be a good cop and arrest the unmanageable menacing teenagers. They could have easily surrendered peacefully, but they chose not to. The young offender who tried to murder Tom, got a slap on the wrist, and spent less than two years in a juvenile detention centre.

It was a horrific experience. We thank God that he survived that savage attack. It was a miracle! This harrowing attack has affected our whole family forever.

Always have an Answer to Defend the Life of the Baby

Scott Klusendorf, a pro-life speaker has this to say about speaking to people who think it is okay to end the life of a pre born baby:

"Arguments based on "choice" or "privacy" misses the point entirely. Would anyone that you know support a mother killing her toddler in the name of "choice and who decides?" Again, this debate is about just one question: What is the unborn?

Is the unborn a member of the human family? If so, killing him or her to benefit others is a serious moral wrong. It treats the distinct human being, with his or her own inherent moral worth, as nothing more than a disposable instrument. Conversely, if the unborn are not human, killing them for any reason requires no more justification than having a tooth pulled.

Remind your critics that you are vigorously "pro-choice" when it comes to women choosing a number of moral goods. You support a woman's right to choose her own doctor, to choose her own husband, to choose her own job, and to choose her own religion, to name a few. These are among the many choices that you fully support for women. But some choices are wrong, like killing innocent human beings simply because they are in the way and cannot defend themselves.[1]

Put simply, there is no morally significant difference between the embryo you once were, and the adult you are today. Differences of size, level of development, environment, and degree of dependency are not relevant, such that we can say that you had no rights as an embryo but you do have rights today. Think of the acronym SLED as a helpful reminder of these non-essential differences:[2]" www.prolifetraining.com

[1] Gregory Koukl, Precious Unborn Human Persons (Lomita: STR Press, 1999) p. 11.

[2] Stephen Schwarz, The Moral Question of Abortion (Chicago: Loyola University Press, 1990) p. 18.

Chapter 15
Millennium, Conferences
and the ABC Link

Since this book was first published, many exciting, poignant and adventurous things have taken place. To God be the Glory!

Millennium, New Years 2000, I was ready for anything. Just in case; for Christmas I had made beautiful paraffin oil candles in fancy tall glass bottles with lots of dried flowers and shells and sparkling stones on the bottom for family and friends. Right after Christmas my Dad called to inform me that Mom was rushed to the hospital with shortness of breath. I flew to Ontario to be with her on New Years Eve. Loaded with a couple of bottles of sparkling cider, we celebrated with her room mates. Incidentally, this was the same hospital where I had my first abortion at the age of 16, many years earlier. Mom was quite ill, fighting congestive heart failure, emphysema, obesity and diabetes; but thanks to God and the prayers of friends, she pulled through and was doing pretty good. She got off the oxygen and was able to be home once again.

To God be the Glory for the great things HE has done! He has opened many doors for me to bring the message that abortion hurts and devastates women, and took the lives of my children. The purpose is to expose the evil and lies of abortion, and proclaim HIS Truth that life is precious; and God has a plan for every person, no matter how small.

While in the Toronto area I was invited to host a "Nite Lite" program on 100 Huntley Street and had the opportunity to minister to many souls on TV from 2-4 AM live! Then the Miracle Channel had me on as a guest on their "Lifeline" program also that year allowing me to share my testimony of God's amazing grace and healing power. I boast in the Lord because over that year I spoke in many High Schools, the University of BC, several Women's Aglow Chapters and churches. Shawn and I drove to beautiful BC as the Lord opened doors for me to speak to hundreds of people and sell more copies of this book. PTL!

The Lord also opened doors for me to share on several radio stations such as CKOV-Kelowna, BC. CHED-Talk Radio-Edmonton, CJMR-Toronto. Again I was invited to speak in prisons, and wherever God opened doors. The Father, Creator of the Heavens, Earth, Seas and all that is therein, hates the shedding of innocent blood, and the Bible says that it pollutes the land.

In late May my Dad suffered a heart-attack, and the Lord provided the airfare for our son Shawn and me to fly back to Ontario. Then in October Dad had a stroke! I flew back again to help out. After much prayer, Dad was healed; he could walk again, talk again, and remember who that nice lady was who had been faithfully looking after him; my Mom. He was doing very well. Many prayed for his salvation. My husband suggested that we ask them to come and live with us… "We've taken in strangers, why wouldn't we have your parents stay with us?" he asked. We gladly invited them to move out west to Alberta and live with us. I was thrilled to have them!

It was just getting to be too much for them alone in that house, in Ontario. Both of them were very independent and yet in such need of help. They were hard workers but years of smoking, financial stresses and all that great food full of cholesterol was catching up with them. It was now difficult for them to do all of the house keeping, laundry, cleaning, cooking, shopping etc. This was a huge move for them; it meant they'd be away from my sister and brother who had lived close by. But they knew it was time to get help. They had no desire to go into a nursing or seniors' home, as that was for the old folks, not them. I was so excited and glad to have them to myself. We were very close. I loved them so much.

God continued to make a way for me to share my pain of abortion at pro-life venues and organizations, Women's Aglow, the University of Alberta, churches, and youth rallies across western Canada. Students commented on my talks with,

"I think that you really spoke from your heart and I appreciate your honesty. People don't tell us of the horror of abortion and you finally spoke the truth, thank you for an experience of a lifetime."

"I think her story forced a lot of people to face what is real-what is the truth and inspired many of us to want to be active and make a difference. I really appreciated it."

"It was very interesting to see how a person can change so much, very impressed by her work and involvement in stopping abortion." "She was an excellent speaker! I'd like us to have her again sometime."

My remarkable Mother had done all the driving from southern Ontario to Alberta with few stops; she looked wiped the day they arrived. It was wonderful having my Mom and Dad around, Mom loved to do some of the cooking and she liked doing the dishes. She wanted to keep busy. Dad liked to read and watch the history channel. I got to take them to weekly doctor visits, shopping trips, the swimming pool, and Jacuzzi whenever they felt like it. It was so nice for Shawn to get to know his Grandparents better too.

About once a month I joined a couple from our church to do prison ministry and was able to share my testimony on those occasions.

In 2002 I spoke in a few churches, a High School, on a radio program and on the Miracle Channel. God had put a burden on my heart to go to the World Conference on Breast Cancer in Victoria, BC. in June. For several years I had heard that there was a significant link to breast cancer by women who had had abortions. I had a lump removed from my left breast in my twenties, and now in my forties another one appeared, and had to be removed. I wanted answers; I wanted women informed of the abortion breast cancer link.

The evidence is clear. Not just one, or two studies, but **over 28 credible worldwide studies linking breast cancer to induced abortion!** The first one was done in 1957! Yet, silence and even denial from the cancer societies and foundations. Why the cover-up, the fear to let women know? Why the denial? Is it because they are afraid of losing millions of dollars in donations to support their executive salaries and expenses? Post abortive women, their families, friends and government will be outraged and angry to learn that they have withheld these studies and information from the public for years. It is unconscionable that they refuse to warn women, of this preventable risk factor. While at the same time they claim to be looking for a cure, walking for a cure, and talking about prevention? Giving birth is a preventable risk factor and women have a right to hear about it.

Fascinatingly, cancer societies seem to dance around the risk factors without using the word "abortion". First, they do agree that delaying a first full term pregnancy creates a risk factor for Breast Cancer. The medical literature does not say that a "little bit" of pregnancy or a partial pregnancy (i.e. one that ends in abortion or miscarriage) is protective. On the contrary, **it is well-established that only a first full term pregnancy is protective.** [MacMahon, B, Cole P, Lin TM, Lowe CR, Mirra AP, Ravnihar B, Salber EJ, Valaoras VG, Yuasa S. Age at First Birth and Breast Cancer Risk. Bull WHO 1970; 43:209-221.]

HELLO; most abortions are done on that FIRST pregnancy, to teenagers and young women. Another risk factor for Breast Cancer is waiting until after the age of 30, to give birth to that first child. Many post abortive women either delay their first full term pregnancy or can't get pregnant until after the age of 30. **In fact, one group of scientists said that women contemplating an abortion have a right to be informed about the risk-reducing effect of a full term pregnancy. They called on doctors to warn abortion-bound women that they will lose an opportunity to reduce their risk for breast cancer if they have abortions. They advised doctors to inform women about the existence of additional research that shows that an abortion will further raise their risk by leaving them with an increase in cancer-vulnerable breast tissue.** [Thorp JM, Hartmann KE, Shadigian EM. Long-term physical and psychological health consequences of induced abortion: A review of the evidence. Obstet & Gynecol Survey 2003;58:1.]

Oxford scientists reviewed 47 **studies conducted in 30 countries. They concluded that by having larger families and breastfeeding our children longer, women in developed nations can reduce the incidence of breast cancer by over one-half.** [Beral V, et al. Breast cancer and breastfeeding: collaborative re-analysis of individual data from 47 epidemiological studies in 30 countries, including 50,302 women with breast cancer and 96,973 women without the disease Lancet 2002;360:187-195.]

A third known risk factor is not having any children at all, and sadly some women abort the only child they could/would ever have. 70 epidemiological studies on the abortion-cancer link have been conducted since 1957 (isn't it strange that the cancer societies didn't want us to know about this large body of research a half-century ago). **Eighty percent report risk increases for women who have abortions.** A 1996 review and meta-analysis of the worldwide medical literature by scientists at Baruch College and Penn State shows a 30% increase in risk for women who have abortions after the birth of a first child and a 50% increase in risk for women who have abortions before the birth of a first child. [Brind J, Chinchilli, VM, Severs WB, Summy-Long J. Induced abortion as an independent risk factor for breast cancer: a comprehensive review and meta-analysis. J Epidemiol Community Health 1996;50:481-496.]

Other studies show that a premature birth before 32 weeks gestation more than doubles breast cancer risk for the mother! Isn't a premature birth biologically the same event as an abortion? [Melbye M, et al. Preterm delivery and risk of breast cancer. Bri J Cancer 1999;80:609-13. Hsieh C-c, Wuu J, Lambe M, Trichopoulos D, et al Delivery of premature newborns and maternal breast-cancer risk. Lancet 1999;353-1239.]

Furthermore, cancer societies state that long term estrogens exposure (as from the Birth Control Pill and Hormone Replacement Therapy) does increase your risk of getting breast cancer. Combined (estrogen plus progestin) oral contraceptives (OCs) is a risk factor for breast cancer according to the World Health Organization they classified OCs, and combined hormone replacement therapy (HRT) as group 1 carcinogens in 2005. [Press Release No. 167, "IARC Monographs Programme Finds Combined Estrogen-Progestogen Contraceptives (the "pill") and Menopausal Therapy Are Carcinogenic to Humans," World Health Organization International Agency for Research on Cancer, July 29, 2005.

Do you know that it is un-refuted that high doses of estrogens can become carcinogenic-capable of causing cancer? That is why Hormone

Replacement Therapy is now considered taboo. When a healthy woman becomes pregnant, naturally 2,000 times the estrogens are pumped into her breasts in the first trimester, to later become milk for the baby.

An induced abortion artificially terminates that pregnancy thus leaving these cells vulnerable to stagnate and possibly become cancerous over time.

I am not a scientist or doctor, but common sense tells me there is a link. Sadly, some of my girlfriends aborted the only children they would ever have! Sandy was forced by her parents to have an abortion at the age of 14; she did not want to abort. She was not given a choice. She knew it was wrong to abort this baby. She felt the pain, guilt and remorse for 2 decades after this abortion. She dealt with years of depression, self-loathing and destructive behaviour for not insisting and fighting harder for the life of this baby. She had so much scar tissue and infections from that abortion that by the age of 22 she had to have a total hysterectomy. At the age of 34 she was diagnosed with stage 3 estrogens positive Breast Cancer, and has now had a relapse at the age of 41 to an advanced stage and is fighting for her own life now. She is livid that women are not being informed about the ABC Link.

One friend had two abortions, fought depression for years, got cervical cancer, and had to have a total hysterectomy by the age of 38. Others have had lumps, cysts and breast cancer. Amanda had two abortions, got cervical cancer, fought depression, and had a nervous breakdown from the guilt and remorse of her abortions.

Dr. Chris Kahlenborn has written a good book on the subject called "Abortion, The Pill and Breast Cancer." Also, Joel Brind, Ph.D. Professor of Endocrinology and Dr. Angela Lanfranchi, M.D. a Breast Cancer Surgeon of The Breast Cancer Prevention Institute have an excellent video/DVD and booklet called, "Breast Cancer-Risks and Prevention" with the explanation and references. The Abortion Breast Cancer Coalition at www.abortionbreastcancer.com has an excellent website with all of the references, rebuttals and outcry to bring awareness and education to the forefront on this issue. It is a crime that young teens and women are not being informed about this deadly risk. I was never told that if I choose to have an abortion, I could be choosing breast cancer down the road. There are now over 2 million women in Canada who've had an abortion over the last 30 years. Now every 30 minutes another woman is diagnosed with breast cancer in this nation. Now we are aging, and this disease is manifesting more and more.

Of course this does not mean that every woman who has had an abortion will get breast cancer, nor does it imply that every woman who had breast cancer has had an abortion. But women have a right to know that many studies do reveal a significant link.

Some studies report that having one abortion doubles your risk. The abortion breast cancer (ABC) connection should be shouted from the roof tops and on every talk show, whether one calls themselves 'pro-choice' or whatever! Now almost one half of women have had more than one abortion. It is not a medical necessity, but a violent form of birth control. It is outrageous that cancer societies are not even erring on the side of caution, but denying this link altogether, implying that all of these studies are unimportant or irrelevant. In my opinion, they think that it is "politically incorrect" to say anything negative about the "a" word, 'abortion'. They fear losing millions of dollars in donations. This is however pathetic when we think of the magnitude of this revelation and the real health and well being of millions of women in Canada and around the world who have had an abortion, and who tomorrow will walk into a hospital or abortion clinic not even having a clue or being informed about the link.

It is especially dangerous for women who already have a family history of breast cancer to abort their baby. May God help us to get this word out in Jesus name, in time to save thousands of women and children!

To my dismay and astonishment, the plenary speakers at this World Conference on Breast Cancer did not even mention one word about the ABC risk factor on their subject of risk factors and prevention of Breast Cancer. Yet they did state that Breast Cancer had become an epidemic in Canada, the USA, Australia and some European countries. Interestingly, these are countries where abortion has been on demand for decades now. In our already under-populated country in 2006, 22,200 women will be diagnosed with Breast Cancer in our nation, and 5,300 will die from it annually.

We had applied to have an exhibit table, but once organizers found out that we were concerned about the ABC link, they forbid us with a lame excuse. They also asked me not to hand out these brochures and to take the banner outside. Kind of reminds me of how the tobacco industry denied any link between smoking and lung cancer, and even paid researchers to deny the link.

While at this conference I randomly met 4 women who were all fighting breast cancer. These women were all in their 50's now. I asked them if they had heard about the ABC Link, none had. I then conferred that I had 3 abortions when I was younger; asking each of them, privately, if they had ever had an abortion when they were younger. Guess how many? Three out of these four women had an induced abortion when

they were younger, and were now fighting for their lives with this deadly disease. The 4th woman had never had any pregnancies, no children. This confirmed my resolve to inform and educate women and the public about this credible information; a matter of life and death.

With conviction, and determined that women have a right to know about this link, I handed out brochures called, "Why Aren't Women Being Told" and held a custom made banner I had designed and purchased stating the fact that 28 studies link breast cancer to abortion with the www.abortionbreastcancer.com website.

While outside I met a wonderful lady from Egypt who was the head Radiologist in Cairo. She was very interested in this information and thought it made sense; she said that every mammogram file should include the question in the history chart on whether they had a previous abortion(s) and when. The effort to warn women goes on!

We may have to launch a class action lawsuit against abortion doctors and cancer societies for refusing to warn women about the dangers and damages of abortion. Please PRAY for us!

If it's not a "baby" then you're not pregnant!

Statistics tell us that 88 percent of clinical abortions happen before the twelfth week of pregnancy. In the Womb shows us a heart cell jolting to life on day twenty-two, arm buds developing in week four, glassy eyes forming in week six, taste buds, purposeful movement, and separate digits on hands and feet by week eight.

As Tallack writes, "The next four weeks [weeks nine through twelve] will see her kick, turn her feet, and curl her toes. She will bend her arms at the wrist and elbow, form partial fists with her tiny hands, and reach up to cover her face with her hands. Her face, with its sealed-shut eyes, will squint, frown, purse its lips, and open its mouth. She will respond to touch."

Tragically, four out of ten women who discover an unplanned pregnancy will choose to abort, we must change hearts and minds.

Chapter 16
Angels All Around

In August of 2002 my Mom had a stroke while she was in the hospital, strangely right after she had a Doppler test on her legs. It became impossible for her to walk anymore. Along with the shortness of breath, congestive heart failure and all those blood tests...her spirit was willing, but her body became weaker. She, being a very strong willed, courageous and brave woman tried physiotherapy, but her heart and physical condition were just too frail...she lost strength. It was emotionally difficult for her not to be able to move much.

Mom would have severe hot spells where she asked Shawn or I to put ice cold cloths on her arms, legs and forehead to refresh her.

She got me to bring in Swiss chocolates for the nurses and doctors. One day, she told me that two Philippino ladies came in and prayed for her, they led her in a 'sinner's prayer'. Praise God she had a spiritual awakening, she was born again! Years of prayer had been finally answered. I was so happy about God's faithfulness. Days later she told me that she wanted to get "water baptized" and celebrate the occasion. She told me to get a Black Forest chocolate cake, and coffee for everyone. She told me to invite Ray and Margo; friends of ours who play guitar and whom I went to prison ministry with. My Dad timidly stayed in the background while Mom got put into one of those wonderful sling machines which lifted her limp body right out of that bed and motored her down to the bathing room. She got water baptized in her gown in a hospital tub, what a site to see. We sang Amazing Grace. It was a time of joy...she said to my Dad... "Hans, let them pray for you too, it's good." He declined, and looking down, shook his head from side to side.

Weeks went by, they transferred her against our wills to another hospital 45 minutes away, Dad and I visited her almost daily. She got a bedsore, and due to her diabetes and lack of sufficient treatment, it got deeper and worse.

Then on the evening of Nov. 13th, while my Mom was at one hospital, my Dad was getting ready for bed, and came to tell me he was getting chest pains, so I quickly called 911. The ambulance came and I followed him to the hospital staying for several hours till he was admitted to the Acute Coronary Care Unit. I was worn out and overwhelmed. I drove to tell Mom that Dad was in the hospital too. When I finally got home I collapsed on the couch with a huge headache, exhausted. My husband handed me two Tylenols and ordered me to rest on the couch and not go back to the hospital that night. I wanted to, but just didn't have the strength. At around 4 AM a nurse called to say that my Dad wanted to see me.

Rested, I quickly got dressed and rushed right over. As soon as I walked into his private room I just knew that he was dying. He was stressing to breathe and looked very pale. An oxygen mask was over his mouth, and tubes of oxygen were going into his nostrils too. I began to cry.

Grasping his hand, I told him, I loved him, over and over. I called my brother and put Dad on the phone; in a weak voice he told my brother that he was so proud of him, of his accomplishments. Then I put him on to my sister and he had a few words with her also. We knew his time was short. I pleaded with him, "Dad, please let me pray for you, this is your last chance, what if I'm right, you will go straight to heaven." "I love you Dad, please," I implored him. He nodded and whispered okay. Wow, I could barely believe it, he had been such a stubborn German, very anti-Christ, now here he was on his deathbed and finally willing to submit to God. I quickly led him in a sinners' prayer. Then I asked if I could read him something from the Bible. He nodded; I turned to Psalm 91, and read it,

> *"He that dwells in the secret place of the most High shall abide under the shadow of the Almighty. I will say of the LORD, He is my refuge and my fortress: my God; in him will I trust. Surely he shall deliver*

you from the snare of the fowler, and from the noisome pestilence. He shall cover you with his feathers, and under his wings you shall trust: his truth shall be your shield and buckler. You shall not be afraid for the terror by night; nor for the arrow that flies by day..."

Then I read that familiar powerful Psalm 23,

"The LORD is my shepherd; I shall not want. He makes me to lie down in green pastures: he leads me beside the still waters. He restores my soul: he leads me in the paths of righteousness for his name's sake. Yea, though I walk through the valley of the shadow of death, I will fear no evil: for thou art with me; thy rod and thy staff they comfort me..."

Next as he was sitting up in that hospital bed, I felt the presence of angels, I cried out, "Dad, look to Jesus, look to the angels..." I was crying, tears streaming down my face. He began to look upwards, his eyes were fixed on something...until his head was tilted right up and he was looking towards the ceiling, then suddenly he was gone. His spirit had gone to be with the Lord! His heart stopped. His body lifeless. He was not there anymore.

The reality, pain of grief and sorrow enveloped me, he was gone. This was my Dad, my Father, the one who made love to our Mother and his seed was planted in her so I and my brother could live. I thank God that she did not abort me. Of course abortion was not as readily available and promoted back then, as it is today, thank God. They were not married, had premarital sex and I was conceived by GOD. Mom was about 8 months pregnant when they finally made that great commitment and got married. They were married for 45 years. Praise God, years of praying for them, finally answered, Dad actually humbled himself/his intellect and asked GOD to forgive him for all of his sins, he was saved~ and just in the nick of time, amen. I had to make phone calls; people needed to know what happened, my brother, my relatives, but first I had to go right to my Mother and tell her the news. I was a mess physically and emotionally, but I had to press on. Alone, shattered, upset and weeping I drove that long way to the other hospital.

Mom shed tears as I told her Dad was gone. I told her the good news that finally he had surrendered and asked God to forgive him, and in faith believe that Jesus was born of the virgin Mary, died on the cross for our sins; so we could be redeemed and reconciled to our Creator/Heavenly Holy Father. I was assured that my earthly father was in heaven now. Mom told me that she wanted to see him one more time and to bring his body there to her hospital. The arrangements were made, she said her good bye. It was so difficult.

A few weeks later Mom insisted that Shawn and I go to Mexico for a vacation; this would be her Christmas gift to us. God knew we sure needed the break. She assured me she would be fine. We had one week of heaven on earth in Puerto Vallarta. Sun, sand and sea. It was restful, it was invigorating! God knew we needed the rest, the time together. Paul my husband had to work; wanted to work. He is such a hard working good man, and I thank God for him. Without his support I could never have the freedom and opportunity to fulfil my calling, purpose and destiny in life.

I called Mom from Puerta Vallarta, she sounded weak, I felt anxious to get back, one week went so fast. On our return December 17th, the hospital advised me that it was impossible to visit her as the ward had been quarantined. A bad flu virus had been spread in the unit, and she had got it. I didn't care; I needed to see her, to massage her feet, her legs, her arms, her hands. I wanted to wash her face and clean her up. I loved her so much. I admired her so much. It was very frustrating, every day I called to see if they would allow me to come to her. I could only pray for her from a distance. Sometimes a nurse would bring a phone to her so we could talk briefly. Then on Dec. 24th the head nurse called to say that she would make an exception because my Mom was down and not doing so well. At long last, I rushed to the hospital, to my dear Mothers side.

It had been a couple of weeks now since I last saw her. First thing I noticed was that the bedsore had gotten worse, it was twice as large, it looked deeper, she was weak and pale looking. I got on the nurses' case and insisted that a specialist take a look and treat this immediately.

A week later they decided to send her to the University hospital in Edmonton for surgery on this bed sore. So on Jan. 1st 2003 I accompanied my Mom to this top of the line hospital. I was shocked as the emergency nurse told me that she was "malnourished," and that they needed to get fluids and proteins into her to boost her immune system before any surgery could be done. The scary thing was that her heart could not handle more fluids, she was already so swollen, that actual drops of water would ooze out of her arms and legs! Her heart was working harder and harder.

Several times a day they would prick her fingers to take blood sugar levels...her fingers were turning blue. Yet, my mother would not complain for months, she was amazing, she was tough. After the surgery January 9th she had about 50 steel staples in her bottom. It was a miracle she survived the surgery. It looked awful. Mom was in pain, she asked me to sleep over with her, and I did...but she would keep me awake, every few minutes calling out my name, and say, "Help." She couldn't eat anymore or even drink. They had put a feeding tube down her throat as they were afraid she might choke and liquids would go into her lungs.

She started to complain about some pains, and one day she told me that she couldn't live like this anymore, she wanted to get rid of some of the medications they were giving her. Too many side effects, the codeine was getting to her. The nurse told me that any changes would have to wait until the morning when the doctors arrived. Mom was getting tired, discouraged, she was giving up, she wanted to go now, to be with Dad; she knew her time was short.

We were praying "Lord, if it's her time to go be with you, take her quickly, but Satan you are not getting her one minute before her time in Jesus name".

The next morning when I arrived, I asked Mom if she still wanted to talk to the doctors about stopping some of the medications, and making changes. She raised her voice saying, "I want to live, I want to live!" It was good to hear her pronounce this. I was glad.

One crisp winter day Mom said, "Denise, I see angels, they are standing on each side of you." I asked, "What do they look like Mom?" She said, "Oh, they are big, huge...and they are waiting for me." I replied sincerely with, "Mom, they can wait...they have eternity." I did not want her to go.

She missed Dad, she was ready to go, she'd had enough, her body was giving up. Just three days later something unusual happened. I woke up at home without that daily urgency to rush to the hospital, and decided to check my emails then go. Suddenly, the phone rang, and the nurse said that my Mom had taken a turn for the worse. I told her to tell my Mom that I am on my way. She was gone before I got there. She went to be with the Lord on Jan. 29th 2003. She had a massive heart attack...the angels had taken her heaven bound. The pain of now losing my beloved mother just two and a half months after my Dad was heart wrenching.

Somehow, with God's grace and the comfort of the Holy Spirit I managed to get through this deep valley of grieving and sorrow in my life. I sure miss them immensely. It is so important to love and be with each other while we are alive, because one day we leave this earth suit and go into another dimension, either hell bound or heaven-bound depending on the choices we make while here on earth. Jesus rose from the dead and made a way for you and I.

Once your parents are gone, you cannot ask them any more questions about their lives, their experiences, their history, thoughts opinions and advice. We can only lean on God and His Holy Spirit to guide and direct our paths if we want to go and live according to HIS will and plans.

In Christ we become a part of the family of GOD, we get new brothers and sisters to hang out with, to grow with spiritually, to love and know.

Some of us think that because we are a 'good person' that we don't need God, or that a 'loving God' would not condemn us to hell. Well, yes, He is a loving God, but He is also a God of justice and He will judge everyone according to their deeds. All have sinned, we all have sinned and fall short of perfection. Have you ever lied, even a little? Have you ever stolen anything, even a pen, or cheated on your taxes? Have you ever looked at anyone with lust in your eyes? Have you committed adultery in your heart? Have you ever hated anyone? Jesus called this, as the sin of murder.

Well, most of us have committed all or most of these things, making us a lying, thieving, adulterous, murderer at heart. God has given us a free will, to choose life or death, blessings or cursings. For we are saved by Faith, it is a gift from God. By faith we can ask God to forgive us for our sins, repent, stop it, change, turn away and do what is right. We can believe that Jesus was born of the Virgin Mary, died on the cross for our sins, was raised from the dead and is alive.

The good news is He then sent us His Holy Spirit to be our teacher, our guide, our counsellor, our comforter in times of trouble. The Holy Spirit gives us the power to be bold and courageous to accomplish whatever God has called us to accomplish. Our time on earth is short. What is our purpose, our calling, our destiny to be on the earth? What does God require of us while we are here? He wants us to love and be loved. He wants us to be salt and light. To preserve His ways, His Truth and His Life. He wants us to destroy the works of the enemy who is out to kill, steal and destroy. He wants us to be over-comers, by the Blood of the Lamb and the word of our testimony. He wants His kingdom to come on earth, and to grow and multiply.

After Abortion "The Pain of Choice"
Artist Shannon Moody, BC

Chapter 17
Canada Silent No More

www.canadasilentnomore.com

Come visit our website! Proverbs 29:18 states, "Where there is no vision, (sight, revelation) the people perish; and he that keeps the law, happy is he." I have a dream, a vision to see the goliath of abortion come down in this nation and around the world. There is a fire in my bones to be a voice for my children, so they did not die in vain. When they asked Helen Keller if there was anything worse than being blind, she answered, "Yes, having eyesight but no vision." We need to see what God's will is on the earth, and then we need to have the faith to believe it, to call those things that are not, as though they were. Having a vision from God means that God has to be a part of it, and it therefore becomes bigger than our ability to achieve it without Him. Sometimes I feel overwhelmed at the enormity of this task. But then the Holy Spirit reminds me that greater is He that is in me, His spirit, than he that is in the world.

The Bible says that Faith, without works is dead. We need to be doers of the word if this vision is to come to pass. We need His wisdom and courage; a vision will die unless it is acted upon. We need to endure, hold up under fire, withstand hardships, adversity, and stress and remain firm till the end. We need to persevere, with God through prayer, His power and wisdom working in and through us to accomplish this great vision that will change history and stop the shedding of innocent blood.

We are on a mission to reach women hurt by legal abortion; to let them know that they are not alone, and help is available. A ministry to let broken hearted women know the good news that they can be forgiven and healed through the precious blood of Jesus Christ. In Luke 4:18 Jesus said,

> *"The Spirit of the Lord is upon me, because He has anointed me to preach the gospel to the poor; He has sent me to heal the brokenhearted, to preach deliverance to the captives, and recovering sight to the blind, to set at liberty those who are bruised, crushed."*

He suffered and died so our penalty of sin would be paid. When we ask God to forgive us, turn from our wicked ways, and are born again, His spirit in us teaches, guides and directs us to be His body, His children, and His people on the earth. Salt and light. It is a process, by His grace.

In the spring of 2003 I had been invited to attend a gathering of post abortive women in Dallas, Texas, and chosen as one to speak at their Media conference. Mr. Allan Parker, an attorney from the Texas Justice Foundation, and a godly man was working to challenge the notorious Roe vs. Wade case, with new evidence that abortion was harmful to women. They had my affidavit testimony along with hundreds more to bring to light the mayhem of legal abortion on women and pre-born babies. I have always felt a connection with the US since one of my abortions was done in a Buffalo, New York abortion clinic, when regrettably my pre-born son Daniel was killed there for $200 cash.

The Lord was prompting me to start up Canada Silent No More, an outreach to the two million women and two million men across Canada who've been hurt or injured by legal abortions. A confirmation from the word of God came to me from the book of Revelations 12:11 *"We defeat Satan by the Blood of the Lamb and the word of our testimony."* A group of post abortive women I knew joined together and we prayed to begin this work. We got a 1-888-777-5503 toll free number, a website, brochures, and began to get the word out. I also felt that we were to collect affidavit/testimonies from women willing to share their pain of abortion and the negative impact it has had on them.

The Holy Spirit gave me verses to stand on, confirming His will "Speak up for those who cannot speak for themselves..." Proverbs 31:8 "Have nothing to do with the fruitless deeds of darkness, but rather expose them." Eph. 5:11 and many, many more in Isaiah, Jeremiah and the books of John. I really believe that if women, who know the sting of abortion, the devastation, and the loss, come forward; the truth will be proclaimed, the evil exposed. I believe that abortion doctors, staff and politicians will have the fear of God come on them as we break the silence; come out of our closets declaring that abortion hurt us and killed our babies!

We cannot be silent anymore. We must be a voice for the voiceless, for our babies who paid the ultimate price with their lives, so we could live as we wish. May they not have died devoid of substance or meaning? May others be rescued? May women be warned of the dangers physically, emotionally and spiritually? More and more studies prove that abortion causes depression, anxiety disorders, suicides, substance abuse and premature births in subsequent pregnancies. See www.afterabortion.org and www.abortionbreastcancer.com and www.polycarp.org

We continue to get more and more calls, emails and letters from women broken and maimed by legal abortion as our ads, billboards and information gets out there into the public square. This will become a huge evangelistic outreach, as we share the good news of hope, healing and forgiveness through the Lamb of God, our Lord and Saviour, Jesus Christ. We need finances to support this work.

Legal abortion killed my children, and has deeply hurt and damaged me also. We hope that young women hearing our stories will understand that abortion is not such a 'safe' procedure and that it took the lives of our babies. One of my girl friends had 2 abortions then got cervical cancer; she had to have a hysterectomy at the age of 38, in addition to fighting depression for years due to her abortions. Many wrestle with deep sorrow and despair afterwards. Here are some excerpts from other women who are brave and courageous enough to share their personal pain of abortion.

Connie from Ontario says, "The fact that I killed my own babies destroyed me. I was suicidal after the abortion and had a nervous breakdown. I struggled with drugs, promiscuity and prostitution because of my poor self identity. The grief is real. Don't do it, you'll regret it, it's your baby!

Roberta from N.B. says it was the only pregnancy she ever had. After the abortion she felt like a piece of dirt, used, unworthy and betrayed by her boyfriend. She became clinically depressed after the abortion and would sleep all the time. She wanted to kill herself. She had deep regret and remorse about the abortion. She had nightmares and has not been able to conceive since. She is now 40 years old. Roberta exhorts teens and young women to "Go to a pregnancy counseling centre, get the facts on fetal development and all the risk factors…abortion is emotionally damaging to women, and the unborn are people too." Her mother and aunt both had breast cancer and she is afraid of her elevated risk due to her abortion.

Vicky had an abortion when she was 23. She was traumatized by the procedure and it brought guilt, remorse and depression. She has also had two cysts removed from her breast and is very concerned about women not being informed about the ABC link.

Kelly from B.C. says that after her abortion she went into denial, trying to block it out, but feelings of emptiness, anger, sadness and remorse began to surface. She hated herself, and says her abortion destroyed her child's life and her life too.

S.H. from B.C writes that for years she tried to kill the pain of her abortion with alcohol. When she discovered the truth about what was developed ten weeks after conception, it traumatized her. They told her it would be painless and over soon. They lied. She cries often and still mourns the loss of that child years later.

Heather from Alberta writes: "After my abortion I had a major sense of loss and guilt, I withdrew from family. I could not bond to my step children, and I had no peace. Abortion murdered my baby, it was wrong, but I thank God for His mercy and forgiveness towards me."

Ann writes: "I still feel physically sick when I remember this period of my life…After the abortion I cried uncontrollably, from the shame, guilt, remorse, sadness, anger and depression it has left me, but as hard as I try-27 years later-it is as fresh as the beginning of the nightmare."

Kathy writes: "My abortion brought tremendous guilt and shame once I discovered the truth about fetal development. It is something I can never undo, I have to live with this for the rest of my life and know that I had my baby killed."

Lorie writes: "Abortion brought major depression, feelings that I was a bad mother. I pretended for many years that I wasn't hurt by the abortion. Yet, I punished others, my husband the father of our aborted child, and our live children. It will affect us for the rest of our lives. We are the parents of a dead baby."

J.D. writes: "I have suffered long term depression, had flashbacks and nightmares of my abortion experience. It affects the way I parent my son, I know that is why I am so overprotective of him…abortion should be illegal."

Linda writes: "Shortly after my abortion, I told my doctor I wanted to be sterilized to ensure that I would never have to go through another abortion. Canadians should protect children in the womb, it is wrong." Linda has sacrificed time in jail for peacefully protesting against abortion.

Lucie from Alberta says her abortion left her physically, emotionally and spiritually crippled. She fought depression and loathed herself after the abortion. She also got a tumor on her left ovary. It affected her sexuality, because abortion is connected to sex!

Bianca from Ontario says she has a badly scarred uterus, and got a tumor called a molar pregnancy. She received an infection, fought depression, and says she is forever linked to those babies as their mother.

Noelle writes: "After an abortion at 19, the guilt was unbearable, my self-esteem was shattered and I was an emotional mess. I went into a depression, couldn't stop crying and had to quit my job. I had severe nightmares, was self-destructive and found myself in abusive relationships. A baby will never hurt you, but an abortion will traumatize you!"

Janelle writes: "I thought it would solve my problem, but abortion made me feel guilty. I felt worthless, I hated myself, I couldn't sleep, I was full of anxiety, and anger, I got depressed and had to go on medication because I aborted my child. Children should have a right to live, they are human beings too. Two wrongs do not make a right."

C.M. from Winnipeg writes: "I tried to pretend it didn't happen and justify it in my mind for ten years after. I was only 14 and my parents pressured me into it. I did experience anger towards them, low self-esteem and depression after the abortion. I have had a lump removed from my breast and worry about the breast cancer link too."

Laurie M. from Saskatchewan writes: "I was pressured by my boyfriend and parents to abort, I got severe depression after the abortion and thought of committing suicide several times over the next 16 years. Not a day went by that I didn't think of that abortion and my dead baby. I went into premature labour with my two sons at only seven months gestation. Abortion hurts women big time, and takes an innocent life."

Sandy was raped, became pregnant as a result, and forced against her will by her parents to have an abortion. She wrote: "I was 14 when I had an abortion. It changed my life forever. I was told it was alright, it would be okay, but I knew it was wrong. This child was innocent!! Instead I looked upon myself every day for more that 2 decades with pain, guilt and remorse. Years of depression, self-loathing, destructive behaviour and counseling followed. The grief is with me still almost 30 years later. The son I had after the abortion was frail and premature. Scar tissue and infections caused me to have a hysterectomy at the age of 22. At the age of 34 I was diagnosed with stage 3 estrogen positive breast cancer and have now relapsed at the age of 41 to an advanced stage. There is not a year that goes by I do not think of the child lost." Please pray for post abortive women.

If you would like to share your pain of abortion please send your story/testimony to dwmountenay@lycos.com or mail it to:

CSNM, 107 Discovery Ave. Morinville, AB. T8R 1N1
www.canadasilentnomore.com

Or call Toll Free 1-888-777-5503

After Abortion "How can I ever forgive myself?"
Artist Shannon Moody, BC

Recent Studies

Abortion is hurting women!

Dr. David Reardon from the Elliot Institute has a wonderful website with all of the most recent studies and research on the damage legal, induced abortions have on women; go to www.afterabortion.org

64% of women reported they felt pressured by others to abort

a. In a record based study of 57,000 women with no known history of sleep disorders; women who aborted were nearly twice as likely to be treated for sleep disorders in the first 180 days after the pregnancy ended compared to delivering women. Numerous studies also show that trauma victims will often experience nightmares and difficulties sleeping. Sleep, 2006

b. A review of Medicaid patients revealed that women who had abortions were 160% more likely than delivering women to be hospitalized for psychiatric treatment in the first 90 days following an abortion or delivery. Canadian Medical Association Journal, 2003

c. The children of women who have had abortions have more behavioural problems and less supportive home environments than children without a history of abortion. This finding supports the view that abortion may negatively affect the natural bonding with subsequent children, disturb mothering skills. Journal of Child Psychology and Psychiatry, 2002

d. Abortion can damage reproductive organs and cause long-term and sometimes permanent problems that can put future pregnancies at risk. Women who have abortions are more likely to experience ectopic pregnancies, infertility, hysterectomies, stillbirths, miscarriages, and premature births than women who never had an abortion. JR Cougle, PK Coleman, Cohort Study of 1995 NSFG.

e. About 10% of women suffer immediate complications; one-fifth are life-threatening: hemorrhage, cervical injury, convulsions, endotoxic shock, infection, embolism, chronic abdominal pain, second-degree burns, ripped or perforated uterus, anesthesia complications, RH sensitization.

f. 31% suffer health complications according to a major medical journal in the USA.

g. 8 weeks after their abortions, 44% of post aborted women reported nervous disorders, 36% had nightmares and sleep disorders, NEY.P.

h. 39% had eating disorder

i. 80% experienced feelings of guilt over their abortion, 83% regret, 79% loss, 62% anger, and 70% depression.

D. Reardon, Aborted Women Silent No More

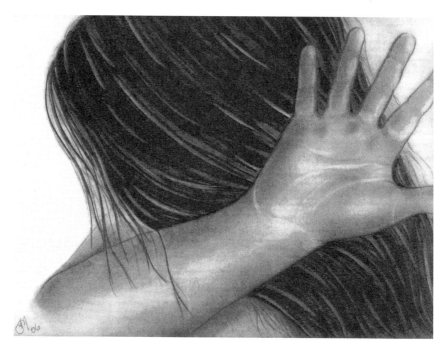

After Abortion "Just leave me alone" Shame/Self-hatred
Artist Shannon Moody, BC

Abortion doctors are not doing women a favor! At least 48 published studies have shown a significantly higher risk of premature birth and low birth weight deliveries among women with a history of abortion! One of the best studies, a record-based study from Denmark, shows that the risk doubled after one abortion. A doubling of risk among an estimated one-fourth of delivering women who have a prior history of abortion would result in a 25 percent increase overall.

PARIS, April 29, 2005 (LifeSiteNews.com) – A new study from France has confirmed that abortion increases a woman's risk of delivering future children prematurely; the risk of very preterm delivery (less than 33 weeks) increases even more dramatically.

After studying data on 1,943 very preterm births, 276 moderately preterm babies and 618 full-term controls, Dr. Caroline Moreau of Hospital de Bicetre and colleagues concluded that women with a history of abortion were 1.5 times more likely to give birth very prematurely (under 33 weeks gestation), and 1.7 times more likely to have a baby born extremely (under 28 weeks gestation) preterm. Their findings were reported in the April issue of the British Journal of Obstetrics and Gynecology, a peer-reviewed medical journal.

Previous research, also conducted in Paris, revealed that the odds of a woman delivering prematurely increase with the number of abortions in her history, with the likelihood doubled in women who have had two or more abortions. Other research corroborated these findings, reporting that "the risk of preterm birth increased with the number of abortions," according to a 2004 study. Preterm births can result in babies getting Cerebral Palsy.

Abortion exposes women to higher risk of depression

By Rosemary Bennett, Social Affairs Correspondent

The Times, October 27, 2006 -- WOMEN who have abortions are risking depression and other mental illness and should be told of the dangers, a group of leading doctors says today.

In a letter to The Times, 15 senior obstetricians and psychiatrists say that new evidence has uncovered a clear link between abortion and mental illness in women with no previous history of psychological problems.

Women who have had abortions have twice the level of psychological problems and three times the level of depression as women who have given birth or never been pregnant, they say.

Their letter, which comes on the anniversary of the legislation of abortion 29 years ago, says that the medical profession can no longer "play down" the links between depression and abortion and that the risk to mental heath must be weighed up in the decisions to approve abortions on ground of a risk to the mother.

Since abortion was legalized in 1967 more than six million abortions have been performed in Britain.

The evidence cited by the doctors was published this year and came after a lengthy study that was conducted in New Zealand.

Although it has been long established that women with a history of mental illness are at greater risk of further instability following an abortion, the New Zealand study established for the first time that abortion could trigger depression and other illnesses in women with no mental problems in the past.

The research prompted the American Psychology Association to withdraw an official statement which denied a link between abortion and psychological harm.

Mayo Clinic Under Fire for Playing Down Abortion-Infertility Link

Rochester, MN (LifeNews.com) -- The prestigious Mayo Clinic is coming under fire for telling patients that abortion does not cause infertility due to endometriosis, despite research showing the contrary.

The information comes in response to a question from a patient submitted to the Q&A section of the May Clinic web site. The questioner asked the Mayo Clinic whether any documented evidence existed between abortion and endometriosis.

Responding for the clinic, an unnamed staff member said "there is no evidence of a link." "Endometriosis is primarily a disease of women who have never been pregnant," the Mayo Clinic writes.

However, according to Deveber Institute in Canada, "No previous births and an earlier abortion put a woman at significant risk of post-abortion complications leading to possible infertility." A 1986 report, "Post-Abortal Endometritis and Isolation of Chlamydia Trachomatis," published in the medical journal Obstetrics and Gynecology says that not only is it possible to contract endometriosis from an abortion, but that the risk is higher for teenagers.

The report says teenagers are 2.5 times more likely than women 20-29 to acquire endometriosis following abortion. Abortion businesses also acknowledge the risk that abortions can have in causing problems for women. In a fact-sheet "Abortion: Questions and Answers" prepared by the Planned Parenthood of Edmonton, Canada for prospective patients, the abortion business acknowledges the endometriosis risk. "Infections can occur from an abortion," PPE writes. "At worst the infection can become a case of endometriosis (the pelvic area becomes inflamed) and the uterus has to be removed surgically." More common is Asherman's Syndrome where the cavity of the uterus is lined by the endometrium. This lining can be traumatized, typically after a dilation and curettage (D&C) done after an abortion, and then develops intrauterine scars which can obliterate the cavity to a varying degree. In the extreme, the whole cavity has been scarred and occluded. Even with relatively few scars, the endometrium may fail to respond to estrogens and rests. The patient experiences secondary amenorrhea and becomes infertile. Sometimes a hysterectomy is recommended.

Abortion is four times deadlier than childbirth.

Abortion advocates routinely claim that childbirth causes six, 10, or 12 times more deaths than abortion. Abortion clinics advertise that legal abortion is many times safer than childbirth. The statistical analysis agency for Finland's government conducted a very accurate and complete study that reveals that out of 100,000 women, there were 281 cases of maternal deaths – 27 were women who had given birth, 48 were women who had miscarriages or ectopic pregnancies, and 101 were women who had abortions.

When the researchers calculated ratios, they determined that women who abort are 3.5 times more likely to die within a year than are women who carry to term. More startlingly, the researchers reported that the risk of death from suicide within a year of an abortion is more than seven times higher than the risk of suicide within a year of childbirth. A Canadian study revealed similar findings, as did a study of Medicaid payments in Virginia.

Sadly, many women have none of this information about the dangers of abortion. Instead, they know only the front-page information that has become conventional U.S. wisdom. Indeed, only a minute number of abortion deaths are classified as such in official data -- which leaves women at the mercy of abortion lies instead of being well informed about abortion realities.

Abortion Leads to Substance Abuse for Significant Number of Women

By Gudrun Schultz

SPRINGFIELD, Illinois, January 23, 2006 (LifeSiteNews.com) – A recent study reinforces previous findings that women who have abortions frequently turn to drugs and alcohol to cope with the aftereffects of the trauma.

Author Pricilla Coleman, professor of Human Development and Family Studies at Bowling Green State University, said studies show women who have abortions are up to five times more likely to use drugs and alcohol, and to smoke, than women who have not had an abortion, in a research review published in Current Women's Health Reviews.

Coleman said studies show women are more likely than men to rely on drugs or alcohol for help in dealing with severe personal trauma, such as physical or sexual abuse, or illness and family dysfunction.

Dr. David Reardon, a post-abortion expert and director of research at the Elliot Institute, a non-profit organization that tracks the impact of abortion, said there are at least 21 studies linking induced abortion and substance abuse, in an Elliot Institute press release.

"Many women who have experienced abortion have unresolved emotional issues related to their abortion," he said. "Substance abuse can provide an easily accessible way to self-medicate their pain and numb their emotions."

Reardon said mental health workers need to recognize the devastating effects of abortion, and find ways of helping women deal with the buried fallout.

"If treatment for substance abuse or other mental health problems fails to address underlying factors such as abortion, the treatment may be ineffective and women are likely to continue to turn to substances such as drugs or alcohol to cope," Reardon said.

Studies have also found significantly higher rates of depression, anxiety disorders, suicidal tendencies, psychiatric hospitalization and poor bonding with and parenting of later children, in women who have had an abortion.

Authors of Finnish Study Fail to Report Relationship Between Increased Suicides and Abortion

January 7, 2005 (LifeSiteNews.com) -- The December 2004 edition of the American Journal of Obstetrics and Gynecology (AJOG) has published a letter to the editor from Dr. Nathan J. Hoeldtke of the Department of Obstetrics and Gynecology, Tripler Army Medical Center, Honolulu, pointing out the failure by authors of a Finnish study to report the relationship between abortion and increased incidence of suicide.

The 2004 study, Pregnancy-associated mortality after birth, spontaneous abortion, or induced abortion in Finland, failed to take into account the higher risk of death by intentional accident after abortion. Abortion advocates routinely scoff at any suggestion of long-term emotional effects of abortion and claim that it is more dangerous to carry a pregnancy to term.

In his letter, Dr. Hoeldtke says, for unclear reasons, the authors excluded deaths from unintentional accidental injuries and intentional injuries in their analysis of pregnancy-associated mortality. The author of the Finish study showed in previous research that a post-abortive woman is 6 times more likely to die from suicide (intentional injury) than women who give birth, and 3 times more likely to commit suicide than the general population.

Dr. Hoeldtke continued that

"A woman obtaining an induced abortion appears to be at increased risk for dying from violent causes in the near future, including suicide. The stark reality underlying these statistics would seem to represent a significant public health concern that warrants further investigation".

1) In 1997, the top Scandinavian medical journal in the field of obstetrics and gynecology published that Finnish women who had an induced abortion had 3.5 times the TOTAL risk of dying as women who delivered in the 12 months after 'the end of pregnancy.' (Acta Obstet Gyn Scand 1997;76:651-657)

2) Fifty studies have found that abortions increase the risk of pre-term babies in subsequent pregnancies. Thus the baby is of low birth weight and much more prone to develop physical and mental problems including Cerebral Palsy.

There have been NO studies done to disprove this. NONE, NADA, ZILCH. Frank Joseph MD.

It is outrageous that women are not being informed about the huge mountain of evidence linking depression, suicides, breast cancer and premature births in subsequent pregnancies after an abortion!

March 23, 2006 Springfield, IL -- This week's prestigious **British Medical Journal reports that women who abort a first pregnancy are at greater risk of subsequent long term clinical depression compared to women who carry an unintended first pregnancy to term.** Publication of the study coincides with anniversary events related to the Supreme Court's January 22, 1973 Roe v. Wade decision legalizing abortion.

Data from a national study of American youths, begun in 1979, was used to conduct the research. In 1992, a subset of 4,463 women were surveyed about depression, intendedness of pregnancy, and pregnancy outcome. A total of 421 women had had their first abortion or first unintended delivery between 1980 and 1992.

An average of eight years after their abortions, married women were 138 percent more likely to be at high risk of clinical depression compared to similar women who carried their unintended first pregnancies to term. Among women who were unmarried in 1992, rates of high risk depression were not significantly different. The authors suggest that the lack of significance in unmarried women may be explained by the higher rate of non-reporting of abortions among unmarried women. Compared with national averages, unmarried women in this study report only 30 percent of the expected abortions compared with married women, who report 74 percent of the expected abortions. This may make the results for married women more reliable, say the authors. Another explanation is that unmarried women who are raising a child without the support of a husband experience significantly more depression than their married counterparts.

Professor David Fergusson, New Zealand researcher at Christchurch School of Medicine and Health, said,

> *"From a personal point of view, I would have rather seen the results come out the other way -- but they didn't. And as a scientist you have to report the facts, not what you'd like to report."*

Fergusson and his colleagues were surprised by the study that followed 500 women from birth to age 25 and revealed that abortive women were one-and-a-half times more likely to suffer mental illness.

> *"Those having an abortion had elevated rates of subsequent mental health problems, including depression, anxiety, suicidal behaviors and substance use disorders," according to the research published in the Journal of Child Psychiatry and Psychology.*

Numerous journals refused to publish the research, but Fergusson defended its relevance saying it would be "scientifically irresponsible" to overlook the findings. "To provide a parallel to this situation, if we were to find evidence of an adverse reaction to medication, we would be obligated ethically to publish that fact," he explained.

WICHITA, January 27, 2005 (LifeSiteNews.com) -- Today, LifeSite-News.com learned that a woman, who was likely undergoing an abortion on January 13 at notorious late-term abortionist George "the Killer" Tiller's abortion facility, has died. Operation Rescue members, who keep a constant vigil outside Tiller's premises, reported that the woman, whose name has not yet been released, was rushed to Wesley Medical Center and died a few days later. 911 transcripts from the day show that an ambulance was requested by Tiller office worker Marguerite Reed, who, according to 911 dispatch records was being "very evasive" and "refused to give any information about the patient." Nothing is known about the identity of the woman and LifeSiteNews.com is attempting to discover if she was Canadian.

In September 2004, LifeSiteNews.com reported that the government of Quebec was using public funds to send Canadian women to Tiller. The report said that only pre-born children older than 24 weeks gestation would be killed at taxpayer expense in Tiller's abortion mill. Quebec Health Minister Philippe Couillard admitted that in 2003, at least 30 Quebec late-term abortions were committed in Kansas and New York. An anonymous source from Tiller's facility said the woman was suffering "severe hemorrhaging." LifeSiteNews.com contacted the hospital but spokesmen refused to reveal any details. Troy Newman, president of Operation Rescue told LifeSiteNews.com that his group has contacted the Kansas Board of Healing Arts and asked that Tiller's license be suspended while this incident is investigated.

More Stats & Facts

Statistics Canada reported in 1994 that the number of teenage abortions in Canada increased from 26% in 1974 to 45% in 1994.

"The rate of chlamydia for Canadian females aged 15-19 is NINE times the national rate for all other age groups." (Health Canada 1995)

STD's represent 36% of all notifiable diseases in Canada. (Health Canada 1995)

In 1994 Alberta taxpayers paid an estimated 5 million dollars for 9,186 abortions (Committee to End Tax Funded Abortions)

In the 39 states in the U.S.A. that removed public funding for abortions, 80% of the welfare-eligible women who wanted abortions were able to obtain them through private funds. (American Journal of Public Health. Sept. 1979)

Henry Morgentaler stated during a 1988 radio interview that "fewer than one-tenth of one percent of abortions are done for serious medical emergencies" (Committee to End Tax Funded Abortions)

In a 1996 study on adolescent sexuality, researchers noted a 54% DECREASE in recent sexual activity one year after teens were taught an abstinence curriculum. (John T. Vessey, Ph.D., Northwestern University Medical School, 1996)

Just like in the garden of Eden, satan is still deceiving women. Instead of saying, "Surely, you will not die," he is saying, "Surely, this is not a baby." Women; Please, no more deception. Be strong and courageous. Stand up for the truth and justice for the preborn, and our children. Giving birth to the kingdom of God and His righteousness. Men; We need your help. Be the husbands/fathers that God has called you to be. The family is the smallest and greatest social unit on earth. Let's keep it that way.

ABORTION IS NOT A BLACK AND WHITE ISSUE…
IT IS BLOOD RED!

The Holy Land

The work goes on. The Lord continues to send me from coast to coast and in 2004 we moved to the mountains and wilderness of beautiful British Columbia.

A producer from The CBC, The National, produced a documentary on the work and the mission of Canada Silent No More. PTL! It was aired on Feb. 22nd 2005. We thank God for opening doors no man could open.

I also feel like the Holy Spirit wants me to take this message to the nations. For the leaf is our nations' emblem, it shall be a healing to the nations. Sadly, many nations pressured and deceived by the pro abortion feminists foolishly have legalized abortion and therefore multitudes of women around the world are now suffering from post abortion syndrome. In 2005, along with Molly White from Texas, we began working on developing the foundation of Women for Life International. Years ago, at a church altar, I remember saying to the Lord, "Here am I, send me to the Nations, Your will be done in my life."

One of my life's highlights was an invitation to attend the first World Pro Life Conference in Israel. Just a week before my trip to Israel, I had been invited to speak at a Messianic church near Edmonton. After my talk, the Pastor and members of the church gathered around to pray for me, and anointed me with oil. Then a man, who I'd never met before, presented me with a beautiful long silver trumpet. Tears rolled down my cheeks, as he believed God wanted him to give me this hand made instrument. It is amazing that this trumpet is exactly like the trumpet we have angels blowing on our Canada Silent No More brochure! For me, this was a confirmation from God.

The Lord provided the way for Shawn, our son, and I to travel to Israel. It was the most exhilarating trip I've ever had! It was so exciting to be in the HOLY LAND, spectacular to wade into the 'Sea of Galilee' then go aboard an old ship, cross the Sea of Galilee praising GOD and singing spiritual songs and hymns! We ate St. Peter's fish, in a beautiful Jewish restaurant on the other side. Amazing. Thrilling! I just had to take my shoes off and go into that water! The weather was perfect too. Imagine, walking where Jesus walked! Being where Peter and Paul were…heroes from the word of GOD. We were on the Mount of Beatitudes, the landscape is a natural amphitheatre, no wonder Jesus could preach to the multitudes there. We went up to the Temple Mount, the Garden of Gethsemane, complete with Olive trees, Mount Carmel where Elijah slew the false prophets of Baal. We visited Capernaum where Jesus taught in the Synagogue and did many miracles. We went to the Wailing Wall, the Holocaust Museum, Masada, and floated in the Dead Sea. The land of His story, so much history. AWESOME! Go, or help send me as a missionary to the unborn Jewish babies and mothers.

Reading the Bible now, is like reading it in three D. For me the most exciting highlight was the afternoon we spent speaking to youth, young adults and store keepers on the streets of Jerusalem. We talked about abortion in Israel, and the truth about fetal development. I quoted Psalm 139, how God had knit us together in our mothers' womb where we were fearfully and wonderfully made, quoting the Torah. We shared the pain of abortion.

Unbelievably, they do 150 abortions a day in Israel! They are actually wiping out their defense army; future troops. They are as deceived as many of us, believing the father of lies, and a murderer from the beginning. We handed out pro-life tracts, and I witnessed about Yeshua/Jesus the Messiah, and prayed for a young Jewish female soldier. During the day we toured, and every evening we attended the conference joined by people from 22 different countries. One night I shared about Canada Silent No More and my testimony.

We repented for the sin of abortion, we wept and prayed and I blew my long silver trumpet in a declaration that the spirit of abortion is coming down in Jesus name! We did this in the Valley of Ben Hinnom where the Bible states that they used to sacrifice their children to the gods of Moloch and Baal, which is an abomination to GOD. I hope the Lord will send me back to Israel one day. We need to bring this message to the Jewish peoples.

Then Shawn and I went to Germany and Switzerland to visit relatives. God miraculously opened a door for me to do an hour long interview on an Austrian TV satellite station covering Europe. A woman translated my words into German. Praise the Lord! (PTL)

Sister Pilar, a mighty woman of God whom I met at the World Pro Life conference, had read my book on the plane on her way home to the Philippines. She runs a convent, many ministries and a pro life centre. A woman of influence with the rich and the poor in her land. She emailed stating that I had to come to share this message with her people. So in February of 2006, Molly and I, along with two other post abortive women from the USA went to share our testimonies. Sister Pilar had us booked solid with talks to hundreds of teens, nurses, politicians and the media.

We only had half a day to be a "tourist". We went to the pearl sellers, where there were about a hundred booths, each with Muslim women selling fresh water pearl jewelry. We got to barter for the best prices; so I made the most of the opportunity and asked these women a few questions about Mohamed and told them about Jesus. I then asked each of them how many children they had. They all had anywhere from eight to twelve children each! And they looked so young. They are multiplying and being fruitful to subdue the earth for Allah. Look at how the Muslim populations are exploding in Europe, the UK, Australia, Africa, Asia, the US and Canada! As of 2005, in Africa almost 50% of the population is Muslim. There are over 51 million Muslims in Europe. Over 1 billion in Asia. Almost 7 million in North America...a total of 1.6 billion around the world, and they do not abort their children.

Mohammed was a descendant of Ishmael. His parents died when he was very young, he married a much older rich woman and began his religion and campaign to kill, steal and destroy if converts did not bow to his Allah. Of course there are many Muslims who are wonderful, God fearing people and who would never kill in the name of Allah. We hope and pray that many will come to know Jesus Christ as their Lord and Saviour one day. Of course we would never blow them up or send in suicide bombers if they didn't.

The Bible tells the history of how God had promised Abraham that he would be the father of many nations. He and his wife Sarah were very old, and she laughed when she heard this. She agreed to let Hagar the maid have sex with her husband, adultery, not God's plan. But nevertheless God allowed that conception to take place and Ishmael was born first. Then came Isaac, the promised son.

Sarah became jealous of Hagar and Ishmael and threw them out into the desert. They were outcasts, abandoned, rejected and deeply wounded by Abraham and Sarah. The seed of Ishmael need to know the Father heart of God, know that they are loved and they need to forgive and not hold on to the anger, bitterness, hatred and resentments passed down from generation to generation. Until this day the seed of Ishmael and the seed of Isaac continue to fight and have strife with each other. When Jews and Gentiles humble themselves and acknowledge Jesus Christ is Lord and that He died for all of our sins, was raised from the dead, sent His Holy Spirit to give those who believe the power to be the sons of God, then there will be peace and unity on the earth. A new heaven and a new earth shall be. God's way is to love them into the Kingdom of God. Jesus paid the price for everyone to enter His Kingdom on earth no matter what tribe, nation, religion or race.

This is the place where David got his 5 smooth stones to slew Goliath.

The Philippines

Philippines~February 2006 Praise the Lord even the Breast Cancer Society of Manila had me speak at a hospital and fund raiser. Dr. Cristina Santos a Breast Cancer Surgeon admitted that women must be warned about the ABC Link and the Philippine Breast Cancer Care Foundation became the first cancer society in the world to acknowledge the ABC link, a huge breakthrough for our cause.

We have been collecting testimonies. Many women have irreparable damage, so many distraught, so many in deep sorrow and anguish due to their abortions. For the last few months, Shannon has been calling me. She is 28 years old now; she had an abortion 4 years ago. She told me that she really wanted a baby, but her boyfriend freaked out on her, and pressured her to abort. Somehow she was paralyzed, afraid, and went into that hospital numb. She had no idea of the pain, the guilt, or the remorse that would follow. She has been in a pit of misery, depression and

Molly, me and Luana at a peaceful protest in Quezon City, Philippines.

suicidal ever since. Her joy has gone, she feels like she is dead too, her countenance has changed, she cannot forgive herself, she feels hopeless, distraught. Please pray for her.

I received this email today from Jodi via our website:

"Your organization is the representation of both Truth and Grace. One without the other is not true Christianity and I praise God for you and your efforts. I had an abortion when I was 15. The 'Planned Parenthood' nurse tried to calm my fears by assuring me "the fetus is not a person until it takes its first breath of air". I know now, that is a lie according to the Word of God, and by the Faith and healing that Christ has given me. I grieve for the millions of women who are suffering in silence because of a law that gives women the free choice to take that life. It does damage the mind- body and spirit- it is NOT in the best interest of the woman OR the child. The choice that I made that day did NOT fix my problem; it brought despair, pain, shame and depression for years afterwards. I cannot go back and change the past, but I can speak up and support your efforts for TRUTH and Grace when it comes to this tragedy for both the unborn and the parents." Jodi K. Saskatchewan

Ladies from the Philippines Breast Cancer Care Foundation &
Breast Cancer Society of Manila

March 27, 2006

Dear Mrs. Mountenay:

The Philippine Foundation for Breast Care, Incorporated (PFBCI) is grateful to you for visiting us, and for being our Guest Speaker February 16, 2006 during our 2nd Breast Care Center-East Avenue Medical Center (BCC-EAMC) Breast Cancer Forum: "The Abortion (induced) & Breast Cancer Link" held at Quezon City, Philippines. This forum was a joint activity of PFBCI, BCSMI, Roche – Oncology Philippines and BCC-EAMC.

We admire your bravery and commitment to advocate the "A BC" Link. On behalf of the board of trustees and members of PFBCI, we acknowledge the abortion and breast cancer link based on the physiologic changes in the breast lobules of a woman who chose to deliberately interrupt her pregnancy (induced abortion) and the risk for breast cancer this will pose to those women.

Here in the Philippines, induced abortion is still illegal...but though glad that it still is, extrapolated data shows that we have some 500,000 - 800,000 victims of induced abortion annually. Alarming to note that in 2004, the Philippines has the highest incidence of breast cancer in Asia...more alarming to find out that the Philippines also has the highest incidence of illegal, induced abortion since 1997. Indeed, women should be made aware of the A BC Link!

Best Regards,

DR. CRISTINA L. SANTOS
President

Sin
Artist Shannon Moody, BC

Sent to the UNITED NATIONS in New York City to be a voice

Left to right is Molly White from Texas, Melony Materi from Saskatchewan and myself.

March 2006 God opened a door of opportunity for us to host two workshops at the United Nations in New York! Molly and I had felt led in 2005 to reach out internationally with our message as most countries around the world now are sadly using abortion as a form of birth control. Thinking it would be wise to have a representative on our board from each continent, I asked Francis B. from Australia if she would be interested. Yes, definitely, she would be honoured, was her reply. Her husband is a lawyer and they won a couple of cases where post abortive women sued abortion doctors for not informing them about all of the negative risk factors including the breast cancer risk. So they are quite aware of our urgency to get this information out to the international community. A few weeks later she asked me if I could host a workshop for her at the UN as she would not be able to attend this year. Sounds like GOD to me I thought, and went into prayer, "Lord, if this is your will, please open doors no man can open, and make a way for me to go, and have your people send me in Jesus Holy Name." I presented this opportunity to my church, and the funds came in to cover my airfare and expenses. Praise the LORD!

I decided to call our workshop "Women's Health After an Abortion", our workshop was packed. We shared our testimonies and how abortion had brought such havoc into our lives. The next day I briefly spoke at our workshop on the Abortion Breast Cancer Link about our concerns as post abortive women on the ABC Link cover-up.

Dr. Joel Brind, PhD did a large meta-analysis on the studies done regarding the abortion breast cancer link and shared his frustration with cancer societies refusing to look at the data, the evidence, and the rebuttals to studies denying the link. As well, Dr. Angela Lanfranchi, breast cancer surgeon and well-known author and speaker on the link between induced abortion and breast cancer, presented medical and scientific information on "The Impact of Women's Choice of Fertility Control and Subsequent Risk of Breast Cancer". She used a power point also to display the physiological implications on the ABC link. It made perfect sense to me. Common sense would say there is a connection just on the estrogen positive factor alone! At a public information meeting, May 10, 2006, on Parliament Hill, sponsored by LifeCanada and Canadian Physicians for Life, Dr. Lanfranchi told the audience, comprised of physicians, Members of Parliament, and members of the public in her own words: "I first learned about the abortion breast cancer link in 1994 from a physician and thought it was a pro-life fantasy. After all, I was a well informed successful breast surgeon. It wasn't in my texts and wasn't spoken about at scientific meetings. But when I looked at the histories of my own young patients with cancer, the association was there. Still not convinced, I didn't look further until a 1996 meta-analysis by Dr. Joel Brind showed that the preponderance of the data which confirmed a positive association. Further study over the next 3 years brought me to the point of certainty in 1999. That was when a Harvard professor, an acknowledged expert in risk assessment, admitted to me that abortion was a risk factor for breast cancer but she would not speak about it publicly. It was only then that I informed my patients of that risk and became a women's breast cancer advocate."

What an honour to meet this wonderful lady. What a huge mission to expose the cover-up on breast cancer. More and more women are calling me who have had abortions and subsequent cancers. God help us save lives!

Abortion-Cancer Research Presented at National Institute for Demographic Studies

The Coalition on Abortion/Breast Cancer reported that British researcher Patrick Carroll presented his research on abortion as the "best predictor of British breast cancer trends" at a conference in Paris sponsored by the National Institute for Demographic Studies on September 7, 2005. Carroll is director of the London-based Pensions and Population Research Institute. The conference was attended by statisticians and epidemiologists.

Carroll provided forecasts of the increased incidence of breast cancers to be expected in Great Britain in the next 25 years. He reported three trends:

1. British upper class women are more likely to develop breast cancer and to die of the disease than are lower class women. Upper class women are more likely to delay the birth of a first child and to abort before the birth of a first child. These are highly carcinogenic abortions.

The disparity between upper and lower class women (called a "reverse gradient") has widened in recent years and is greater in England than in Scotland, a situation Carroll attributes to a higher abortion rate and later age at first birth in England. Carroll expects a widening of the disparity between classes in England and Wales for the next four years.

2. Geographical variations in breast cancer rates across the British Isles can be explained by the abortion rate, but not the birth rate, although childbearing reduces breast cancer risk. Ireland, which prohibits abortion, has the lowest breast cancer rate in the British Isles. London and the Southeast, where abortion is most prevalent, have the highest breast cancer rates.

3. Breast cancer rates between 1971 and 2002 increased approximately 70%. Carroll studied breast cancer rates for women ages 50-54 born in the years 1926-1946 and found that breast cancer rates were highly correlated with abortion rates and less highly correlated with fertility and other factors.

> *"Despite the best efforts of the U.S. National Cancer Institute to cover up evidence of a link during the last half-century," declared Karen Malec, president of the coalition, "women will ultimately learn the truth."*

The Abortion Breast Cancer Link
a personal testimony

By Jeanette Joyce, R.T. (R)(M) 2005

I am by profession a mammography technologist. As a registered radiographer, I have worked exclusively in mammography for the past 12 years. I also travel nationwide teaching mammography and breast disease. My office walls are lined with breast imaging and cancer books for reference.

In 1998, I asked my friend at work to do my routine screening mammogram. At the age of 42, I had no reason to suspect a breast problem in view of my good health and lack of family history for the disease. However, working in mammography afforded me the opportunity to see other women diagnosed and I was convinced that a screening mammogram could detect early curable breast cancer.

Following the routine 4 films, I stood at the film processor ready to grab my films as they dropped into the bin. I set them up on the view boxes, took a quick look and immediately pulled them down in order to check the patient's name on the films. There was no mistaking that these were my films and I had breast cancer. I laid my head down on the counter and reminded the Lord that I had small children at home who needed a mother. Additional films were necessary so we walked back to the x-ray room. As my friend set up the machine, I sat with my head down between my legs because I feared passing out. The new films confirmed my suspicions. I had breast cancer. This was confirmed 2 days later with a breast biopsy.

My research into the risk factors associated with breast cancer began to expand. As I uncovered more and more information, I found extensive research that had been conducted confirming a link between abortion and breast cancer. The thought haunted me. Could it have been possible that I actually caused my own breast cancer? Up until this time, I had never disclosed an abortion in my past. At the age of 18, I found myself pregnant. My boyfriend told me that he was not ready for marriage or a family. Although I knew abortion was wrong, I decided to buy into the lies of the feminists who told us that we had ultimate control over our own bodies and we should never permit a man to determine our future. I scheduled the appointment at the abortion clinic and never discussed the event with anyone.

24 years later when I was sitting in the office of a surgeon discussing my lack of options for treatment. I was told my only choice was a modified radical mastectomy. Three years later, I decided to have a prophylactic mastectomy on the opposite breast in order to reduce my risk of another cancer in the future. Today I am breast cancer free, and on a mission to expose the truth.

If only I had known then, what I know now, about the link between abortion and breast cancer. The most vulnerable is the young woman under the age of 18 who has never experienced a full term pregnancy and decides on an abortion. These women are most at risk for developing breast cancer later in life. An early first, full term pregnancy actually has protective factors and lowers a women's risk of breast cancer. I found a study conducted by **Dr. Janet Daling** who found that young women who abort their first pregnancy and also have a family history of breast cancer are at an incalculable increase in risk.

Women deserve better! This is much more than a pro-life/pro-choice issue. The ABC connection is a pro-woman issue. It is a matter of informed consent. Women who are approaching 50 years of age are the first generation since abortion on demand. We are approaching an age when the risk of breast cancer begins to accelerate. Many health experts will agree that we could have an epidemic on our hands in the years to come as the number of newly diagnosed cases of breast cancer explodes. My message is simple. Choose life! Jeanette Joyce is a mammography technologist and the owner of a mammography medical education business. Today, she is an avid pro-lifer and sits on the board of the Abortion-Breast Cancer Coalition.

Legal Implications of a Link Between Abortion and Breast Cancer

Andrew L. Schlafly, Esq. Lawyer

Journal of American Physicians and Surgeons
Volume 10 Number 1 Spring 2005

Dozens of studies have shown that the greater the number of abortions, the higher the incidence of breast cancer. Three states expressly require physicians to disclose to patients seeking abortion that the procedure may increase the risk of breast cancer. Three other states have more general disclosure requirements about abortion.

There is a legal obligation of **informed consent** for any medical procedure. With the majority of studies showing that abortion increases breast cancer risk, and even the minority studies reinforcing the well-established principle that childbirth is protective against breast cancer, patients seeking abortion have an obvious right to this information. The patient who had an abortion and later develops breast cancer may have a valid claim against the provider. Already, there have been at least two settlements in the United States in lawsuits brought for such failure to disclose. Unfortunately, misinformation has circulated in the media following an article published last year in the British medical journal. The article did not deny that increased abortions result in greater incidence of breast cancer. Rather, the article merely claimed that abortion does not increase the risk of breast cancer, compared to the risk of someone who delayed pregnancy altogether. The article and data are consistent with the prevailing medical view that the more abortions in a society, the greater the number of breast cancer cases.

The BRIDE of CHRIST…and birth control?

How does the Kingdom of GOD grow? The Bible tells us that one way is through Godly families… "Train up a child in the way he should go, and when he is old it shall not depart from him." Proverbs 22:6 Also, Acts 11:14 declares that "You and your household shall be saved." God wants His people, His children to multiply and be fruitful and subdue the earth for the Kingdom of God.

Yet, despairingly, many Christians are not trusting in God, not exercising their faith, but operating and consumed in fear and the world's rhetoric and philosophies. Many Christian couples have become self centered. After one or two children they have turned to sterilization to prevent the Kingdom of God from growing. Husbands have vasectomies (a surgical operation in which the vas deferens from each testis is cut and tied to prevent transfer of sperm during ejaculation) and wives tubal ligations; (a sterilization technique in which a woman's fallopian tubes are tied to prevent ova entering the uterus). Multitudes are on birth control pills and other man made inventions to put a stop to the body of Christ increasing in numbers. Unimaginably, some decide not to have any children, and have aborted their babies.

There is not one scripture exhorting God's people to use birth control. Abstain, for a time for fasting and prayer, yes. Several scriptures declare that children are a blessing, the heritage of the LORD, a GIFT from God! It breaks the Father heart of God to see His children reject the greatest gift He has for them, children created in His image. His word reveals that even before we were born, He knew us and predestined us for a purpose. How many great apostles, prophets, evangelists, teachers, nurses, doctors, mothers, mechanics, musicians, speakers, husbands, scientists, and pastors are missing because we never permitted them to be born? We, the church!

The other way the Kingdom of God grows is for one to be born-again. How can anyone be born again, unless he or she is first born?

May we repent from our fear and self centeredness? May we walk in the light as He is in the light? May we make an impact while we walk on this earth for the Kingdom of God and His righteousness? "Righteousness exalts a nation, but sin is a reproach to any nation." Proverbs 14:34

Please pray for me, my family and Canada Silent No More. Together we can stop this silent genocide; we need your support and help. May God's will be done, may His Kingdom grow on the earth. Hope to hear from you. "Do not grow weary in well doing, for in due season you shall reap a harvest, if you faint not." Galatians 6:9,10 GOD loves you so much, you are precious! Thank you for taking the time to read this book. Now put on the full armour of God and help us be a voice for the voiceless!

After Abortion "How could I have done this?"
Artist Shannon Moody, BC

Abortion Recovery

"Screams of anguish come from Ramah, Weeping unrestrained: Rachel weeping for her children, uncomforted-for they are dead."
Matthew 2:18 TLB.

HEALING after an abortion: If you have had an abortion, you may have felt an immediate sense of relief, then felt the pangs of grief, guilt, remorse and regret for years.

To grieve is a normal, healthy response to a death, a major loss to you. Grieving is a painful process, but it relieves us of the deep sorrow following an abortion. Many women attempt to bury their grief, numb themselves with alcohol or drugs, or push down their emotions, and run from God. But sooner or later, we come to the realization that abortion ended the life of our unborn baby.

Women who have a miscarriage or stillborn suffer grief as well. They may feel guilty because they don't know why their baby died. Women who have an abortion feel anguishing guilt because they know that they played a part in their child's death. Some women will stay in a place of denial for months or years, still trying to justify the abortion or deny it was a 'baby'. But eventually it hits you.

Once out of denial many women become angry, because we were never told the truth about fetal development. We are angry at the people who encouraged us to abort. Angry at the abortion doctors and staff for not informing us about all of the negative emotional and physical complications, the damage to our bodies, the risk of Breast and Cervical cancers. How could they kill our little baby? They know it's a baby with a beating heart, arms, legs, fingers and toes! Why didn't anyone encourage us to have the baby, support us, or give him or her up to a loving couple who could never have their own children? At least our child would be alive! Why didn't the baby's father try to talk us out of it, support us, love us enough to be a man about it, and take responsibility for his actions? Why didn't we listen.

After Abortion "Depression/Isolation"
Artist Shannon Moody, BC

"Blessed are those that mourn, for they shall be comforted." Mat. 5:4 In order to be healed and to move on with our lives, first we must repent, turn from our wicked ways, believe in a loving God, who sent His Son Jesus to die on the cross for the penalty of our sins. "Surely God is my salvation; I will trust and not be afraid. The Lord, the Lord, is my strength and my song; He has become my salvation." Isa. 12:2 "For I know the plans I have for you, declares the Lord, plans to prosper you and not to harm you, plans to give you hope and a future." Jer. 29:11 "If you confess with your mouth the Lord Jesus Christ and shall believe in your heart that God raised Him from the dead, you shall be saved." Rom 10:9 Ask God to forgive you for this sin, and for all of your sins and short comings. Repent, change your life.

"Confess your faults one to another and pray one for another that you may be healed." James 5:16

"If we confess our sins, He is faithful and just to forgive us our sins, and to cleanse us from all unrighteousness." 1 John 1:9

You may want to pray and ask God to give you a name, or vision of your child, or children, have a memorial, or write a letter, in faith, ask your child to forgive you for having them aborted.

Then as difficult as it may be, not that they deserve it, but we must forgive those who pressured or coerced us into it. We must forgive the boyfriend or husband who got us pregnant, the abortion doctor and staff, the politicians who allow this to go on. "For if you forgive men their trespasses, your heavenly Father will also forgive you." Mat. 6:14 The most difficult thing is to forgive ourselves. By faith just do it! Let go and let GOD.

Many women suffer shame, self condemnation and self-pity. They want to punish themselves. Isolation, depression and suicidal tendencies are a strong force in post abortive women. But, "Looking unto Jesus, the author and finisher of our faith, who for the joy set before Him, endured the cross, despising the shame, and is set down at the right hand of the throne of God." Heb. 12:2

What happiness for those whose guilt has been forgiven! What joys when sins are covered over! What relief for those who have confessed their sins and God has cleared their record. There was a time when I wouldn't

After Abortion "GOD's forgiveness and GRACE"
Artist Shannon Moody, BC

admit what a sinner I was. But my dishonesty made me miserable and filled my days with frustration. All day and all night your hand was heavy on me. My strength evaporated like water on a sunny day, until I finally admitted all my sins to you, and stopped trying to hide them. I said to myself, "I will confess them to the Lord." And you forgave me! All my guilt is gone." Psalm 32:1-5 TLB.

"What benefit did you reap at that time from the things you are now ashamed of? Those things result in death! But now that you have been set free from sin and have become slaves to God, the benefit you reap leads to holiness, and the result is eternal life." Rom. 6:21,22

"So if the Son sets you free, you will be free indeed." John 8:36

"For the Lord is good and His love endures forever; His faithfulness continues through all generations." Psalm 100:5

Meditate on the Word of God, get to know who you are in Christ, as a child of the King, as a daughter, a woman of God. When you have a spiritual awakening, you are born again, and see good and evil with clarity. When you surrender your life, your will to God, and grow in the knowledge of Him, getting to know HIM, Jesus the Lamb, the Light, the Bread of Life, our Healer, our Shalom, our Peace, then your light will shine, the Holy Spirit will fill you with His love, wisdom and power so you can fulfill your destiny and purpose in this generation. Find a good alive, Bible believing church. Together we can change history, expose the lies, proclaim the truth, and ... "Defeat Satan by the Blood of the Lamb and the word of our testimony." Rev. 12:11

The Vision

One night, at the age of 31, while soaking in my bathtub, I began to weep for the loss of my children. Suddenly, I sensed that Jesus was about to come into the bathroom with my three children. I imagined that He was going to bring in three tiny babies wrapped in soft blankets… He didn't.

He walked through the door with three children in front of Him. The first was a girl. She was tall, slim, had long beautiful hair and looked alot like me. I just knew that her name was Jennifer. With tears in my eyes, I told her that I was so sorry, and asked her to forgive me. "It's okay Mom, I forgive you," she replied in a soft angelic voice. Next to her stood Daniel, a handsome young lad, with golden brown hair and hazel eyes. Sobbing now with remorse, I told him how sorry I was, and asked for his forgiveness. He said, "It's okay Mommy, I forgive you, we are with Jesus." Then, with floods of tears cascading down my cheeks, and barely able to speak, I looked at Rebecca, and told her that I was so sorry for what happened. She was adorable, with long curly dark hair, wearing an ivory coloured gown with a gold belt. In a sweet child's voice she answered me, "Mommy don't cry, we love you, I forgive you too."

As I shut my eyes, crying aloud now with emotion, they disappeared. What peace to really know they were with the Lord.

Shawn Paul made it! He is God's blessing to us and this world, despite our faults.

Speaking Out

Denise Mountenay continues to share her story in churches, conferences and schools. A grade ten High School teacher writes: "Denise Mountenay is a dynamic and interesting speaker who effectively advocates for the pro-life movement. This presentation was a challenge to us to critique our culture and to individually and corporately speak out against injustice. I wouldn't hesitate to recommend her." G. Jewett.

Another High School teacher writes: "Mrs. Mountenay was able to keep the attention of this group of forty. Her emotional testimony was a reminder to the students that babies are not the only victims of abortion. Following her visit the students continued to talk about the session for several days. Mrs. Mountenay is to be commended for the courage she shows while discussing such a painful experience, and for the care and concern she possesses for the unborn and their unfortunate mothers." L. MacSween.

This is what the students are saying: "I think that you really spoke from your heart and I appreciate your honesty. People don't tell us of the horror of abortion, and you finally spoke the truth. Thank you for an experience of a lifetime."

"I think her story forced a lot of people to face what is real-what is the truth, and inspired many of us to want to be active and make a difference. I really appreciated it."

"She was an excellent speaker! I'd like us to have her again sometime."

"I really enjoyed it and appreciated that she was willing to share her experience with us. I've never had someone get so deep with me about a serious issue."

"My parents are very glad that I was exposed to what truly goes on and are also very grateful to Denise that she takes the time to talk to people like me!"

A High School Teacher Writes

June 15, 1999

Dear Mrs. Mountenay:

It is truly my pleasure to be writing to you today to thank you for having shared your story with both of my religion classes last week. The teachers and students in attendance were deeply touched by your painful experience with abortion, and by your courage to speak out about the horrors experienced by women and unborn babies in hospitals and clinics across this country.

Your message is not one of judgement for girls and women who are very often victimized by greed and lies, but one of truth, and hope in the confusion that prevails in our secular society. The facts must be made known to our youth! They want to know the truth, and they respond to it. Many of the so-called 'pro-choice' students in my class realized that their arguments were based on false information, and that the prolife options are respectful of the lives of all involved.

Several of us are in the process of reading your new book. Best of luck in distributing it. Innocent lives, I pray, will be saved as a result of it. We hope to see you back next year! Thanks again, and God's blessing.

Sincerely Yours,
Suzanne Foisy-Moquin
High School Teacher

What Can You Do?

PRAY! From Genesis to Revelation is the continuing saga about the seed of the woman, and the seed of the serpent go to WAR. We have a Holy God, and the Bible says that the wages of sin is death. Sure men wrote the Bible, but they were inspired by the Holy Spirit. The Bible consists of sixty-six different authors from all walks of life, who lived over a period of two thousand years. Some were Kings, farmers, a doctor, some fishermen, a tax collector, Prophets, Priests and teachers etc. Yet, all of their writings line up. They all talk about the Creator of the universe, the Messiah, and the evil one. They warn about God's judgment and proclaim the love of God toward us.

The good news is that we have Jesus, the Messiah, born of the virgin Mary, dying on the cross for our sins and defeating death, the final enemy. He rose from the dead, and is alive. He sent His Holy Spirit to teach, guide and give us the power we need to overcome the evil one. God wants His children to lay hands on the sick and they shall recover, cast out demons and pray for miracles, His will to be done.

But **faith without works, is dead**. The Lord has given me courage, many answers to prayer, and I know, that I know-Jesus is real. So many people are lost, deceived and miserable. We are on a mission, for God has called us for such a time as this to expose that which is evil. For when the light hits the darkness, the darkness must flee. Ephesians 5:11 "Have nothing to do with the fruitless deeds of darkness but rather expose them." Ezekiel 33 States that we must warn the wicked of their wickedness or the blood is on our hands. *Together with the knowledge of the WAY, THE TRUTH, and THE LIGHT we can make a difference for righteousness in our Nation of Canada and throughout the whole world.*

If you or someone you know has gone through the trauma of an abortion please seek counsel from a "Born-again" Pastor, Post Abortion Counselling Centre, or Pro-Life Centre. Please write me if you have been hurt or damaged in ANY way due to an abortion! We need this vital information to uncover the pain women suffer from this procedure.

If you or someone you know is pregnant and thinking of having an abortion, *please do not*. You will regret it for the rest of your life. **Let your baby live. He or she will bring the greatest joy in your life.** How you feel when you are pregnant, and how you will feel holding that precious baby in your arms, are two totally different feelings. **There are many support groups to help you;** Pregnancy counselling and Crisis Centres, Right to Life, Pro-Life Groups, churches and Aid to Women. Financially, practically and emotionally they are there to help you and so am I.

If you have been inspired and motivated after reading this book, please do something to help stop the holocaust in this generation. Please write, and let me know! **Together we will make a difference for a better Canada.**

Remember this: "For we wrestle not against flesh and blood but against principalities, against powers, against the rulers of the darkness of this age, and against darkness." Ephesians 6:12. So pray for our Government leaders, the abortionists, their staff and women. *Pray the churches wake up from their complacency, and pray that they will no longer tolerate that spirit of Jezebel, Molech, Baal and lawlessness.* And pray for the spirit of wisdom and revelation in the knowledge of Him, the eyes of your understanding being enlightened; that you may know what is the hope of his calling..." Ephesians 1:17,18. Secondly, we must **talk** about this abhorrent issue openly and publicly since little lives are at stake. We need to **keep writing letters** to editors, politicians and leaders. **Join Pro Life** groups. **Get involved**. Volunteer, picket, join peaceful protests and give financially to the cause of the fatherless. Vote for Pro Life candidates on all levels of Government.

Be a voice for the voiceless. It's a matter of life and death!

BE A PART OF THE FELLOWSHIP COMMITTED TO DOING WHATEVER IT TAKES...

I am a part of the fellowship committed to doing WHATEVER IT TAKES!

I have Holy Spirit Power. The die has been cast. I've stepped over the line. I am out of the comfort zone. The decision has been made. I'm a disciple of His. I won't look back, let up, slow down, or back away. My past is redeemed, my present is focused, and my future is secure. I am finished and done with sight walking, small planning, smooth knees, colourless dreams, tame visions, mundane talking, chincy giving, and dwarfed goals. I no longer need preeminence, prosperity, position, promotions, or popularity. I don't have to be right, first, tops, recognized, praised, regarded or rewarded. I now live by His presence, lean on faith, love by patience, lift by prayer and labour by His strength. My face is set, my gait is fast, my goal is Heaven, my road is narrow, my way is rough, my companions' few, my Guide reliable, my mission clear. I cannot be bought, compromised, detoured, lured away, turned back, diluted, or delayed. I will not flinch in the face of sacrifice, hesitate in the presence of adversity, negotiate at the table of the enemy, ponder at the pool of popularity, or meander in the maze of mediocrity. I won't give up, shut up, let up, or burn up-till I've prayed up, preached up, paid up, stored up, and stayed up for the cause of Christ. I am a disciple of Jesus. I must go on till He comes, give till I drop, preach and teach till all know, and work till He stops. And when He comes to get His own, He'll have no problem recognizing me because I have dedicated my life to being a part of the fellowship committed to doing … WHATEVER IT TAKES!

Annonymous

Finally

Love! God is love. *"Love has been perfected among us in this: that we may have boldness in the day of judgment; because as He is, so are we in this world. There is no fear in love; but perfect love casts out fear,"* 1 John 4:17,18. The power of love is greater than the power of fear which brings torment. Women usually have their babies aborted because of fear. Fear of the unknown, fear of failure, fear of isolation, fear of rejection and fear of the pain in childbirth. We must show them love. *Love is patient, kind, long-suffering, does not envy, is not puffed up, does not behave rudely, does not seek its own, is not easily provoked, thinks the best, does not rejoice in iniquity but rejoices in the truth; love bears all things, believes and hopes all things, endures all things. Love never fails.* 1 Corinthians 13:4-8

For it is by love and knowing the truth that you will be set free. Jesus is the way, the truth and the life, and He loves you. He was born of a virgin teenager, a single Mom, until Joseph married her. King Herod the wicked Prime Minister sanctioned by Parliament, passed a law legalizing infanticide/abortion and had all the male babies from birth to the age of two murdered. Yet God made a way of escape for Mary and her baby. The only thing you need to do is take a little step in faith, believe and trust in God. It will change your whole outlook for life. *"For whosoever is born of God overcomes the world. And this is the victory that has overcome the world – our faith!" Who is he that overcomes the world, but he/she who believes that Jesus is the Son of God?"* 1 John 5:4,5

"Behold, children are a heritage from the Lord, The fruit of the womb is a reward. Like arrows in the hand of a warrior, so are the children of one's youth. Happy is the man who has his quiver full of them; They shall not be ashamed, But shall speak with their enemies in the gate." Psalm 127:2,3 Also read Gen. 9:1,5. 1 John 3:16-18, and the whole Bible, it's the greatest book ever written in His story.

Recently, Theresa Burke, PhD founder of Rachel's Vineyard, healing retreats for Post Abortive women wrote: "While public witness is not something that everyone is called to, there are many who, after experiencing healing of their trauma, feel a calling to speak about their experience, in the hopes of educating the public about the trauma of abortion.

Stories encourage and empower the listener. They reveal the possibilities for changing direction. They encourage others to forge through what seems insurmountable, to discover their strength. Stories help us relate the pain of the past into the transformation we long to achieve in the future. The choices and situations we may regret can become moments of opportunity for defining our depth and courage, enabling us to find new vantages from which to make sense of our pain. Certain stories are retold because they are turning points. They reveal what is true. By understanding our stories, we can begin to see some of the bigger picture of God's plan and purpose for our lives. Listening to and connecting with the emotional life hidden within the tapestry of the past can be challenging. Too often we may feel tempted to escape from the reality of the truth hidden in the human soul.

We can choose disconnection and numbness from our stories, but by doing so; we miss out on valuable moments of learning the wisdom our stories have to teach us. Numbness and denial will always conceal the truth. We can ignore these stories or we can learn from them and deeply enrich our lives in the process. If we don't learn from difficult life experiences we are destined to repeat them, in endless patterns of trauma and crisis. The repetition is actually a symptom - a disguised way of communicating a story that has never been spoken, listened to, or understood.

Telling our stories gives us an opportunity to explore the rich textures and colors of emotion and experiences that have touched our lives. This is certainly a generous gift we give to ourselves when we begin to seek healing, but it can also be a charitable gift to the thousands of men and women who suffer in silence and isolation. Your voice can stir the longing for freedom and healing in their hearts and inspire them to reach out for help. By laboring through the pain of what our stories have to teach us, we open ourselves to traveling a new path directly into the arms of life. A life embraced and fully lived. A life of meaning. A life of truth. A life of faith, hope and compassion. A life that provides a quilt of comfort and hope for the suffering of others. This is the fruit of healing, which frees us of the shackles of the past by reawakening awareness of our true identity in the present. A journey into our own stories allows us to feel the dark night of the soul and open our hearts to the light and destiny that God longs to share with us."

On writing letters to politicians; be brief and courteous, addressing only one issue at a time. Find out who your Member of Parliament is, who your Member of the Legislative Assembly (Provincial) is and the current names of Ministers of Justice and Health. Meet with your representatives. For the Prime Minister and Federal Ministries, write to the House of Commons, Ottawa, Ontario, Canada, K1A 0A6. Check your telephone directory for provincial representatives, and do please write.

So, my friends for Life, *"Do not grow weary in well doing, for in due season you shall reap a harvest, if you faint not."* Galations 6:9, 10. Keep being a voice for the voiceless. Keep supporting Pro Life/Pro Family organizations, and keep giving your time and money to defend the cause of Pre-born children as well as helping broken women. May the Lord Jesus Christ bless you all!

END NOTES-Bibliography

1. Pat Robertson, Excerpts from "Spirit Filled Life Bible" pg. 142
2 Dr. Samuele Bacchiocchi, "Wine in the Bible-A Biblical Study on the Use of Alcoholic Beverages. pg. 149
3. The Barrier Performance of Latex Rubber. C.M. Roland; chemistry division, Naval Research Lab. Washington D.C., 1993 pg. 153
4. Planned Parenthood STD and pregnancy stats, Alliance for Life and Statistics Canada pg. 155
5. Scriptures taken from King James, New King James or Amplified versions

For Speaking engagements, or if you would like to share your pain of abortion please contact Denise at 780-939-5774 or Toll Free 1-888-777-5503
Email: dwmountenay@netscape.net or dmountenay@msn.com
Website: www.canadasilentnomore.com
For more copies of this book, $20.00 each
send cheque or money order to:
Together for Life Ministries
107 Discovery Ave., Morinville, AB, Canada T8R 1N1

Dear Television/Movie Producers; this needs to be made into a movie.
It's a matter of life and death!